# YOU

## and

# THE NEW WORLD ORDER

## HOW YOU CAN INFLUENCE THE ALARMING AND GROWING INTERNATIONAL AND DOMESTIC PROBLEMS

## RICHARD HOBBS

ColDoc Publishing, Sparks, Nevada

To Diane, Deanna, and Christian
with the hope that there will be a just order in the world in
the years ahead

# Books by Richard Hobbs

La Grande Illusion, La Victoire Totale
Notebook and Readings for International Relations,
   "Operation Statesman," Co-Editor
Readings in International Relations, 2 Volumes, Editor
Operation Statesman, Focus on Southeast Asia, Editor
THE MYTH OF VICTORY   What Is Victory In War?
THE NEW WORLD ORDER   Tribalism, Nationalism,
   and Religious Fundamentalism
WORLD WAR IV   China's Quest for Power in the 21st
   Century

Published by:

**C**  **ColDoc Publishing**
**D**     Post Office Box 50682
**P**     Sparks, Nevada 89435-0682 USA

Copyright © 1995 by Richard Hobbs

**Library of Congress Cataloging-in-Publication Data**
Hobbs, Richard  1931-
   You and the new world order: how you can influence the alarming
and growing international and domestic problems / by Richard Hobbs
First Edition
      p.    cm.
   Includes glossary and index.
   ISBN 0-9647788-6-6 : $19.95
   1. World Politics -- 20th Century.          I. Title.
   2. International Relations.
   3. International Relations -- United States.
   4. United States -- Politics and Government.
Library of Congress Catalog Number 95-70416
D443.H652    1995   909.82

# CONTENTS

# DISCLAIMER

The purpose of this book is to educate and to entertain. The author speaks for no organization, political party, or government, US or foreign. The author and ColDoc Publishing shall have neither liability nor responsibility to any person or entity with respect to any loss or damage caused, or alleged to be caused, directly or indirectly by the information contained in this book.

**If you do not wish to be bound by the above, you may return this book to the publisher for a full refund.**

# PREFACE

The euphoria of the end of the Cold War has evaporated and we now are faced with new challenges around the world. The terrible threat of a nuclear Armageddon is hopefully behind us, but we have found, instead of a peaceful world with the great peace dividend, an unstable world in disorder. There is a **new order** in the world; our problem is to try to define it and then to address it intelligently to make some sense out of it and hopefully provide a better world for ourselves to live in and as our legacy for our children.

For those of us who lived through all of the Cold War, the death of the Soviet Union was both amazing and unbelievably rapid. The last great empire in the world collapsed in a very short period. The ramifications of that monumental event will be with us well into the next century. It was an Evil Empire and it is necessary to remember it and the old world order we lived in for so long to understand where we were and where we are going.

The drama of the tearing down of the Berlin Wall, the emancipation of the states of Eastern Europe, and the lowering of the old Soviet flag over the Kremlin on Christmas 1991 were key events of the final years of the 20th Century. But as with all great events, they were only the introduction to the next era. How will that drama play out? Can a Russia with no history of democracy or free enterprise really make that great leap or will it fall back into its traditional autocratic ways?

Will the new states survive or will they tear themselves apart?

The threat of major nuclear war has waned but the world is still a very heavily armed place. There is the threat of stolen or sold nuclear devices falling into the hands of the rogue states. We have to ponder nuclear blackmail or nuclear terror. What are the conflicts around the world and what is the likelihood for war? What are the most dangerous regions in this new world? What are the threats?

We have witnessed a ferocious new tribalism erupting in the world, from the former Soviet Union, to the Yugoslav tribes, to Asia. As Yogi Berra said, it's *déja vu* all over again as we see shades of Neville Chamberlain as Europe sits on its hands watching the massive catastrophe in Bosnia as nationalist thugs rape, torture, pillage, and destroy their countrymen in what was Yugoslavia. They claim a militant nationalism, ready to kill to form the new Greater Serbia or Greater Croatia. Added to the beastiality of their actions is the intolerant religious hatred they demonstrated.

Religion, along with language and race the most divisive elements in the world, continues to set men apart. Of the numerous wars or disputes around the world, two-thirds of them have a religious basis. The frustrations of the Muslims with their difficult economic troubles and a feeling of hopelessness toward Western liberal actions have led to the rise of Islamic fundamentalism. The bombing of the World Trade Center brought the outrage of these people to our shores. But there are others too: Jewish fundamentalists, Christian fundamentalists or Christian Zionists, and others who wish to impose their parochial views.

The bipolar world is gone but is it really a unipolar world? The US is the only major power for now and it threw out its president because the candidate said he spent too much time on foreign affairs and not enough time addressing the problems of the economy. Now that new president is mired in world affairs without any basic philosophy or program to deal with them. The US has been called upon to be the world's policeman but it does not want the job.

The nation state is in turmoil as international frontiers cannot provide the protection of yesteryear. International boundaries have been sacrosanct for decades but now they are changing. Has Pandora's box been opened?

There is growing strife around the world. Overpopulation is making the poorer countries poorer. There is less food now which may lead to more famine. Jobs are not being created as fast as new babies grow up. AIDS is threatening a massive attack on the world economy. Terrorism is on the increase and more disputes are exploding into larger confrontations. It is a very disorderly world.

America seems to be in as much disarray as the world. The great melting pot is boiling. Racial troubles increase as there is less assimilation, more disillusionment, and more equal but separate division. Where is America going? Where does it want to go?

If the US does not wish to be the world's policeman, then we must grant the United Nations the capability to take up the role. We have become quite aware of UN force actions in the 1990s, starting with the large peacemaking operation in the Persian Gulf to force Saddam Hussein out of Kuwait. But the peacekeeping operations in Somalia, Bosnia, and Haiti have soured the American feelings toward helping some of these peoples. The UN needs its own force; these intractable situations need to be placed under UN Trusteeship, and the UN needs an International Court to deal with war criminals and other gross violators of human rights.

There is a lot wrong with the the US and with the world. Like the huge national debt we are leaving to our children, we are leaving other major unresolved problems because we do not have the courage to deal with them. They are our **terrible legacy** to the next generation.

The US needs to get serious about its internal problems and address them. It also needs to act like a major power and lead. The world needs a leader; unfortunately, we are the only candidate. If there is going to be a new world order to our liking, America must lead; the rest of the world will follow.

**You** are key to that future.

RICHARD HOBBS

Reno, Nevada
May 1995

---

*Every man ... should periodically be compelled to listen to opinions which are infuriating to him. To hear nothing but what is pleasing to one is to make a pillow of the mind.*

-- St. John Ervine

# ABOUT THE AUTHOR

Richard Hobbs graduated from the United States Military Academy at West Point in 1954 and entered the Infantry. As a paratrooper, Ranger, and Pathfinder, he had various troop assignments, including attending the British Jungle School in Malaya during the Emergency and in charge of Tropical Training for a Division in Hawaii.. He was selected as one of the original Olmsted Scholars and attended the University of Lyon in France receiving the degree of Docteur de l'Université in international law and international relations.

Two tours were spent in Viet-Nam (one year each) advising Vietnamese paratroopers, serving as Executive to the Deputy Commander in Viet-Nam, managing a large fire base, and commanding a US infantry battalion. Instead of attending the Army War College, he was an Army Research Associate at the Center for Strategic and International Studies in Washington. During that time he worked on a conference about the Western Mediterranean and reworked his thesis from Lyon which was later published by Westview Press as *THE MYTH OF VICTORY What is Victory In War?*

After serving in the Pentagon, his last assignment was as Politico-Military Advisor in the Bureau of Near Eastern and South Asian Affairs in the Department of State in Washington. He was responsible for politico-military activities in international relations and military assistance to the Middle East during the period after the 1973 War. He retired from the Army as a colonel after 27 years.

Entering the business world, he joined Teledyne serving in various positions for over 10 years including Vice President -- International where he worked with the Departments of State, Commerce, and Defense and the embassies on international policy questions and export licenses. During those years, he continued to work with the Middle East, travelling to the area, particularly Egypt, every few months and extensively through Africa.

He established his own consulting firm, Service International Ltd., for international business development which he moved to Reno in 1991. There he ran an export-import company for a while, built a slot machine, and taught courses in international politics and international conflict for undergraduate and graduate students at the University of Nevada, Reno. In addition to the large amount of teaching in the military, he had served as Assistant Professor of International Relations on the faculty of the Department of Social Sciences at West Point.

With an ongoing interest in national and international affairs, he wrote this book for citizens in an effort to emphasize that they can play a role in the momentous decisions of our times. His desire is to encourage people to take part in the political process and make their voices heard so that the active few cannot impose their views due to the apathy of the many.

# Chapter 1

# IS THIS WHERE WE ARE GOING?

> *We are living through such a frightening peace because the Cold War has not yet rid us of its legacy. The war is over. Beware the peace.*
>
> -- Eduard Shevardnadze
>
> *Decreasingly able to mobilize support and form coalitions on the basis of ideology, governments and groups will increasingly attempt to mobilize support by appealing to common religion and civilization identity.*
>
> -- Samuel P. Huntington
> "The Clash of Civilizations"

You, a concerned American citizen, always wanted to visit Washington, D. C. and see what makes it tick. You saved your money and took the pretty wife to the nation's capital for a vacation. You had seen the sights, been up to the Hill to meet with your Congressman and your Senators, and even had a special tour of the White House that your Senator arranged. You were staying at one of the best hotels in the city and since it was such a beautiful evening, you decided to take a little stroll even though the doorman had repeatedly warned you not to.

Nonsense, you said to yourself, why shouldn't I go for a walk in the capital of the only superpower in the world? You had not gone too far when you noticed that the sidewalk was full of skimpily clad ladies, some of whom brazenly propositioned you even though your wife was holding your arm. Having escaped the gauntlet of street walkers, you notice a group of men under a street light. They are busy doing some kind of business and making some exchanges. You are not sure what they are doing and you quickly walk past them. They do not speak but they all turn and stare, and you think you hear one of them whisper to another, "They gotta be honkies from the Midwest!"

You continue along and note that the houses are all brick and were probably very elegant back in the 1930s, but they are quite rundown now. There are broken windows, some boarded up, and there is trash everywhere. Maybe this is not such a good area after all. You are approached by a young girl, she can't be a day over 14, with a baby on her hip. She asks if you can spare some change for her and her baby. You are appalled and quickly give her a buck and she disappears into the night.

You hear some shooting in the distance and sirens wailing. You decide that perhaps the doorman was right and you turn to head back to the hotel. Just then two young punks suddenly appear and demand your wallet. Being a tough old veteran, you quickly deck one and put a good karate chop on the other and turn to run. But you hear the rapid burst of an automatic weapon (the first time you've heard that since Viet-Nam) and then the hammer like thuds in your back. You see yourself and your wife falling into the gutter and sliding through the garbage and you swear you can hear the young punks laughing.

You sit bold upright in your bed in a cold sweat. Thank God, it was just another nightmare and your wife is safe beside you! But your nights in Washington have been full of nightmares. You have been reading *The Washington Post* and watching the evening news and much of it is disconcerting and your imagination has been running wild.

You always thought the Europeans were civilized; your grandfather went over there to France in World War I and your father again in World War II. Fortunately, European Communism seems to be quite dead but Europe has given us some of the worst authoritarian and totalitarian governments we ever had to face.

With neo-Nazis resurging in Germany, were we seeing a replay of the 1920s? Could Germany fall back into its old black boot ways and go back to dictatorship? The Russian Communists taught the world the fine points of totalitarianism. Could the new Russia really become democratic when it has absolutely no tradition of democracy or a free market economy and a very deep culture of strong rulers?

The Balkans have caused trouble before; you remember where the First War started. It bothers you that there are wild men trying to build a Greater Serbia. And just like the 1930s, the Europeans are sitting on their butts. Will we have to go bail them out again? You went to Viet-Nam and you don't want your son to go to war.

The rabid tribalism and nationalism exhibited in Bosnia are not the only examples. The collapse of the Soviet Union only seemed to create new problems. There were numerous old scores being settled with fighting throughout the Caucasus including the mess in Chechnya. Africa continued to tear itself apart with the tribes (clans) in Somalia, the seemingly endless fighting in Angola and Liberia, and the unbelievable tribal slaughter in Rwanda.

And why was China building up its military so strongly when all the rest of the world was cutting back? China was booming economically under a capitalist surge, but it was still run by Communists and Tiananmen Square had shown that democracy was not yet the order of the day in China.

Some religious crazies had blown up the World Trade Center in New York and we had our own loonies in Oklahoma City. You had become accustomed to the religious fanatics who took over Iran and held our people hostage. These weird people killed like the Inquisition of old in the name of God. You had heard about Salmon Rushdie and the warrant for his death by these so-called men of God and also Taslima Nasrin from Bangladesh who was also threatened with death  for having the audacity to write anything these characters did not approve.

Was Algeria going down that slippery slope with the continued slaughter of people there?  Were these wild fundamentalists going to take over other Arab countries? Why did they hate us so much? How could Hindus and Muslims slaughter each other so easily? What is there about religion that people can be so pious and yet so terribly intolerant and murderous?

The Cold War was over and we supposedly won. But where was that great peace dividend? Was the US going to have to be the world's policeman? We did not seem to want the job and you did not seem to want to send your children off to fight the world's battles, particularly if it meant some of them getting killed. Yet there seemed to be growing numbers of boundary disputes. Was there going to have to be a realignment of the world? The nation state seemed to be in trouble. Was it going to survive?

Why couldn't the UN take care of these problems? Particularly since we did not want to. But the UN was becoming a laughing stock and was constantly humiliated. It was hideous to see the UN being treated like a Third World puppet by those thugs from Serbia. But what did we do about it? Yet sanctions were proving ineffective. The UN really had no force of its own and the troops it was given were often held hostage or treated with contempt. Those miserable thugs in Serbia needed to be brought to trial as war criminals but there was no real vehicle to deal with international crimes.

Your nightmares were getting worse. You had trouble visualizing a world of 10 billion people. How would countries take care of them when they cannot take care of the 5.7 billion people in the world now? How would we feed them? Would we see famines again? There are not enough jobs now, how would the growing problem of unemployment be handled? Would diseases like AIDS increase? Where would all these people go? Would they start crossing borders to try to find better lives? What would that mean to Europe and the US which have terrible immigration problems now?

Strife seems to be growing in the world. There is more terrorism. Must we expect only more? Will the population pressures and the other difficult problems facing many governments push them into wars? Your family has served its country, now will your children have to die for the country also?

How will all this affect America? We have enough problems here already with growing crime and drugs. Our melting pot is boiling as some of the minority groups are not assimilating. The country is breaking up into ethnic groups and disillusionment is growing.

The world seems to be degenerating into chaos. The nation state is proving incapable of dealing with the problems of the 20th and 21st Centuries. A new form is needed but we cannot even clean up the mess at the UN and give it enough authority to help solve the problems.

Here at home, our economy is going bankrupt with a staggering debt that is not being controlled. People are working harder and making less. The working people in America are falling behind not getting ahead. Our political leadership is morally bankrupt in that it cannot get above special interests to deal with the national interest. The country is leaderless and there is no likelihood of any improvement.

Our own population growth is out of control being led by the least productive parts of our society. We have permitted the destruction of the family and are now saddled with teenagers with babies out of wedlock, millions of women with babies and no fathers helping to raise them, and an unmanageable welfare monster. Crime and drugs have taken over so that many of our streets and inner cities are war zones controlled by our own urban terrorists.

Is this the world your grandfather fought for to make the world safe for democracy? Is this what your father bled for in the great crusade to stop the tyranny of Germany and Japan? Is this what you waded through the mud of Viet-Nam for during the Cold War when you were stopping the spread of world Communism?

Will these internal problems destroy America? Will these problems around the world spill over and affect our trade interests, affect our economy, or even worse drag us into wars?

Is this disorderly world drifting toward anarchy, toward total disorder? Is that where we are going? What is to be the **New World Order**? Can it still be shaped to make the world a better place to live, a better place to raise your children, a better place for mankind?

The 20th Century was the most deadly century in history with the carnage of world wars and the scourge of Communism. This may not be the dawn of the Age of Aquarius, but it could be the nightmare that dawns as the 21st Century.

**NO**, the world does not have to go to hell in a handbasket. **YES**, you can do something about it. The world does not have to collapse into disorder. The future will not be determined by great figures with enormous wisdom. It will be determined by plain, ordinary, common people in Washington, Moscow, Paris, London, Berlin, Tokyo, Beijing, and thousands of other cities.

They are not particularly intelligent, rarely wise, generally selfish, often arrogant, they respond to pressures, and if properly pushed they even can make some wise decisions. But most of them are opportunists and they go with the tides.

**YOU** must become part of the tide that pushes them toward wisdom.

**YOU**, as that concerned citizen, must remind them from whence they came, that they have no God-given right to power, and that they are responsible to the people.

YOU must remind them of what is good for the country and the world, not just for their political futures.  If you do so, you have a chance to stop your nightmares and have an impact on the New World Order and make this world a better place.

In the chapters that follow, we will look at some of these problems and try to determine some of the options and possible actions to deal with them.  This then can serve as your **citizen's handbook** for addressing some of the problems of the world.  But first, we should take a brief look at how the world got into this mess.

> *It is clear that we have entered a new world of disorder, and our inability to formulate either coherent policies or strategies to deal with ethnic conflicts and NATO expansion has led to a cross-Atlantic fear, confusion, incoherence and recriminations.*
>
> -- Senator William S. Cohen

> *If this [Bosnia] goes on, there will be no global stability and no security in Europe.  We will have to fight again.  You cannot take holidays from history.*
>
> --Manfred Woerner
> Secretray General, NATO

# Chapter 2

# HOW DID THE WORLD GET INTO THIS MESS?

*Freedom is still expensive. It still costs money. It still costs blood.*

-- Harry S. Truman

*As long as capitalism and socialism exist, we cannot live in peace: in the end one or the other will triumph.*

-- Lenin

The end of World War II dispelled the dreams of Japanese Empire and the 1,000 year Third Reich. It also signalled the pending demise of the British, French, and Dutch Empires. China was already locked in civil war with Mao's Red Army. With America having come to the rescue of the Soviet Union, what could have been a golden age of cooperation was not to be. A new world order evolved but it was not what we expected.

## THE OLD WORLD ORDER -- Tense But Relatively Stable

The Soviets refused the Baruch Plan by which America, which then had a nuclear monopoly, offered that all atomic development and control would be under the United Nations, and they also refused aid under the Marshall Plan.

Either the Communist dogma of world domination arguments by Marx and Lenin were too deeply ingrained or Stalin's thirst for power too great; either way, Stalin led the USSR into confrontation.

### A Bipolar World

With most of the modern world exhausted from the war and concentrating on rebuilding their economies, only two countries were left to play major international roles. The United States was left standing with the strongest economy and soon took to helping in the reconstruction, particularly via the Marshall Plan.

Soviet Russia, exhausted but under a powerful dictator who saw great opportunities for expansion, pushed to increase its world position. Even though the United States was the only nuclear power at the time (the USSR conducted a crash program to end that monopoly which they soon did in 1949), these two "**super**" powers were destined to enter into world competition.

Confrontations arose early and soon all of Eastern Europe was under Moscow's domination, and a great **Iron Curtain** came thundering down. The Soviet role in the Greek Civil War awakened President Truman to the new reality of Communist intentions and the invasion of South Korea on 25 June 1950 brought us into the era of proxy wars.

Thus, two centers of power evolved based in Washington and Moscow. The Moscow doctrine of **Wars of National Liberation** was basically that any country that was not already in the Communist camp was fair game and subversive activity took place in many countries around the world. The US was then forced to respond or let those countries go Communist.

Each power tried to attract other nations to its side whether it was in debates in the United Nations, political or economic groupings, or in confrontations. The **Containment Policy** was developed to keep the Communist empire from expanding and various regional organizations (NATO, CENTO, SEATO) were formed. The massive Russian invasion never came but the wars of national liberation continued for forty years.

The Bipolar World also provided opportunities for leaders with their own agendas which often had nothing to do with either Communism or Democracy. It was not unusual for a country to try to play one superpower off against the other. The forces of nationalism rebounded and the international order took a different tack from rigid bipolarity.

## Neutralism and Non-Alignment

World War II accelerated the death of European imperialism, except of course Russian. Anti-colonialism was a strong movement in the post-war years. It began in Asia where Raj India became India and Pakistan and post-colonialism became the major influence for Asian foreign policy, led by India.

The result of the Cold War and post-colonialism was neutralism and non-alignment. Thus a non-aligned movement evolved initially under the leadership of Jawaharlal Nehru of India. Leaders like Nehru first had to clearly establish their independence; therefore, non-alignment and trust in the United Nations seemed preferable to alliances.

Despite their economic and strategic dependence, the choice of non-alignment was based on neutrality. Some nations did not relish the idea of having to align themselves with one of the two superpowers, either from philosophical differences or concern that being too close to one might cause dangerous fall-out if the two behemoths ever came to blows. Thus, the non-aligned movement evolved.

They learned to exert influence by means of conferences around the world and by their voting in the UN General Assembly. This newly independent world grew to over 150 separate states with various power centers. It was bipolar only in the sense of major power relationships and danger of major war.

## Cold War

The "Cold War" or the Communist War, since it was often "hot," was perhaps the greatest war in the history of mankind and was total war in the sense that it was all-encompassing in that every facet of human life and thought was exploited. The Communists tried to impose their ideology on the world and directed all their massive energy against the Free World.

Yet, it was also a limited war in that many limited wars were fought throughout the world. It was not that the stakes were limited but the means employed by the belligerents were limited. In a military sense, it was a race for bases, allies, raw materials, and prestige. Although the Soviets and Americans generally tried to avoid direct conflict between themselves, this did not prevent war by proxy, through satellites, subversive organizations, guerrillas, or many other forms.

The long hoped-for peace after World War II never came. The Communist War was extremely expensive, costing trillions of dollars, and precluded a return to normalcy. No clearcut line between war and peace existed in the Cold War period.

Communist Russia, which had proved to be an impossible ally in war, quickly increased its uncooperative policy in the early postwar years. The Communists, with their intent to seize control of the globe, were the self-appointed enemy of the world. It should be remembered that our enemy in the Cold War was not Russia or China but the Communist Parties.

Without the Communist Party, there would have been no Cold War. The propaganda diatribes about the struggle between Communism and Capitalism were nonsense. The true issue in the Cold War between the Communists and the Free World was **freedom versus force.**

We tend to forget what was at stake during the Cold War. It was a struggle between those who believed in freedom of the individual and a pagan ideology that counted the state supreme over the individual. These differences were irreconcilable.

The impetus for the conflict came from Communist imperialism. Not satisfied to remain in their area, they were intent on trying to convert the world to their system, by force if necessary. The major battleground of this war was the minds of people. Never has the world seen such an egotistical breed of plotters.

The Communist War was an ideological struggle unlike any wars of the past, even the religious wars. The Communists were at war with everyone, including their own people. It was clear that ideas were as important as weapons and that the survival of ideology was more important than the survival of people.

An extremely important phase of this war was the call for "**peaceful coexistence.**" This was well designed so that the Westerner looked upon it as honest competition and a reduced threat of war. However, for the Communists, it was merely a continuation of the conflict with a reduced emphasis on military operations due to the nuclear threat.

Peaceful coexistence was the source of great confusion in the West due to the Western differentiation between war and peace that was so unclear in the Communist War.

With the growth of the Russian (and Chinese) nuclear capability and the ever present reluctance of the Americans to use theirs, there developed a nuclear stalemate, often referred to as the "**balance of terror.**"

The "cold" war was a combination of psychological war, the weapons of which are the emotions; of economic war aimed at destroying financial stability; of guerrilla war, the most primitive form of war; and civil war, the most brutal form. The Cold War was the true **"protracted conflict"** and continued until the 1980s before a combination of events finally brought about changes at remarkable speed.

In the Cold War, then, peace was a very deadly state of affairs; it was waged much like war but in a more subtle and insidious manner. To the Communists, peace was synonymous with war.

The Communists started from a premise that what's mine is mine; what's yours is negotiable. This war involved every imaginable aspect of potential conflict: economic, emotional, and social. The name "Cold War" itself helped them by prolonging the idea that it was not a shooting war, thereby leading us to underestimate its importance.

> *The Western military experts are not sufficiently freed from traditional conceptions, and keep wondering whether war will come, when it is raging all the time.*
>
> -- Raymond Aron

The Cold War was characterized as a period of intense anti-colonialism and fiery nationalism. The machinations of the Soviet empire on the world scene since the late 1930s present examples of world power politics incomparable with any others in history.

The Cuban Missile Crisis was one of the watersheds of the Cold War. Khrushchev lost face but turned defeat into political victory. Although the Cold War encompassed all forms of conflict, it was often quite "hot" in various forms of armed conflict from guerrilla warfare to the limited (but large) wars in Korea, Viet-Nam, and later Afghanistan. The list of these small wars is quite long - over 500 conflicts since World War II.

The two antagonists rarely fired a shot at each other and never became directly engaged in an admitted shooting war. The significance of the threat was obviously the potential of nuclear and thermonuclear war to cause cataclysmic damage to each other and the world.

The USSR quickly developed massive weapons of its own with its first explosion in 1949. England and France joined the nuclear club followed in 1964 by Red China. India exploded a nuclear "device" and Israel developed an arsenal. Numerous other states were at various stages of nuclear development programs.

Soon the United States and the Soviet Union were threatening each other with nuclear annihilation and confronting each other all over the world; any change in some other part of the world could upset the delicate balance. This was quite different from the nineteenth century balance of power which relied on the interaction of five great powers, each of which had an interest in the survival of the others.

The Americans and the Russians had little real interest in the survival of the other because each would have felt the world safer without its antagonist. Therefore, except for mutual fear, there was no powerful external restraint to keep them from destroying each other.

The Cold War meant that the world was an armed camp on constant alert for a possible nuclear exchange. The nuclear warheads grew from the 20 KT (kilotons) of Hiroshima (the equivalent of 20,000 tons of TNT) to thermonuclear weapons of hundreds of megatons (millions of tons of TNT). Warheads were refined so that they were small enough to put in artillery shells, landmines, small land, air, and sea missiles, and torpedoes. The explosive power grew beyond the capability of human minds to comprehend.

The policy became **MAD (Mutual Assured Destruction)** which meant that the two sides each had enough firepower to destroy the other, even after absorbing a first strike. The world was truly sitting on the threshold of Armageddon.

We will never be able to forgive the Communists for the terrible waste of the cost of the Cold War. In 1946, the US military was reduced to no deployable army divisions or air wings. We had to completely rearm at a cost of trillions of dollars over the next forty years. Just think what that money could have accomplished if it had been used for peaceful measures!

## World Order During the Cold War

There was no agreement on the nature of the world

order throughout the Cold War since it was in flux. Communist doctrine was that all non-Communist states were to be liberated and added to the Communist World.

The West, if it had a doctrine, would probably have agreed to an order founded on the equality of states and independence. The Third World had no clear agenda either but searched for self-expression, independence, and the opportunity to develop their states.

So long as international relations were based on the nation state, the prevention of war and the basis of a world order could only be secured by powerful states. They formed the United Nations but since there was so much suspicion, it could have only limited power.

The United Nations was an improved version of the League of Nations, but it still had to exist in the real world of sovereign states, particularly the superpowers. The reality of the veto in the Security Council became a nightmare in practice as Russia feared the UN would become an extension of American policies. This quickly reduced the potential of the peace-keeping mechanisms even though there were numerous UN operations around the world.

The form of the emerging new international order was still unclear and changing in the mid-1980s. The three blocs that were established in the 1950s and 1960s were fairly clear: the Western or Free World, the Communist World, and the non-aligned or Third World, the latter being quite loosely organized. It is probably preferable to call the world order "polycentric" because there were many centers of power and they included not only blocs but also individual states and international organizations.

The Cold War, despite its horrendous potential for destruction, did actually provide a degree of stability. The two superpowers developed great respect for their power and developed complicated control procedures to ensure that no wild subordinate could initiate a nuclear war.

Even though there were occasional "limited" wars, even backed by one or both of the big two, they were very careful to keep them limited and not permit them to escalate to the nuclear threshold. This was **deterrence** and what later became known as **Détente**. We are beginning to appreciate some of the stability of the Cold War only now that it is over.

The Old Order, in retrospect, was rather hierarchical and surprisingly ordered though not structured. The two superpowers stood way above the other states due to the combination of their large populations, major economies, modern technology, and massive standing land, air, and naval forces that could project their power to almost any part of the world. They were truly the only two "**world**" powers.

As the Cold War continued, the two became more respectful of each other and the enormous responsibilities they held in their hands. Even though their philosophies were still antipathetic, their mutual interests came closer together. It was difficult for them to work together, but they realized that they were not going to permit some other country to force them into a showdown not of their choosing. This resulted in pressure from the two to keep some of the countries on their sides "in line" in a sense adding to world stability.

## IT WAS AN EVIL EMPIRE

Marx and Engels wrote in the 19th Century that Russian foreign policy had one constant objective -- world domination. Stalin tried to suppress those writings. Alexis de Tocqueville observed that the conquests of the Americans were by the ploughshare and those of the Russians by the sword. The history of the Russian Empire is one of conquests and blood.

### The Russian Empire

What was to become a great empire evolved erratically over centuries by accident, anarchy, and aggression. The fertile steppe area north of the Black Sea was repeatedly invaded by nomadic tribes from Central Asia over thousands of years. A people known as the East Slavs began settling in the dense forests to the north around 500 AD. Occupying an area from present day St. Petersburg to Kiev, they shipped furs and honey down the Dnieper River to Constantinople.

According to old chronicles, the Slavs sent a delegation to Scandanavia in 862 to meet with a tribe called the Rus, part of the Vikings, asking them to come rule over their land which was rich but had no order.

Thus a Viking Rus called Rurik established control in Novgorod (south of St. Petersburg) and the region became known as "**the land of the Rus.**" Rurik's successor, Oleg, is considered the founder of "Russia." The Northmen had united the Slavs and now started to expand.  Prince Oleg invaded the Eastern Roman Empire in 907 and wreaked havoc in Constantinople.  There were many of these forays and after each a successful trade treaty was brought home to Kiev, which became the first Russian state, Kievan Russia.

Oleg's successor, Igor, was killed in battle and his widow Olga was regent for 17 years for her grandson Sviatoslav.  She was the first famous Russian woman, first Slav ruler who converted to Christianity, and the Orthodox Church made her its first Russian saint.  But she was a tough woman who buried alive or burned to death representatives from her suitor, the prince of the tribe which had killed Igor.

Kievan Russia prospered until the Mongol Empire led by Batu, grandson of Genghis Khan, invaded in 1240.  Kiev resisted and Batu burned it and killed all its inhabitants.  Batu continued his quest and conquered Hungary and Poland before withdrawing.

The **Mongols** or **Tartars** of the **Golden Horde** dominated Russia in a harsh manner for over two centuries.  Russia was isolated and missed the Renaissance in the West.  The decline of the South caused emigration and the North grew, particularly Novgorod and the nearby town of Moscow.  The Russian Orthodox Church moved to Moscow in the 14th Century.

Ivan III, who became known as "the Great" (1462-1505), gathered in Novgorod and extensive lands to the northeast as well as attacking the Lithuanians.  He saw himself as more than a prince; after marrying the niece of the last Byzantine Emperor, he took the title of Russian Emperor and referred to himself as **Czar**, or ruler.

The Golden Horde dissolved into the three khanates of Kazan, Astrakhan, and Crimea.  The first two khanates disappeared after Ivan's grandson, **Ivan the Terrible** (which means awesome in Russian, but he was pathologically cruel), invaded Kazan in 1552.  The onion-domed St. Basil's Cathedral on the edge of Moscow's Red Square was built by Ivan to celebrate that victory.

Tartar rule was significant because it brought contact with the East, Asiatic customs, increased cruelty toward slaves and the conquered, bureaucratic ideas and the efficient Eastern financial system.  Moscow, which was the natural terminus of the trade routes to the East, became Russia's leading city.  It became a strategic center after the construction of the Kremlin, the strongest fort in Russia at that time.

The expansion into Siberia was led by the church not the government. Monks went into the forests to establish new monasteries. Behind them came trappers and hunters, fortune hunters, and tough frontiersmen called **Cossacks.** The weak Tartar Empire could not stop them.

It only took 80 years to conquer this frozen wilderness and the Cossacks were on the Sea of Okhotsk by 1647. They moved on south to the Amur valley where they met soldiers from the Manchu Empire of China and were stopped at Manchuria.

**Czar Peter the Great** commissioned a Danish shipmaker, Vitus **Bering,** to explore east of the Kamchatka Peninsula. After eight years of crossing Siberia, building a ship, and sailing across the strait that now bears his name, he saw the mountains of Alaska on 18 July 1741. Russia took over Alaska and set up forts down North America as far as California.

The Czar defeated King Charles XII of Sweden in 1709 at Poltava. With this significant victory he was able to consolidate his gains, dissolve the Cossack state, and fully incorporate the Ukraine. This led to Russian control of Estonia and Latvia on the Baltic, a key opening to the West. In the swamps at the mouth of the Neva River, much harsh labor built what became the parks and canals of St. Petersburg.

Expansion to the West continued under **Catherine the Great.** She invaded Poland and with plenty of bribes managed to have one of her discarded lovers (there were supposedly 21) elected King of Poland. She defeated Turkish intervention and acquired Poland and Crimea.

**Alexander I** had inherited the alliance against France and the invasion by Napoleon. The allies pursued Napoleon all the way into France where Alexander and the Prussian king made a triumphant entry into Paris in July 1813 and Napoleon was forced into exile. Russia received Finland and Besarabia, and Persia was forced to cede Baku.

**Alexander II** (1855-81) emancipated the serfs in 1861 (the American Emancipation Proclamation was in 1863). Recurring threats to Alaska from England and France led the Russians to consider selling it rather than adding defense expenditures which might not be sufficient. Thus Russia sold Alaska to the US in 1867 for $7,200,000 a sum considered exorbitant by America but adequate by the Russians.

The Social Democratic Party was organized in 1898, but the growth of the Socialists was slow due to the small industrial proletariat. Strikes called in 1896 and 1897 were failures. The Socialist split in 1903 when the "majority," or **Bolsheviks**, under Vladimir Ulyanov (later known by his pseudonym **"Lenin"**), seceded leaving the "minority," or **Mensheviks**, who continued to work through evolutionary and parliamentary means.

**Nicholas II** (1894-1917), was the last of the Romanovs. His reign was a period of industrialization but only limited progress in democratic reforms. The Trans-Siberian Railroad was built. There were wars as always, including the significant defeat by Asians in the Russo-Japanese War in 1904-05. The Socialists gained strength and a general strike called by quickly formed revolutionary councils (called *soviets*) paralyzed the country in   October 1904.   One of the new leaders was **Trotsky**.

The Triple Entente with France and England guaranteed that Russia would be drawn into the differences with the Triple Alliance (Germany, Austria-Hungary, and Italy) and eventually into the First World War, which was to be a disaster for Russia. While the war was raging at the front, the unrest was boiling at home resulting in the October Revolution in 1917 by which the Bolsheviks seized power.

## The Soviet Empire

Lenin took Russia out of the war and gave up Estonia, Latvia, Lithuania, Finland, Poland, and the Ukraine. Much of the old empire (which was actually larger than the eventual USSR because of the inclusion of Finland and Poland) was gone.   German puppet regimes were installed but after Germany was defeated, the Soviets reconquered the Ukraine.

While the Bolsheviks consolidated their power, there were various independence movements in Belorussia and Turkestan. Armenia,  Azerbaijan, and Georgia established a Transcaucasian Federation but it soon fell apart.

The Bolsheviks, by means of cajoling, negotiations, and military force,  recovered Armenia, Azerbaijan, and Georgia. The independence movements were quelled in Central Asia, Belorussia, and the Ukraine (except the western part was still in  Poland).   The Baltic states and  Finland kept their independence due to British and German help and the French managed to keep Poland free from the Soviets.

On 30 December 1922, the Union of Soviet Socialist States held its first congress. There were four union republics: the Russian Soviet Federated Socialist Republic, the Belorussian Soviet Socialist Republic, the Ukrainian SSR, and the Transcaucasian SSR.

Rising Georgian nationalism (remember Stalin came from Georgia) led in 1924 to dividing the Transcaucasian SSR into three union republics and in 1925, Central Asia was broken into five states based on languages: Kazakhstan, Kirghizia, Tadzhikistan, Turkmenistan, and Uzebekistan (all five became union republics by 1936).

Hitler granted Estonia, Latvia, and Lithuania plus eastern Poland and Bessarabia (in northeastern Romania) to the USSR by a secret agreement with Stalin in 1939 (the Communist Party only admitted it in 1989). Stalin added the part of Poland to the Ukraine and added Bessarabia to the Moldavian Autonomous Republic and changed it to the Moldavian SSR.

Thus the Union of Soviet Socialist Republics, or the Soviet Empire, with a long history as the Russian Empire, was under new and stronger management. The old Muscovite practices of intrigue, deceit, exploitation of disunity after fomenting it, unnoticed penetration, and secret usurpation were also Soviet methods. Czarist Russia's objective of world domination continued as the Soviet objective.

| *We will bury you.* | -- Nikita Khrushchev |

The Soviet goal of world domination was also the aim of worldwide Communism. Communist leaders from Lenin on stressed that since the Soviet Union was the first homeland of Socialism, all Communists should follow its policy lead. Communist Parties around the world owed their support to the Soviet Union and it was always a Soviet-inspired unanimity that was prescribed for all parts of the Communist bloc. The independence of Tito, growing nationalism, and the Sino-Soviet split were not helpful.

Stalin and Khrushchev insisted that the Soviet Union had the right to extend its power by all expedient means and to demand from all Communist nations and Parties subservience to Moscow. All non-Communist lands were considered as future conquests: by intrigue, exploiting disunity, unnoticed penetration, secret usurpation, and "peaceful competition."

*Communism is the corruption of a dream of justice.*
                                        -- Adlai E. Stevenson

Communism with its goal of economic justice and a classless society and its dogma of class struggle and the dictatorship of the proletariat, permitted the Soviet Party-State to rationalize totalitarianism -- total power over all the people and every aspect of society. The implementation was so different from the theory that if Karl Marx had ever visited the Soviet Union built by Josef Stalin, he would have proclaimed, "I'm not a Marxist!"

One cannot understand Russian policies without being aware of **geography**. Russia is a very large continental land mass, but with a key element in that it had no natural frontiers. There are no significant physical features as one goes from Moscow out across the Central European plain. The central region was indefensible, so the frontiers ebbed and flowed according to the power of the central government.

Lack of easily defended frontiers left the country vulnerable to attack and also encouraged the Russians to expand for security. The Muscovites expanded from the region around the city of Moscow to the natural boundaries of the Arctic and Pacific Oceans and in all other directions where they either subdued or fought with their neighbors.

This imperial foreign policy required centralization of control and unity of effort which Czarist Russia accomplished fairly well despite a vast area and a large population. The USSR, which had to rebuild the old Russian empire, was a conglomeration.

It was made up of 15 republics, 20 autonomous republics, 6 krays, 123 oblasts, 8 autonomous oblasts, and 10 autonomous okrugs. It was not a nation state but a patchwork of something like sixty nationalities with 169 ethnic groups and over 200 languages.

About one fourth of the people were non-Slav, mostly Asiatic. Only about half the population was Russian. Most of the Asiatic Republics are Muslim. This vast area covers about one sixth of the land surface of the world and spans 11 time zones.

## Extended Empire

There was also the extended empire of states over which Moscow exerted varying degrees of control or influence, the main part of which was Eastern Europe, but the Kremlin also played significant roles in Outer Mongolia and North Korea.

Rather than incorporate these "colonies" directly into the Soviet Union, Stalin elected to try to establish puppet regimes that, hopefully, he could control. So he created a satellite empire of legally separate entities but under the aegis of Moscow's influence by the presence or threat of Soviet military forces, the insidious role of the Communist Parties, totalitarian controls, and unequal economic arrangements.

Finland was permitted to remain independent, provided that it pursued "correct" policies. The Yugoslav problem was different in that Tito was a loyal Communist but felt Yugoslavia's needs were different from Russia's and did not bow to Stalin. Yugoslavia was expelled from the Cominform in June 1948.

One year after the war, Albania, Bulgaria, Czechoslovakia, and Yugoslavia had Communist prime ministers. Peasant Party leaders held the position in Hungary and Romania, socialists in Finland and Poland. All had coalition governments with only Helsinki and Prague showing any true distribution of power. The Communists did poorly in the July 1948 Finnish elections and were omitted from the government. However, Communist control grew elsewhere during 1947-48.

Stalin molded each satellite to a general pattern to align them as closely as possible with the Soviet Union by all means short of incorporation. They were to be People's Democracies but not Soviet Republics.

In terms of building an empire, Stalin's political control by means of **puppet regimes**, was only the beginning. He then embarked on **economic exploitation** and **Russification**. He worked to make the satellites economically dependent on the USSR and to make sure they did not have balanced economies. Trade treaties were implaced so that arms were sold to the satellites in return for goods at favorable prices to the USSR, so it was difficult for the satellites to get out of debt.

The satellite economies were counted as sources and markets for Soviet planning and specific Soviet requirements were "tasked" to particular satellites. The major industries of the satellites were placed under Soviet-controlled binational corporations with strong Soviet financial controls. Managers, advisors, and experts were assigned by Moscow to control key industries in the satellites as well as all the agencies overseeing political reliability and efficiency of workers and managers. Finally, Moscow controlled their trade with the outside world and was the main buyer, seller, broker, and clearing house for all of the Soviet Empire.

Stalin tried to force as much Russian cultural change as he could. Russian was required in language training and there was an enormous amount of propaganda of all forms emanating from Moscow into the initially controlled media. Also, much of the history was rewritten, particularly to emphasize the role of Russia in liberating the peoples in the area.

Tito survived his dispute with Moscow because he had genuine national roots, unlike many Communist leaders who had lived longer in Russia than their native lands. He was the war leader who had successfully fought the Germans and the Italians, and he was able to offset the Communist economic blockade by Western aid.

Perhaps most important, Yugoslavia had no frontier with Russia. Many other puppet leaders who displayed any independence were not so successful and there were purges, trials, "confessions," and executions.

New systems were created for Communist integration for economic assimilation and military coordination. These measures were not fully developed until after Stalin's death but they eventually changed the relations between the Soviet Union and its satellites.

The Council for Mutual Economic Assistance -- known as **COMECON** -- was created in January 1949 to offset the Marshall Plan. Bulgaria, Czechoslovakia, Hungary, Poland, Romania, and the Soviet Union were the founders, quickly joined by Albania and a year later by East Germany. The members were sovereign states in form because the Communist propaganda then was attacking the Marshall Plan as a US means of usurping European sovereignty.

However, there was no question of sovereignty in COMECON as the USSR dominated it. It was basically an anti-US device of Russian foreign policy and lay dormant for ten years. After 1956, twelve regular commissions were set up in various capitals, China and Yugoslavia were granted observer status, a constitution was in place by 1960, an international executive in 1962, and there were regular meetings of these groups.

After the 1956 revolt in Hungary, COMECON organized financial and material assistance. Joint planning and investment efforts grew and there was broader multilateral cooperation such as for power distribution and pipeline construction.

The Soviets controlled the satellite military forces by officers who had been trained in Russia and were trustworthy. Marshal Rokossovski's assignment in Warsaw as Minister of Defense was a very public move but there were many similar assignments of Russian officers at lower levels. A military coordinating committee was established in 1952 under Marshal Bulganin as chairman and a combined general staff was created under a Russian general with headquarters in Cracow.

Numerous military facilities were installed in the satellites. At that time, the satellites were providing about 1,500,000 men to military and security forces with an accompanying financial cost, plus they had to totally align their industrial capacities and their economic planning to the military needs of the Communist bloc as defined by Moscow.

There was no formal defense treaty until West Germany's entry into NATO led to the formation of the **Warsaw Pact** in May 1955 which claimed to be a regional defense agreement under Article 52 of the UN Charter. It was essentially a formalization of existing arrangements with little new except it did establish joint organizations in Moscow. However, it introduced, like COMECON, the concept of cooperation which was in increasing demand by the satellites and later gave Moscow a means for altering relations when they were under pressure.

Unrest grew in the satellites and there were problems in all of them but particularly acute crises in Hungary and Czechoslovakia which resulted in Soviet invasions.

For years, we considered Communism to be monolithic. Of great significance was the Sino-Soviet split which evolved in the late fifties. Mao conducted a long revolution and did not feel beholden to Moscow. Khrushchev conducted public campaigns against the Chinese and this disturbed the satellites when he tried to make them take sides. These disagreements grew until China became an outright opponent of the USSR.

## Peripheral States

There were several other states that were beholden to the Soviet Union to varying degrees. Outer Mongolia had been in the Russian sphere since 1921 and was yielded to Russia by the Allies at Yalta. It was a point of contention with China but Russia maintained control over it. The Soviets were designated to accept the Japanese surrender in Korea above the 38th parallel. Thus was born the Communist regime in the North where Stalin installed Kim Il Sung. Stalin also removed much Japanese industrial equipment from Manchuria after the war, much to Chinese disgust.

The Suez invasion of 1956 permitted the Soviets to move into the **Middle East**. Nasser's Egypt did not become a full satellite but was supportive of Moscow until Sadat ejected them before the 1973 War. Iraq became closely aligned with the Soviet Union and remained so until the end. Syria and Egypt later split the United Arab Republic and Syria maintained close ties with the Soviets.

The Russians were interested in South Yemen because of the base of **Aden** which was key to the entrance to the Red Sea and the Horn of Africa. Eventually there developed a republic in North Yemen and a Communist regime in the People's Democratic Republic of Yemen (or South Yemen).

The Russians supported the regime in **Somalia,** then in one of the more bizarre events of the Cold War, after the revolution in **Ethiopia** which ended the rule of Haile Selassie, Ethiopia left the American camp and joined the Soviet side. Somalia made the opposite shift.

On the other side of Africa, both China and the Soviet Union became involved in **Angola**, each supporting a different faction. A new player entered that scene when Cuba sent troops there to fight as proxies for the Soviets.

Castro took over **Cuba** in 1959 and pronounced himself a Communist. He became almost totally dependent on Moscow and was a part of the Soviet Empire even though far away. Confrontation with the US came early on during the missile crisis of 1962 which brought the superpowers to the brink of nuclear war. Castro remained in the Communist camp and was one of those who suffered the most when the Soviet Union collapsed and ended its support.

The Soviets intervened in **Afghanistan** in 1979 which

turned into a quagmire of religious fundamentalists of various factions and the West returned the favor of Viet-Nam and provided military aid to the rebels. The Soviets pulled out as the Soviet Union was crumbling in 1989.

That was the conglomeration of republics, satellites, and other states with varying degrees of subservience to Moscow with its massive nuclear arsenal, missiles deployed in Eastern Europe, naval forces in the major seas including missile submarines patrolling off American coasts, and supporting subversion throughout the Third World that President Ronald Reagan referred to in 1983 as **the Evil Empire.**

## THE END OF EMPIRE - THE SOVIET DISUNION

The Cold War had gone on for so long and become so much a part of the world situation that when the Soviet Union started to disintegrate, the world in general was caught by surprise and truly amazed at the speed of these spectacular events. The threat of nuclear war had abated, mainly due to the maturity of the superpowers and their respect for the devastating power they controlled.  Leaders on both sides concluded that they could not win a nuclear war even though they continued to build more of these awesome weapons, always fearful of losing an advantage.

US-Soviet relations had gone up and down.  There was a partial nuclear test ban treaty in 1963, the non-proliferation treaty signed in 1968 and SALT 1 (Strategic Arms Limitation Treaty) in 1972 and SALT 2 in 1979 (and five months later the Russians invaded Afghanistan).  There was still the occasional confrontation.  The key event, however, was the rise to power of Mikhail Sergeyevich Gorbachev in March 1985.

| *A state that deserved to die* | -- Strobe Talbot |
| --- | --- |

Richard Nixon, the supreme anti-Communist who had the famous "kitchen debate" with Khrushchev in Moscow when he was Vice President, led the way with the continued hard line toward the Communists.  However, he developed pragmatic policies and pursued détente and talks toward arms control.  He persisted in the long, difficult SALT negotiations and opened the door to China.

After the drawdown from the Viet-Nam War, Jimmy Carter started rebuilding the US military and started the planning to send US missiles to Europe in response to the Soviet deployment of SS-20 nuclear missiles. He also supported the Afghan guerrillas in their war against the Soviets and urged Moscow to respect human rights within the Soviet Empire.

Ronald Reagan had to deal first with Leonid Brezhnev who was ill and died in 1982 and was replaced by Yuri Andropov, the KGB chief who was a hardliner but who knew the system needed reform and evidently wanted a new détente with Washington, but he died after only 15 months. He was followed by Konstantin Chernenko who lasted only 13 months in power. Reagan was frustrated and complained that he could not work with Soviet leaders because they kept dying on him.

## The Great Arms Race

The Cold War grew into an extremely expensive business. The modern implements of war became astronomically costly. The Soviets basically stayed on a war footing after World War II and continued to emphasize development of their heavy industry over consumer production. The US, with its booming economy, was able to provide both guns and butter with less dislocation in what became a 45-year arms race.

The US felt its atomic advantage was adequate deterrence from any Soviet adventures after the war and did little rearming until the expansion for the Korean War. In an effort to preclude fighting another war like Korea, the US announced a policy of **massive retaliation** directly on the Soviet Union in the event of another proxy war against the Free World.

There followed years of buildup of large missiles which led to a degree of parity, a rather academic concept in the age of **mutual assured destruction,** an assumption that either side could absorb a first strike attack and still have adequate forces survive to conduct a fatal second strike on the opponent.

The arms buildups of both the US and the USSR peaked in the mid-1980s and there were internal pressures to reduce expenditures. The Soviets, by their totalitarian control over their people, had been able to continue their military production, but it became increasingly clear that, even though the USSR was a nuclear superpower, economically it was a Third World country. The arms race had also become an economic competition and the Soviet economy was not up to it.

## Cold War Resurgence

The late 1970s had shown real progress in East-West relations. The Viet-Nam War was over, Mao had died, and the US and China had established diplomatic relations, China and Japan had signed a peace treaty and Jimmy Carter and Brezhnev had signed SALT 2. However, in 1979, China invaded Viet-Nam, the Communist-backed Sandinistas overthrew the Somoza government in Nicaragua, and the Soviets invaded Afghanistan.

In 1980, Iraq invaded Iran, there were strikes in Poland, and Ronald Reagan won the presidency and pursued a hard line against the Soviets. Superpower relations plummeted after Reagan's denunciation of the USSR in his "evil empire" speech on 8 March 1983. Reagan initiated his Star Wars program and deployed *Pershing II* nuclear missiles to Western Europe, and the Soviets shot down a Korean airliner which had strayed over Russian territory killing all 269 aboard.

The Soviets conducted a vicious propaganda campaign against the deployment of the US medium-range *Pershing II* missiles to Europe even though they had initiated the escalation by introducing the SS-20s, a triple-warhead mobile missile, in Eastern Europe in 1977, Also the US invaded Grenada to oust a Marxist government. There were even rumors spreading in Moscow of war with the United States.

1984 saw Reagan pressuring the Soviets in regional conflicts by supporting the Contras in Nicaragua, the *mujahedin* in Afghanistan, and other anti-Communist groups. Relations began to improve with Chernenko, but the real break came when Gorbachev took over in March 1985.

## The Walls Came Tumbling Down

Relations warmed in the late 1980s as Gorbachev called for *glasnost* (new openings) and political reforms. The Americans and the Soviets signed the INF Treaty to eliminate intermediate range missiles. Then the Soviet troops started withdrawing from Afghanistan and Reagan made a successful summit visit to Moscow. British Prime Minister Margaret

Thatcher proclaimed, "**The Cold War is over.**"
The **Tiananmen Square** massacre got 1989 off to a blazing start for a momentous year. The feelings were rising though and the infamous **Berlin Wall** came down in November and people were dancing in the streets. The barriers to the West collapsed. The Czech parliament announced the end of Communist dictatorship and called for free elections. Shortly thereafter, Ceaucescu's Communist regime in Romania was ousted.

Moscow did not move to intervene. By January, the Communist Parties in Bulgaria and Yugoslavia had lost their monopolies. In February, the Communist Party in Poland dissolved followed in March by the end of the monopoly of the mother of them all the Communist Party of the Soviet Union. East and West Germany reunited into the German state in October.

There was a conventional forces agreement in November and then the Warsaw Pact itself was dissolved in July 1991 as well as COMECON. President George Bush announced in September the removal of all land-based tactical nuclear weapons from Europe and sea-based nuclear cruise missiles and took the Strategic Air Command (SAC) off alert for the first time in decades. Gorbachev took similar actions.

The policies that Gorbachev introduced set new trends in motion. *Glasnost* was bound to open up old questions such as Russian domination of the Communist Party and all the republics and the forced use of the Russian language in official work, newspapers, and schools. The republics quickly attacked this Russian cultural imperialism. *Perestroika,* or restructuring, was eagerly awaited but it never came.

With the satellites gone, the fever burned in the Soviet Empire itself. Azerbaijan declared its sovereignty in September 1989. Most of the other Republics made similar declarations in 1990. Estonia, Latvia, and Lithuania announced their independence from the USSR followed by Byelorussia, Ukraine, and Georgia and then Moldavia

Gorbachev struggled to hold his empire together fighting for his idea of a Union of Sovereign States. But there were no takers. Gorbachev and Russian President Boris Yeltsin agreed there could be no union of any type without Ukraine.

Finally the Presidents of Russia, Ukraine, and Byelorussia (the slavic core and founding republics in 1922 of the old union) met outside Brest on **7 December 1991** for a last try.    Evidently they had not planned to end the old union and form a new grouping, however, after unsuccessful talks, they pronounced the death certificate:

> **"The Union of Soviet Socialist Republics, as a subject of international law and a geopolitical reality, is ceasing its existence."**

They also announced the formation of a new Commonwealth of Independent States.

On Christmas Day (ironic for the atheist state), Mikhail Gorbachev resigned as President of the Union of Soviet Socialist Republics which was disbanded and the hammer and sickle was lowered and the old Russian white, blue, and red tricolor rose over the Kremlin.

An empire died.   But it had been dying for months and was generally referred to as the "former Soviet Union." Nevertheless the speed of its fall was spectacular. Never had we seen a powerful government disintegrate so rapidly. Normally empires fall in war or if they overextend themselves. The Soviet Union imploded.

---

*I could have lived like an emperor for 10 years and not given a damn about what happened after me.  Is there another case in history when a man, having acquired so much power, has given it up?*

-- Mikhail Gorbachev

---

Mikhail Gorbachev is the most important man of the second half of the 20th Century.  In his 6 1/2 years in power, he changed the world.   Not all the changes were intentional; he certainly did not want to destroy the USSR.  But he ended the Cold War, the most dangerous in history, and he liberated the external empire and his own people from Communist tyranny and the most brutal totalitarian system ever devised.

### Significance to the World

The Soviet Union and the Communist ideology were so pervasive that they reached into every corner of the world. Communism was not based on the nation state but on class struggle and saw as its mission the reorientation of all the working people in the world. The Utopian aspects of the ideology were soon discarded under the totalitarian boot. In place of the former USSR, we now had 15 foreign policies, four nuclear powers, and quite a few hot spots both internal and some on international frontiers.

The immediate effect of the collapse of the Soviet Union was the liberation of the "colonies" in Eastern Europe permitting them to try to get back on the road to recovery from World War II that was interrupted by nearly forty years of Moscow's dominating influence. There were unresolved differences and problems between some of the Eastern European countries and the former Soviet Union, including border disputes and residual industrial and pollution problems of the years of occupation.

The key element in attempting to spread Communism around the world was the Communist parties in each country which Moscow tried to control. This eventually failed with the defection of Tito in Yugoslavia and the Sino-Soviet split; however, most of the parties around the world took their ideological guidance from Moscow and received significant financial support in return.

The discrediting of Communism led to most of the parties running away from the word "Communist." They quickly changed their names. The harsher reality was that they no longer had a power base and most of them disappeared. The few exceptions were in Cuba and Asia and they experienced enormous problems. The Communist movement, except for those few diehards, basically died.

The great collapse was also an enormous shock to the clients of the Soviet Union which had depended on it for foreign aid. With the Cold War over, the global network of regimes that the Kremlin had built friendly relations with since the 1950s was dismantled. Support ended for Afghanistan, Iraq, Syria, Nicaragua, India, Ethiopia, Angola, Cuba, North Korea, and Viet-Nam. Centralized world Communism and its support for its allies were dead.

The Free World had spent a great part of its fortune to attain this great day; now what did it mean? The Cold War with its threat of a nuclear Armageddon was finally over and the great ideological war of Communism against Freedom was also over. But from there on, it was not too clear.

The end of the Cold War removed most of the rationale

for the major military forces of the West and their alliances, deployments, and base agreements worldwide which had been created to contain the Communist threat. With the evil empire gone, who was the enemy now?

For the foreseeable future, the military forces of the West would have to be ready for contingency operations against various undefined threats. These ranged from fairly large military commitments such as in Iraq to dealing with terrorists or supporting UN peacekeeping operations.

Also, in this new order, it would be hard for non-aligned states to bargain for advantage between East and West. The "losers" of the Cold War were the poor countries that did not receive any more foreign aid.

The first confusion was the US relationship with Russia and the republics. Were they enemies or friends, even allies? The Americans, despite their own economic problems, provided aid to Russia. The tricky questions were not how much aid, but what kinds and where and to whom to release it to gain the best return.

The joy of the end of the Cold War led to great hopes that there was going to be a peace dividend, money that could now be used to address the problems of the environment, the homeless, medicine, in other words, more humane uses for the money. The sad answer in the first few years after the end of the Cold War was that there was **no peace dividend**.

The important problems on the international scene and world politics will be fundamentally different for the future. Russia will not disappear, and its interests in Europe, Asia, and around the world will reemerge. Russia is a great nation with talented and resourceful people and much natural wealth. She was able to find a Mikhail Gorbachev when she needed him most and therefore should be able to produce others who can build a new future for Russia.

With the subsiding of ideological battles, we saw long-suppressed ethnic, religious, and tribal or clan conflicts reappear. Even without the Cold War, the world was still a turbulent and dangerous place. The Cold War had provided a degree of stability, even if it was accompanied by a balance of terror.

Regardless, no tears should be shed for the death of the Union of Soviet Socialist Republics, a regime that was based on imperialism and totalitarianism, a regime based on fear, a regime based on contempt for the rights of the individual, a regime that killed millions of its own people in the purges, famines, and the collectivization program, a regime that wanted and tried to instill its outdated and inefficient system on the rest of the world.

Karl Marx had it all wrong except for the key role of economics in politics. America and its allies spent trillions of dollars ($2 trillion in the last decade for defense alone in the US) in the Cold War to keep the USSR from destroying the world. A fraction of that amount would keep the new grouping from tearing itself apart or perhaps returning to old ways. The new Commonwealth of Independent States will require outside aid, both money and technology, if there is to be any hope for political stability during this difficult transition.

## THE POST-SOVIET TRANSITION AND ITS EFFECTS

The world was very much in transition after a bipolar Cold War and the evolution of a still undefined new world order. The key to that transition was what happened to the Union of Soviet Socialist Republics.

### The Commonwealth of Independent States

The USSR had been built by Lenin and Stalin with each of the republics a dependent part of the Union but not organized to stand alone. They were tied to each other by the central planning system of quotas and directed markets. That left them specialized in certain areas and totally lacking in others.

The system collapsed. America announced that US Air Force planes would start flying food into Moscow, St. Petersburg (changed back from Leningrad -- many names changed as we will try to note as we go along), and other cities.

The three republics that set up the CIS agreed to try to stop the drift toward economic war. They agreed to coordinate radical economic reforms for free enterprise and to maintain the ruble as the common currency at least for the near term. They decided to let prices float and to introduce a value added tax. Obviously, that was a lot and the details were not worked out in one night so they were to be added later.

These leaders were trying to stop the slide toward anarchy and create some way to start a semblance of reintegration. They agreed to cooperation in many areas of government from security to education to foreign policy. They called for equal rights to be guaranteed to their citizens and to respect each republic's territorial integrity, no small matter when they were facing war among the various ethnic minorities. They also agreed to try to liquidate all nuclear weapons under strict international control.

Kazakhstan (about 40% ethnic Russians who might have rebelled against an independent Muslim state) and the other Central Asian republics (which simply could not survive on their own economically) quickly joined the CIS at another signing session in Alma Ata (also seen as Almaty). Except for the Baltic states which had already gone their own way in September, the remaining former Soviet republics joined except for Georgia which was under siege (Georgia did join later in exchange for Russian help).

Thus the CIS replaced the USSR but it was nothing like the old union. To accentuate that it was not a new Russian empire, the offices to coordinate CIS policies were to be set up in Mensk (new spelling for Minsk), a bland city in Byelorussia, rather than the traditional Moscow. (However Yeltsin moved CIS headquarters to Moscow in February 1995.)

Coordination of such a conglomeration was not going to be easy. There were too many grudges borne from years gone by, too many old scores to settle, and too many miserable problems that had never been resolved.

### The Infancy

The death of Communism liberated factory managers from the tyranny of the central planners, but they also lost their secure and predictable economic environment. Although freed from the five-year plan, they were deprived of that key capitalist tool, a reliable monetary system.

The government lost control of the monetary supply around 1988 and the central bank wildly printed money with little restriction thereafter. The Soviet debt skyrocketed to 800 billion rubles, 15-20% of their Gross National Product or about four times the American level.

The result was the beginnings of a trade war. Newly independent states and many members of the CIS resorted to economic nationalism and protectionism to protect their peoples from deepening economic chaos. They turned to export quotas, customs controls, and national currencies.

Trade slumped and the once specialized economies of each state refused to buy each other's shoddy goods and COMECON closed its doors.

The horde of central planners faded away, but unfortunately they were replaced by a new group of local bureaucrats and customs officials. For 1992, the effects were painful: 2,500% inflation, 19% drop in Gross Domestic Product, and increased unemployment. The US and the West tried to help.

Inflation was raging, the government was so unstable and weak that it was unable to collect the taxes, there were very few managers knowledgeable in modern business methods, and even though it had made great efforts in space projects, it was somewhat primitive at home where basic commodities were absent or in short supply and many hospitals lacked even bandages and aspirin. Food prices outstripped wage hikes and nutritional levels dropped and disease rates climbed.

The brutal social experiment of collective farming was plowed under. The USSR, which had been an exporter of food, was spending billions of dollars on imports. In January 1992, Yeltsin offered 25 hectares (about 62 acres) for people to start private farms. The numbers increased dramatically. As we recall, the private plots of the Soviet era outproduced the state farms. The problem was 70 years of taking orders with no creativity and total destruction of the concept of private property. It will take time to change that legacy.

The country was woefully unprepared for the economic revolution underway. People were talking about "privitization," "free markets," and "liberalizing prices," but few had any idea what they mean. After 70 years with no one in the country who really knew or understood free enterprise, it was difficult to attract investment from abroad when the basic laws and protections for business were not there.

A few billion dollars were not going to solve these problems. The Germans had estimated that it would take $100 billion per year for a decade to bring the former East Germany up to 75% of the living standards of West Germany. The population of Russia is about 10 times that of East Germany and is much less developed. A straight line projection, $1 trillion per year for years, was so enormous that Western leaders did not want to even contemplate it.

There was much pessimism but the alternative of the

nuclear armed former USSR returning to authoritarian control and a renewal of the Cold War kept the West searching for ways to help.  Russia needed to join the Western market system; for that it needed access; for that trade to flow, the tax and legal codes required reforms to assure foreign businessmen they could make money and repatriate profits.

Yeltsin had a major problem with the old Russian parliament and the conflict came to a head when Yeltsin called in the tanks and burned the White House ending the revolt by the parliament and putting the leaders in jail.

There was some regret and some people were doing poorly; salaries had risen 1,300% but inflation was 2,500%.  But some Russians were happy with Yeltsin's free-market reforms which had created a new class of entrepreneurs (plus hucksters and criminals).   Although everything was more expensive and there was more crime, there was a good side: there was more food in the stores, Western consumer goods were widely available, there were more jobs in the high-paying private sector, there were no restrictions on foreign travel, and the Communist Party was no longer in power.

## A New Russian Empire?

As the old Soviet Union fell apart, many of the pieces were picked up by the Russian Federal Republic.  This was not surprising since Russia was the largest republic by far in both land and population (147.4 million) and the major part of the Soviet economy.  The Soviet Empire was in most ways really the Russian Empire; it was dominated by Russia and Russians.

In fact however, Russia was less prepared to be independent than the other republics.  Since Moscow was the capital of the Soviet Union and Russia, many of the bureaus of government were not duplicated for Russia but controlled directly by the central government.  The governments of most of the republics were larger than Russia's which controlled only agriculture, its budget, education, law, etc.  There was not even a separate KGB office for Russia as there was in each of the other republics.

Yeltsin solved that problem by taking over numerous ministries and industries from the Soviet government plus the property of the Soviet Communist Party within Russia, the KGB, and the Kremlin itself.  Not surprisingly, other republics followed suit and seized union property in their areas.

However, when Yeltsin acted as a Russian nationalist and reserved the right to challenge existing borders by claiming the coal-rich areas of the Crimea and the ethnic Russian areas of neighboring republics, he quickly alienated the leaders of the other republics, particularly Ukraine and Kazakhstan.

When Yeltsin's State Secretary insisted that Russia should be the "successor state" to the old Soviet Union, that intensified the fear of the other republics of being absorbed into a new Russian Empire. Yeltsin spent the next couple months repairing the damage from such incidents that had strained the relations with the other republics. He finally reached agreement with them that existing borders were inviolable but many of their suspicions of Yeltsin lingered.

> *Boris Yeltsin bluntly warned the Estonians not to misinterpret "Russia's goodwill." Moscow, he pointed out, had "ways of reminding them" of geopolitical realities.*
>
> -- July 1993

With the fall of the old Soviet Union, Russia inherited the permanent seat in the UN Security Council, most of the nuclear arsenal, the large army of the former superpower (and the obligation to feed it), plus thousands of international obligations including the largest part of the foreign debt. Soviet military industry was mainly on Russian soil but now it had little to offer to its neighbors.

The **Russian Federal Republic** was smaller than Russia under Peter the Great (who died in 1725). The region around **Kiev** was the "land of the Rus" which is considered the historic heartland of Russia and Kievan Russia was the first Russian state. That area is now in the Ukraine as well as Belarus (the new name for Byelorussia) which had no history of independent statehood.

The other "Russian" area was the **Crimea** which, after the centuries of wars with the Ottoman Empire, Russia had annexed from Turkey at the end of the 18th Century the Black Sea coast including Odessa and the Crimea (that drive to warm water ports). Without the Black Sea and Baltic Sea ports, Russia has limited sea trade with the rest of the world. Russia has been cut off from direct contact with the rest of Europe; all the railroads to Western Europe go through the Baltic states, Belarus, Ukraine, and Moldova (new name for Moldavia).

The crowning blow to Yeltsin came from the referendum in the Ukraine when Russians in the Ukraine voted for independence with the Ukraine. Thus failed the Russian plan to gain real control over the former Soviet Union.

There will be continued problems. For example, republics within the Russian Republic also press for independence. Tatarstan and Bashkiria, which are the heart of the Soviet petrochemical industry, located southeast of Moscow, have larger ethnic minorities and longer histories of pre-Russian statehood than Moldova. There is a question of logic then in having granted commonwealth status to Moldova and not to Tatarstan and Bashkortostan. Incidentally, the Supreme Soviet of Tatarstan had already declared itself a member of the CIS.

It is difficult for a loose confederation to function. It did not take a week for the first major problem. Yeltsin had assured the Soviet military leaders that the military would remain under unified command. Then President Kravchuk of Ukraine announced that all military units (except those controlling the nuclear weapons -- he moved on them later) and the Soviet Black Sea fleet were now the Ukrainian army and navy under his command. The whole subject of the nuclear forces was complicated because they are deployed in four republics: Russia, Belarus, Ukraine, and Kazakhstan.

It appears inevitable that Moscow will attempt to rebuild some form of central authority. In February 1995, Yeltsin was elected Chairman of the CIS, moved it to Moscow, and a senior Russian minister was charged with working out the details of economic union. Also the members signed a collective security agreement and discussed a joint air defense system to be managed by Moscow.

The members of the CIS have declared themselves equals, but Russia will clearly be the *primus inter pares* in whatever the CIS does. Russia will be a great power for the indefinite future. It is unlikely to be a superpower, but it will continue as a great military power and a major part of the world strategic balance.

Economic problems consume the republic leaders for now, but as foreign policy and security matters resurface, there will be a tendency for Russia to try to lead. If the republics are not able to cooperate and develop common policies, the CIS may have a short life.

## The Future of the CIS

The United States and many other countries quickly recognized the 15 former republics of the old Soviet Union as independent countries. There was little agreement on joint efforts as there was always the lingering fear of a return to Russian domination. The fighting or threat of fighting between the ethnic minorities in the republics was the greatest cause for unrest.

## Russia

Many of the internal republics in the Russian republic want more autonomy or independence. It is important to recall that Russia is a very large country with 89 provinces and republics, most of which are ethnic. If they became independent, the map of Russia would look like a piece of Swiss cheese.

In addition to the autonomy desires of the Tartar and Bashkir Republics, and the Chechens and the Cossacks, there was unrest in the North Ossetia region in the Caucasus Mountains of southern Russia, and in Yakutia in the Far East.

Russia is 82% ethnic Russians but the 18% minorities often are not happy with Russian domination. Another problem is the nearly 24 million ethnic Russians who were urged or forced to move to the other republics and now live in foreign countries.

When any of these minority groups of Russians is slighted or mistreated by the new states, there is pressure on Moscow to come to their rescue. Any intervention by Moscow is seen by the new states as resurrection of the old Russian Empire.

Russia is rich in resources but weak in effective government and the managerial force required to move it into a free-market economy. It was still difficult to make and implement the reforms needed. As Harvard Sovietologist Marshall Goldman said, "Russia is not Poland; it is not a Western country. It is a country riveted in the past. This is a society that doesn't lend itself to immediate solutions."

Therefore, it would not be surprising if a supernationalist, xenophobic, autocratic Russian dictator emerges to try to recreate an inward-looking, new imperial Russia.

> *They want a good czar to put things in order.*
> -- Moscow journalist

If Russia can survive until a new managerial class is developed, it could slowly move forward as a modern state. That "if" is critical because the country has a history of authoritarian leaders and no history of democratic philosophy or institutions. It will take a major effort by the Russian people themselves as well as any help the West can provide to try to keep Russia oriented on democracy while it goes through this painful period of transition.

## Belarus and Ukraine

These two republics had a special place in the USSR as they had in Russian history. They were the leading edge in contacts with Eastern Europe and around the Black Sea and Stalin adjusted their boundaries as he pushed to the West, particularly in Poland. Also, at the time of the formation of the UN in 1945, Stalin insisted on and received membership for Byelorussia and Ukraine.

Since these were the forward parts of the Empire, nuclear weapons were deployed there both for defense and to extend the maximum ranges. The possession of these weapons became the key to their successes as they quickly learned how to use them politically.

Both were blessed with resources and had developed higher standards of living than in Russia.  But it was the nuclear weapons that made them important.  The weapons in Eastern Europe were all under Soviet control and could be removed.  However, the systems deployed in Belarus and Ukraine could not be easily moved so they stayed with the new states at independence.

At first, both agreed that all the weapons would be destroyed, but it soon became clear that the US was very interested in them, but really only for that one reason.  It did not take long for them to play their trump card.  They delayed destroying weapons or agreeing to START 2 or other agreements.

In addition to taking over the strategic weapons, Ukraine also took over the Soviet Black Sea Fleet which was the heart of the Soviet Navy.  That caused immediate consternation for Yeltsin. With a 300,000-man army, its own currency, customs officials, etc., Ukraine appeared determined to be a modern nation state.

President Kravchuk made a deal with Yeltsin to sell the Ukraine's share of the Black Sea Fleet and relinquish its nuclear warheads to Russia in return for forgiveness of its multi-billion dollar trade debt. The deal stirred up considerable opposition in the Ukraine.

These two states are capable of surviving independently. The key is the relationship with Russia. Russia probably will feel that it has to have at least a strong relationship with these two because of their positions on the European and Black Sea fronts.

Russia can probably tolerate the CIS as long as these two stick with Russia. If they go their own ways, there will be heavy pressure in Moscow to bring them back into the "fold."

## Moldova

Fighting broke out in the Trans-Dniester region of Moldavia as the old USSR died in December 1991. The nationalist government, which had a strong Romanian majority, had been in power two years and had made the Romanian language mandatory.

This upset the mainly ethnic Russians and Ukrainians in the **Trans-Dniester**, a strip of land of 600,000 people in eastern Moldavia next to the Ukraine, which had proclaimed itself a separate republic the previous year and now voted to secede. Their concern was that Moldavia would unite with Romania, which had controlled all of the country, except Trans-Dniester, before World War II.

President Mircea Snegur declared a state of emergency in March 1992 after continued fighting in the breakaway Trans-Dniester republic. The area is valuable to Moldova due to its relatively advanced industrial base and because it supplies most of Moldova's electricity. Trans-Dniester President Igor Smirnov raised his own militia of over 11,000 volunteers, mainly Russian and Ukrainian Cossacks.

To add to Snegur's problems, another separatist group, the Turkic-speaking Christian minority in Gagauz in the south reacted by declaring its own emergency and threatening to retaliate to any Moldovan attack. In August 1993, the parliament failed to ratify membership and Moldova left the

CIS. Moldova is a candidate for fragmentation or assimilation into other states. The concept of inviolability of borders is good but mainly to protect the status quo. Moldova will remain independent only if the countries around it want it to be.

## The Caucasus

The Caucasus Mountains include Armenia, Azerbaijan, Georgia, and parts of southern Russia (including Karachai-Cherkess and Kabardin-Balkhar which wanted to separate, Chechen-Ingush which separated and Chechnya declared its independence in 1991, and South Ossetia in Georgia which wanted to join Russia). The region had some of the worst ethnic fighting in the old USSR.

Georgia, like the Baltic states, refused to join the CIS. At the time of the creation of the CIS, the President of Georgia was under siege from the opposition which was trying to oust him. They were successful in January 1992 but they left their capital, Tbilisi, a shambles. Eventually former Soviet Foreign Minister Eduard A. Shevardnadze returned to his native land to lead the country.

In August 1992, the western province of Abkhazia, a tiny mountainous strip of land, a former resort area, between the Black Sea and the Caucasus Mountains declared its sovereignty. Shevardnadze sent troops in and they battled for a year with over 2,000 people killed. Numerous peace accords failed but a ceasefire was reached in August 1993 and UN military observers were sent in to monitor the withdrawal of all troops and help reestablish civilian government. This was the first significant UN contingent to arrive in the former USSR.

Georgia's entire cabinet resigned on 6 August after parliament refused to approve the national budget and the country was on the brink of disintegration. Most of Abkhazia fell to the rebels and the former president opened a new front by attacking the port of Poti. Shevardnadze took Georgia into the CIS and asked Yeltsin for peacekeeping forces even though he had accused the Russians of supporting the rebels.

Moscow had claimed to be neutral in the civil war but evidently Russia supplied weapons, intelligence, and operational military support to the Abkhazi separatists. The US became involved when it deployed US Army Special Forces to Georgia as security advisors.

A CIA representative, Fred Woodruff, who was sent to

provide anti-terrorist training to top Georgian officials, was assassinated in August 1993. The US offered "good offices" to ex-Soviet republics in settling disputes with their neighbors. Georgia's neighbors, **Azerbaijan** and **Armenia** had been fighting for over five years. They battled over another residual of the Soviet Empire. The enclave of **Nagorno-Karabakh** was predominantly Armenian Christians and was totally within Muslim Azerbaijan. The fighting had cost 15,000 lives and there were about a million refugees, including hundreds of thousands in Baku, capital of Azerbaijan.

Armenia, next door to Turkey, which was no friend due to their own historical hatred, a landlocked country with its trade routes cut off, factories closed down for lack of fuel, and with food and medicines scarce, was facing economic disaster.

The Caucasus had maintained their martial reputation from over the Centuries. Russian forces attacked **Chechnya** in December 1994. This Muslim area was known for its bitter feuds and hatred of Russians. The fighting went poorly for the Russian Army and television coverage only added to Moscow's problems. Despite heavy attacks, the Chechens were not subdued.

The key element was what role the former Soviet army would play. If Russian troops were successful in establishing peace in any of the republics, it would strengthen Yeltsin's hand and the role of Russia. There appeared to be no near term solution to the disputes and there was little the CIS could do to help.

Azerbaijan has oil so that assures it at least some opportunity if it is not too badly diverted by internal fighting. Armenia seemed to be waiting to see if the Europeans planned to play any significant role in the area.

## Central Asia

**Kazakhstan** was like Belarus and Ukraine in that it had nuclear weapons on its soil. But Kazakhstan is much different: four times the size of Texas with vast natural resources that were exploited by the Kremlin for decades, it was one of only four republics, along with Russia, Armenia, and Turkmenistan, that did not declare independence from the USSR.

Many years under Stalin's purges and deportations taught them to be cautious. The area was so diverse that there was no real sense of nationhood and so vast that it could not fight to secure its borders.  It needed Moscow; only 3% of its exports went outside the USSR.  It had no foreign exchange and very little contact with the West.  It has large untapped oil fields, ICBMs, the Semipalatinsk nuclear test site, and the Baikonur Cosmodrome which is a major satellite launching facility.  It produced almost 10% of the grain for the old Soviet Union and nearly 6 million Russians live there.

President Nursultan Nazarbayev was not invited to the meeting in Brest which set up the CIS but he quickly indicated he wanted to join and another signing was held in his capital of Alma Ata along with the other four republics in that area, **Turkmenistan, Uzbekistan, Tajikistan** (new spelling), and **Kyrgyzstan** (was Kirghizia).   These republics have been isolated for so long that they cannot go it alone.  They will remain with the CIS, or whatever grouping that Moscow can put together, for the indefinite future.

The most volatile problem in the area was the Tajik civil war which broke out after the fall of the USSR.  Russia backed the government made up of former Communists and regional leaders that ousted a loose coalition of Islamic fundamentalists and democrats in 1992.   The significance is the role of Russian troops who are defending Tajikistan's border with Afghanistan.

In the Summer of 1993, Russian troops asserted the right to attack targets inside Afghanistan to block rebels from launching raids across the border.   Russia and the other republics want to keep out drugs, weapons, and Islamic fundamentalism.

With most parties ignoring its pronouncements, the future of the CIS was unclear, but some arrangement among at least some of the former Soviet republics is almost definitely going to continue at least in the South and perhaps in other areas if foreign policy crises flare up.

## Significance of the CIS to the World?

Confederations, commonwealths, and such loose joinings of sovereign states have a poor record in history for being able to coordinate foreign policies and face difficult problems in concert, so it should come as no surprise that the Commonwealth of Independent States has had very limited success.   Following an extremely centralized totalitarian regime and the constant suspicion of domination by Russia made the likelihood for active cooperation by the CIS that much more difficult.

Regardless, from what was once an empire, we now have 15 countries, 11 or 12 of which are loosely joined in the CIS, each with its own foreign policy, four inherited nuclear weapons, and there are numerous areas of violence, both internal and on international borders. If the CIS is going to be a 16th actor on the world stage or a substitute for any combination of the 15, then it is important.

There were numerous residual problems and disputes left over from the Soviet Empire. The two most likely places to look for resolution will be in Russia or at the CIS, which is the "successor state" or more accurately successor organization to the Soviet Union, though Russia has actually taken over most of the old Soviet roles.

Considering the weakness of both initially, it will be difficult. However, times do change and we should expect Russia to eventually regain some of its strength and the CIS, or whatever might replace it, to also play a more prominent role.

The CIS provides a forum to address questions of security, foreign policy, international law, differences among members, nuclear and space matters, the environment, and major economic matters. Many of these questions are larger than the individual republics and will either be taken over by Russia or dealt with in a joint forum.

Dealing with the former USSR is already much more difficult in that the US and other countries have to deal with each of the now 15 governments, and they are inexperienced in conducting their own foreign affairs. That has particularly complicated military matters and compliances with the treaties that were signed by the Soviet Union. For example, Ukraine requested a new agreement with the US and Russia about keeping missiles in the Ukraine. That would upset the 1991 START 1 treaty which Ukraine has not ratified.

Another aspect is sheer numbers. There are now 15 entities to deal with in place of one. All foreign trade was controlled by Moscow. Now anyone dealing with the area has to make separate arrangements for each republic which includes customs and currency clearances, plus new problems in transportation. If there is any CIS or any other organization among the republics, then it will be important and an additional player.

This was a very brief background review. For

additional details, see my Special Studies in the Resource Directory at the back of the book.

Let us now look at the order or disorder in the world that has followed the end of the Cold War.

---

To be a politician is but to feign ignorance of what you know well, pretend knowledge of what you are totally ignorant, decline to listen to what you hear, attempt what is beyond your capacity, hide what ought to be exposed, appear profound when you are dull-witted, and to justify ignoble means by claiming admirable ends.

-- Pierre Augustin Caron de Beaumarchais
*Marriage of Figaro* (1778)

---

**Man's worst pollution of planet Earth is the increased number of human beings placed on it!**

# Chapter 3

# TRIBALISM AND NATIONALISM

## Man Is Still His Own Worst Enemy Or Has Mankind Yet Evolved from the Jungle?

*The ethics of international politics reverts to the politics and morality of tribalism, of the Crusades, and of the religious wars.*

-- Hans J. Morgenthau

*Nationalism as an articulate force issued from the volcanic fires of the French Revolution.*

-- G. P. Gooch

The end of the Cold War did not signal the end of warfare as man continued to battle his fellow. However, the foundering of the Soviet Union did seem to unleash a new phase, what can be called a return to tribalism.

Yugoslavia was an example. It had returned civil war to Europe for the first time since the fighting in Greece in the 1940s. It had extremely bitter disputes between different tribes that went back centuries concerning religion, language, and territory.

These tribes wished to stay free of the control of others, dominate others, or simply wanted to kill each other. The one constant was a deep hatred of their neighbors.

What we see around the world in many of the insurgencies or struggles for secession by regions that want to separate themselves from various countries is violent expressions of tribalism. We might speculate as to whether it is the wave of the future.

Three of the most divisive forces in the relations among peoples are **language, race,** and **religion.** All three appear repeatedly in the new tribalism. Before we pursue the idea of a return to tribalism, we should take a brief look at a few basic concepts to clarify the vocabulary we will be using.

## CONCEPTS

Attitudes and beliefs held by the members of a society have a basic influence on the behavior of states. Customs and traditions lead to attitudes which lead to beliefs. Attitudes and beliefs combine to determine the "**values**" people hold and the ends they seek. Values are the ends of human actions, the standards people consider right and desirable. Political action is driven both by and toward values.

"**Community**" between states is the degree of **shared values,** the extent of agreement about attitudes and values among two or more states. Peoples and leaders hold opinions or attitudes on most matters in international affairs, such as war, peace, nuclear weapons, capitalism, socialism, race, religion, foreign aid, ethics, etc.

Attitudes and thus values are shaped by **perceptions**. It is difficult (if not impossible) to view the world with total objectivity. First, there is never complete access to the facts. We are just now learning many new facts about the Cold War since we have gained access to the files of the Kremlin and the people who played significant roles. In war, it is called the "fog of battle."

Second, even when we have facts, our comprehension of reality is influenced by our prejudices and preconceptions. We develop stereotyped images: "the military mind," "the Soviets," "foreigners," "Arab terrorists."

Community then is based on shared values. When these values conflict, the result is "**politics**" through which "**power**" is expressed either by its physical capability or its relational strength yielding "**order,**" both domestic and international. Order provides "**justice**" to a society or among nations.

We define justice as value fulfillment. On the international scene, if there is relative fulfillment, nations are generally satisfied and they do not seek changes, they prefer to continue with the **status quo.** If there is relative unfulfillment, then there is a mood for **change** which can be brought about two ways: either peacefully or by revolution.

A community that has all these attitudes and values in common needs a game plan, a road map, of how to put them into action. "**Ideology**" is the grouping of those ideas concerning political, economic, and social values and goals into action programs to attain those goals. Democracy is an ideology with emphasis on the individual, freedom, and government of the people, by the people, and for the people.

Communism is another ideology with quite different views of historic conflict, classless society, "dictatorship of the proletariat," and the subordinate role of the individual and freedom. Those extreme differences made the Cold War so intense and so important.

A "**nation**" is a community of people who share common values, interests, and beliefs. A nation is not necessarily a "**state**." We may think of the Palestinians or the Kurds as nations, but they are not states. States are the principal actors in international politics. There are four requirements for a community to become a state: people, territory, government, and sovereignty.

The Palestinians have people, territory, could have a government (have the outlines of one ), but do not control the territory, even though the people respond to the PLO, thus do not have sovereignty.

Nevertheless, Palestine proclaimed itself a state in November 1988 and was recognized by some 122 states, a large majority of the world. Each of the 50 US states has the first three but does not have sovereignty, so they are not "states" in international politics.

A state can have several nations (or nationalities); the USSR was such a state, or empire, with many different nations or nationalities included. However, the two words, state and nation, are used almost interchangeably. The common expression is the "**nation state**" whereby the people of a nation desire to have their own state to govern their lives and not be responsive to any other nation's views or directives (that is to have **sovereignty**).

States in their routine international relations have interests. The "**national interest**" is the combination of all the national values or the general and continuous ends for which the nation acts or the aspirations of the state in applying specific policies.

One state can have an interest in another state's trade policy because of the effect on its economy. States can link their interests by treaties. Social conditions can induce action. The West has poured billions of dollars into countries suffering from famine or natural disasters or sent troops in to try to help such as in Somalia.

## THE NEW TRIBALISM

As man evolved and started to gather into larger groupings, there was a tendency for people, families, or clans descended from a common ancestor to group together. This community was a tribe with recognized ancestry and common leadership. The tribe had the same language, the same religion if there was one, the same ethnic background of traditions, history, and culture: basically a homogenous group.

The tribe can grow and tribes with similar interests or values can join together and eventually become a nation. But a nation tends to introduce more diversity: different people, different languages or dialects, greater territorial coverage which may introduce ethnic diversity.

Thus the tribe is a relatively pure ethnic unit; a nation can be, such as Japan, but generally is not. The mobility of man over the centuries has left almost all nation states with some degree of internal diversity: the Arab states have Shia and Sunni Muslims plus, for example Copts in Egypt. Races have become mixed with migrations from one continent to another.

The new tribalism is characterized by violent hatred of neighbors. Before the age of the nation state, most wars were fought between monarchs or some such powerful leaders for territory, economic gain, or power for the despots.

Much of the fighting in the world now is based on grudges that go back for many years or centuries. The young people who do the fighting and dying do not have first hand knowledge of these grudges but were raised on them as they were passed down from the older generations, thus keeping the hatreds alive.

Africa is replete with tribal differences, partially from history, and partly from the way the states were created by Europeans often crossing tribal boundaries: Afars and Issas in Djibouti, Hutus and Tutsis in Rwanda and Burundi, Ethiopia with several tribes and religious splits, various clans which tore Somalia apart, Sudan split between Muslim North and Animist South, Mozambique, Mali, Liberia, and many others.

The states tend to be internally divided along tribal lines which yield differences in language, religion, and cultural background. For example, Zaire, with a population of 40 million, has 6 major ethnic groups and some 450 tribes. Fortunately, most of the fighting in Africa is low intensity, probably more due to lack of capability and finances rather than desire. An exception was the brutal massacres of over 500,000 Hutus by Tutsis in Rwanda, yet most of the killing was done with machetes. Modern technology is arriving: one massacre of women and children in Liberia included chain saws plus the machetes. The fighting in Europe and east to the former Soviet Central Asia is tribal. Most of it resulted from the demise of Communism in the last great empire, the Soviet Union. We tend to forget the Protestant-Catholic violence in Ireland since the late 1960s and the occasional outbursts by the Basques in Spain.

## The Former Soviet Union

Part of Stalin's legacy was his attack on the nationalities and the ethnic minorities. Of the 23 borders between the former Soviet republics, only three are not contested. The borders were established by Stalin not in the normal sense of nationality but to deliberately set one people against another to prevent the rise of national unity in any one region.

As one of his means of repression, Stalin deported hundreds of thousands of Balts, Crimean Tartars, Ingush, and other peoples to Siberia, Kazakhstan, and other remote areas. Also, nearly 24 million ethnic Russians were encouraged to move into the various republics, now foreign countries, where they usually had the best jobs and controlled the Communist Parties and governments.

Major fighting broke out in the **Caucasus**. The war between **Armenia** and **Azerbaijan** continued for over five years with more 15,000 killed and created over a million refugees. The Armenians were another minority, somewhat like the Kurds, who had not been able to establish their own state. They were massacred by the Turks in their failed nationalist movement in the last century, but finally got their own republic in the USSR. The Armenians are Christians. The problem is **Nagorno-Karabakh**, which is an autonomous Armenian enclave completely inside Azerbaijan, their oil-rich, Muslim neighbor.

The Armenians supported the separatists in Nagorno-Karabakh and sent troops into Azerbaijan to help their compatriots, seizing Azeri towns in the area and driving back the Azeris. The dispute threatened to expand as **Turkey**, which is a secular Muslim state, sympathized with the Azeris who speak a Turkic language and demanded that the Armenians withdraw from occupied parts of Azerbaijan. Turkey had been cautious due to the risk of confrontation with Russia. **Iran** (Muslim) also borders Azerbaijan and sent troops into the border area. Turkey and Iran have been competing for influence in oil-rich Azerbaijan and other Muslim former Soviet republics.

Tribal geography continued as the Turkish prime minister (a woman) asked Parliament to wage war if Armenia invaded **Nakhichevan**, an Azerbaijani enclave on the Turkish border, separated from Azerbaijan by Armenia. Turkey and Russia announced in September 1993 that they would work together to try to stop the fighting.

There was a similar dispute in **Georgia** where **South Ossetia**, an autonomous region of Georgia, was fighting to secede and join **North Ossetia**, which is part of Russia. There was fighting for over a year, the Georgian government had fallen, and the Russians were drawn into the fighting.

Unrest in the **Caucasus** was complete. To keep it complicated, North Ossetia borders another enclave, **Checherno-Ingushetia**, inhabited by two Muslim tribes. Russia conquered them in the 19th Century. Stalin deported hundreds of thousands of them during World War II to Kazakhstan for supposedly collaborating with the Nazis. They worked their way back to their old homeland in the late 1950s and want to be independent. The Ingush also claim a part of North Ossetia which they once controlled.

The 160 tribes (clans) in **Chechnya** regularly fight among themselves, but they are united in their hatred of Russian domination. Many have taken the *"gazavat,"* or oath of holy war against invaders. The tough, self-reliant Chechens have a traditional, clan-structured society that still pursues blood vendettas (predecessors to the Hatfields and the McCoys!). They have historically preferred to withdraw to the hills in guerrilla bands rather than submit to Moscow. Chechnya declared itself independent in 1991 but no foreign government recognized it and little was heard from Moscow.

The Kremlin accused Chechnya of stealing Russian military equipment, supporting organized crime, and being a haven for drug runners, criminals, and arms dealers. The Chechens said those charges only hide Russia's desire to impose its rule. Then in December 1994, Russia attacked

Grozny, the capital, in a bloody fight that upset the Russian image and brought concern to the world. "According to Muslim tradition, before a man dies he must raise a son, plant a tree and kill a snake," explained one Chechen fighter. "I have already had my sons, and I have planted many trees. Now I am killing snakes."

In addition to the many disputes in the former republics, there are numerous areas of tension in the Russian republic itself besides Chechnya. There are several of the internal republics of Russia that want more autonomy or independence, including the **Tartar** and **Bashkir** Republics as well as the **Cossacks** and the **Chechens**.

The **Tajik** civil war was more volatile even though it was more remote from world view. Fighting broke out after the collapse of the USSR and Russia backed the government which was composed of former Communists and regional leaders that ousted a loose coalition of Islamic fundamentalists and democrats in 1992. Some 20,000 people have died with 600,000 displaced, including an estimated 80,000 who fled to Afghanistan. The main element was the role of Russian troops who were defending Tajikistan's border with Afghanistan.

In the Summer of 1993, Russian troops asserted the right to attack targets inside Afghanistan to block rebels from launching raids across the border. In July, Russian artillery struck some Afghan border towns and Russian warplanes were reported to have strafed an Afghan village. In August, the troops drove Islamic rebels back across the border and killed more than a 100 and threatened to strike their bases in Afghanistan.

Many Russians were concerned that, as their military was becoming involved in Russia's largest military operation in the region since the Soviet's costly and unsuccessful 1979-1989 Afghan War, they were sliding into another quagmire. However, Russia and the other republics wanted to stop the influx of drugs, weapons, and Islamic fundamentalism from Afghanistan.

Boris Yeltsin met in the Kremlin with the leaders of Tajikistan, Kyrgyzstan, Uzbekistan, and Kazakhstan. They agreed to cooperate in defending the Tajik border as well as to seek talks with Afghanistan and help from the UN. Afghanistan's fractious Islamic government denied involvement and wanted talks to ease tensions.

There are numerous other disputed areas that are left

over from the Soviet Empire. Stalin was not concerned about such problems. As it did not bother him to move whole populations, it also did not bother him to gerrymander areas to permit some degree of autonomy to keep the peace because all the area was under Soviet control anyway.

The breakup of the former Soviet Union left a map with leopard spots of enclaves all over it. The disputes between the ethnic minorities are so widespread that, as one writer put it, the map of the conflicts in the old Soviet Union would be 5 yards long. It will be basically impossible to sort out that mess on a nation state basis and have any rational organization.

## The Yugoslav Tribes

Nowhere is the new tribalism more violent than in the fighting over what was once Yugoslavia, particularly in **Bosnia-Hercegovina**. The tribal hatreds have mixed sources. We tend to forget that most of the 23 million people in **Slovenia, Croatia, Bosnia, Serbia, Montenegro, and Macedonia** are of common Slav background. Even the Muslims of Bosnia are Slavs; they were converted by the Ottomans.

The name of the country, Yugoslavia, means Land of the South Slavs. Their only common element is ancestry. Every other element of a nation is missing: history, language, alphabet, religion, even economic potential.

The **Serbs**, at 10 million, and the **Croats**, at 4.5 million, are the center of the problem. Since the Serbs are the most numerous (and as we shall see also the most militant), they have settled outside their home area, forming significant minorities in Croatia and Bosnia. The Serb-Croat rivalry started long before the Muslim problem.

As the Christian Church split centuries ago, the Croats stayed with Rome, while the Serbs became Eastern Orthodox opposed to the pope. Serbs took up Eastern ways, which explains the Russian affinity for Serbs. Croats took up Western traditions. The two speak roughly the same language, not like the Slovenes and Macedonians, but Serbs use the Cyrillic alphabet like the Russians, while Croats use the Roman one.

The **Ottoman Turks** invaded the Balkans in the 14th Century putting the Serbs under their control for 500 years. The Croats were able to maintain their relationship with the

**Habsburgs.**

The Serbs, even under the Ottomans, were the major Slav power in the region. The Croats never really had any independent status. When the Turkish siege of Vienna failed in 1683, Islam's threat to the center of Christian Europe faded. Ottoman hegemony settled back to a line curving through the Balkans which some 2 1/2 centuries later would be Yugoslavia.

The culture clashes are seen best in Bosnia where the republic sticks like an arrowhead into Croatia because that was the frontier between the Ottoman and Habsburg Empires. The proposed partition of Bosnia gives almost all of the frontier areas to Serbia and Croatia. Serb communities are located all along that frontier because the Habsburgs brought in Serbs to man the front lines because of their military prowess.

But that is not enough to explain the bitter hatreds among the tribes. In addition to schisms of Catholic and Orthodox, Christian and Muslim, Habsburg and Ottoman, there was a poison of West European fascism, ethnic nationalism, and populist demagoguery injected after World War I. It was the Nazis who planted the idea of "ethnic cleansing" and the Communists who started Yugoslavia toward destruction.

The Serbs gained their freedom from the Ottomans in the 1800s and thus felt they were the major partner when the Allies formed the **Kingdom of Serbs, Croats, and Slovenes** in 1918; also they had fought on the winning side. Croats did not like the oppression of the dictatorial King Alexander I, the Serb who took over the Yugoslav throne.

Serbs began assassinating Croat members of the Yugoslav parliament in 1928. King Alexander was murdered in 1934, with the support of **Ustashe**, a secret Croat terrorist movement. Jealous neighbors turned into murderous enemies.

That assassination was key to transforming the chronic mistrust between Serbs and Croats into the paranoid fear and hatred evidenced in the current war. The catalyst was World War II. Hitler and Mussolini invaded Yugoslavia and turned Croatia and part of Bosnia into a puppet state headed by Ustashe members. The Ustashe started a massacre of Serbs and executed hundreds of thousands along with many Jews.

In revenge, the **Chetniks**, Serb royalists, killed thousands of Croats, while Tito's partisans, which included many Serbs, fought the Germans and the Ustashe. At the end of the war, there was no group left except Tito's Communists and he built the second Yugoslavia. Tito was a Croat and had a simple rule: to have a strong Yugoslavia, Serbia had to be weak. He played off the ethnic groups to enhance his own power.

After Tito's death in 1980, there were inadequate institutions to hold the country together or the tribes apart. With the death of Communism in Eastern Europe, Yugoslavia, whose economy was already in shambles, fell apart. **Slovenia** and **Croatia** were both richer than **Serbia** and wanted off the sinking ship.

**Slobodan Milosevic**, the Communist President of Serbia, decided that Serbs, wherever they were, should stick together and could not be left under Croats or Bosnians. Thus was born his effort to seize the land of "**Greater Serbia**" quickly followed by a "**Greater Croatia.**"

To establish those two "Greater" areas required carving up Bosnia where Muslims outnumbered both Serbs and Croats. The tribes shifted alliances as fast as the old European countries in the days of the Balance of Power.

The Croats initially supported the Muslims against the Serbs in Bosnia. Then the Croats turned on the Muslims as the Serbs and Croats divided up Bosnia between themselves leaving the Muslims only a small part while the West sat by and did nothing.

The intense feelings are demonstrated in the stabbing of Monica Seles, the 19-year-old girl who was ranked number 1 in the world when she was attacked during a tennis match on 30 April 1993 and has not played competitively since. Seles was born in Serbia but she is ethnic Hungarian.

Gunther Parche, who attacked her, told the German judge that he considered the Serbs the "worst and greatest danger for Europe." He told the judge he would not have plunged the kitchen knife into her back if she had been an American or a German.

The intensity and bitterness of the feelings in that area are astounding for what we consider to be civilized people. Unfortunately, we are seeing more of this in various parts of the world.

Only **Serbia** and **Montenegro** are left in what was **Yugoslavia**. The others are independent except that Bosnia has been torn apart and is being partitioned into three different areas, none of which will be viable economic entities. The saga is not over yet.

## Asia

The wars in Asia are mostly tribal also. The ideological wars left over from the Cold War are still raging in Cambodia, have degenerated into religious tribal war in Afghanistan, and have faded in what is left of the Communist insurgency in the Philippines.

Tribal insurgencies continue with Buddhist rebels in the Chittagong Hill Tracts of Bangladesh, Aceh guerrillas in Indonesia, and Kachin, Karen, and Shan rebels in Myanmar (old Burma). Peoples are trying to secede in Assam, Kashmir, Manipur, Mizoram, Nagaland, and Punjab in India; East Timor and Irian Java in Indonesia; Bougainville (famous to Americans in World War II) in Papua New Guinea, the Tamil region of Sri Lanka; and the Kurds in Iraq, Iran, and Turkey.

The old tribalism has been with us throughout history and will likely remain with us. The new tribalism is more shocking because we are seeing it in the more advanced cultures such as in Europe and it is showing an unexpected violence and immorality which we thought those societies had risen above.

At the same time that some advanced states are grouping together to enhance their power, such as the European Community, we see the continued fragmentation of the world into more, small political entities.

## NATIONALISM

The nation state evolved from the tribe, city-state, feudal lord, church, etc. which had earlier claimed supreme loyalty. Nationalism is a body of ideas and beliefs which entail a commitment to the value that the nation should form the state (**self-determination**) and the nation should be preserved and augmented. As a political force, it combines an ideology about the idea of nationality with the political institutionalization of that ideology into a nation state.

Nationalism is a "**state of mind.**" It is a "feeling" of belonging to the nation and of loyalty to that nation -- **MY country** -- the feeling that the country is paramount and more important than ethnic or religious origins.

Nationalism is one of the most dynamic forces for political change and action in international relations. It shaped Europe and America and caused many wars. It ended empires and brought independence to many new states. It can also generate parochial attitudes and barriers to trade, communication, and collaboration.

Leaders of every state consider the national interests, which only they can define, as supreme and loyalty to the state more important than any other earthly obligation. Nationalism often supersedes or melds with moral and religious beliefs. National Socialism in Nazi Germany was an example. It can be carried to the extreme of total blind allegiance; some of the most inhumane acts of man have been perpetrated in the name of nationalism.

Writers tried to define the evolution of nationalism. One listed the successive stages of nationalism as humanitarian, Jacobin, traditional, liberal, and integral. Quincy Wright listed in his *A Study of War* medieval, monarchical, revolutionary, liberal, and totalitarian nationalism.

Modern nationalism originated in the 17th and 18th Centuries in Northwestern Europe and America. It spread across all Europe in the 19th Century and to the whole world in the 20th Century.

Modern nationalism has deep roots in the past but it is a development of the last two centuries and is directly linked to the nation state system, which is relatively new in history even though we sometimes feel it was always there. The nation state system became institutionalized after the Peace of Westphalia in 1648 and became more effective in the late 18th and early 19th Centuries.

Early nationalism was monarchical. Even after Westphalia, international relations were still mainly relations between sovereigns, thus the flourishing of court diplomacy and wars of that period were often only dynastic struggles.

Most of the forms of modern nationalism came from the three great revolutions -- the Industrial, the American, and the French -- which shaped the modern world. The French Revolution and the Napoleonic Wars accelerated the evolution of nationalism. It became such a powerful force that it could not be stopped and it even turned on its creators for it carried the Revolution into uncharted areas and stimulated reactions in other peoples of Europe against the French invaders.

Nationalism has many roots: language, literature, religion, race, symbols. Nations can develop without a common language, Switzerland has four, but facility of communication is a major factor in passing ideas, values,

objectives, history, and traditions to following generations.
**Languages** can be very divisive for a country. India, for example, has 14 major language groups, with over 1,600 regional languages. To find a common language in India, they had to turn to a foreign language, English.

Different languages are a typical problem across Africa with different tribal languages. There are some 6,000 languages in the world (there were probably 10,000 to 15,000 languages in prehistoric times) but they are dying off fast and probably half will disappear in the next century.

Scholars, historians, poets, and philosophers play important roles in fostering nationalism. We do not think of William Shakespeare as a propagandist but note, "This blessed plot, this earth, this realm, this England." (*King Richard II*).

**Religion** can play a major unifying role; its biggest problem is when it tends to become a theocracy. **Race** is particularly evident in Africa. Heroes, like Washington, Jefferson, and Lincoln in the US; national shrines such as the memorials in Washington, the *Arc de Triomphe*, Westminster Abbey; slogans; national flags; and anthems all represent feelings of attachment and loyalty to a nation.

The great French philosophers and our Thomas Jefferson discredited the feudal concept of the divine right of kings and held that there were natural laws which should govern men. They were the source of liberal or humanitarian nationalism and the democratic concept best expressed in Jefferson's words in the American Declaration of Independence.

When he stated that it was the people's right to change their government, the concept of national self-determination was clearly enunciated from liberal nationalism and democracy. When a people no longer wanted to remain part of the state that controlled them, they had the "right" to choose how or by whom they would be governed. That soon swept away the "old order" in Europe, the Spanish and Portuguese colonies in America, and on to Asia.

The liberal nationalists saw a world order made up of independent governments which provided legal protection to private property, free enterprise, and free trade. However, strong states emerged at the end of the 19th Century and as nationalism developed mass support, many states became more nationalistic and less liberal. Between the two world wars, there was increased protectionism and economic nationalism.

That period brought us Communism in the Soviet Union, National Socialism in Germany, and Fascism in Italy and totalitarian nationalism. In each case, the rights of the individual were subordinated to the supreme power of the state. Statism and dictatorship replaced the humanitarianism of the liberal nationalists. The brutality of the Nazis and the Fascists led us into the terrible ordeal of a total war. The struggle with the Communists went on for another 45 years in the Cold War.

The right of self-determination became the battle cry of the new nationalism of the non-Western World after World War II. Anticolonialism was the main feature in addition to political equality. As the colonies strove to break away from the old empires, the desire was for independence even if they were not really ready for the responsibilities.

There was little national consciousness among people who were mainly from tribes, villages, castes, clans, or small areas. There were few shared values except anticolonialism and the desire to be independent.

Many of these new states became one-party regimes with dictators. The number of independent states increased from about 50 to over 150. Some of them are still not viable economic units.

## The Dangers of Nationalism

As you should have gathered by now, it is difficult to define precisely some of these terms such as nationalism. Patriotism and nationalism are often used synonymously. Both are emotions.

**Patriotism** is the love and loyalty or zealous support of one's own country, especially in regard to other countries. Nationalism would seem to be more attuned to the basic common interests of the group while patriotism is more of an attitude toward the state itself.

Russians could still be patriotic even if they hated the Communists. When Stalin was losing in World War II, he appealed to the people on the basis of their love for Mother Russia rather than for Communism or the Soviet Union.

Patriotism can be a powerful emotion and a major element of strength for a nation state. But like any emotion, it can be carried to extremes which can be quite dangerous.

**Chauvinism** (not the male chauvinist pig!) is militant, unreasoning, and boastful devotion to one's country or fanatical patriotism. Another term is "**jingoist**" which came from a refrain of a patriotic British music hall song of 1878, a person who boasts of his patriotism and favors an aggressive, threatening, warlike foreign policy. We have seen too much of these in recent years.

Two other emotional factors can turn nationalism into a negative role: **racialism** and xenophobia. Race can be an important element of nationalism, but if it is used to find scapegoats or add to hatred, then it detracts.

Another emotion that can be linked with racialism is **xenophobia**, the fear or hatred of strangers or foreigners. These were particularly evident in Africa, a recent example being the murder of an American student in South Africa because she looked like a "settler." We have seen more racial hatred, particularly as economic times are bad, such as the attacks on North Africans in France and on foreigners in Germany.

Nationalism was originally associated with liberty and democracy. We soon discovered that it could actually threaten them and even was supportive of authoritarianism and totalitarianism and could restrict human freedom rather than improve it.

We are forced to conclude that humanitarian and liberal nationalism are compatible with liberty, democracy, and internationalism but that totalitarian nationalism subverts individual rights and is not compatible with those concepts.

Since any form of nationalism can change to totalitarian nationalism, we must further conclude that nationalism, regardless of its form, makes peace insecure and we must therefore find ways to bypass nationalism, at least the totalitarian form. This would appear to be a major problem of our time.

Nationalism is generally considered to be an evil force since it has developed into some intolerable forms and been a major cause of wars. It certainly does not facilitate international cooperation. The aim of traditional nationalism was freedom of the nation from foreign rule and to permit it to be a state.

That goal was felt to be the right for all nations. Then once all nations had their own states, there would be a society of satisfied nation states which could find in the legal and moral principles of self-determination the appropriate means to preserve that society. The result could more accurately be called international anarchy since each nation state is sovereign and does not answer to any outside power.

## Options

• Continue to do nothing and let international anarchy run rampant until it eventually impinges on our direct national interests and then we will react.

• Try to lead the world into a better life before we are drawn into new disasters.

## Possible Actions

• Contact your government officials and urge them to work harder to stop such terrible disasters as Bosnia via regional organizations (NATO or the CSCE) or the United Nations.

• Commit US troops if necessary.

• Urge stronger US leadership to provide more humanitarian policies in the world.

• As you will see throughout this book, if the US is unwilling to be the world's policeman and if the major powers are unwilling to act on major international problems, then the only alternative to anarchy is to provide authority to an international organization such as the UN.

• Pull all the UN troops out (England and France are afraid to act because of threats to their troops in the UN force) and commit NATO to clean up the mess in Bosnia and bring the war criminals to justice.  (Russia is blocking action by supporting Serbia and France and Russia are pushing for lifting the sanctions on Iraq.)

• After the high price in blood and capital the US paid for bailing out the Europeans before due to their temerity and appeasement in dealing with problems early on, we have the right to demand that Europe stop the Serbs and Croats and protect the sovereignty of Bosnia.

For those who believed (or hoped) the 20th Century would become the age of internationalism, they were disappointed as it turned into the age of virulent nationalism and a fallback to tribalism.  The two world wars stemmed from nationalism and the Communist nationalism carried on late into the century.

There are a few signs of progress in the growth of internationalism for all of us are faced with surviving together in an anarchic and dangerous world.  However, nationalism and tribalism remain with us as major impediments to man's ability to live together in peace on this planet.

President Bill Clinton
The White House
1600 Pennsylvania Avenue, N. W.
Washington, D. C. 20500
White House Comment Line:  (202) 456-1111
Fax: (202) 456-2461

Secretary of State Warren Christopher
Department of State
Washington, D. C. 20520
State Department Public Information Line: (202) 647-6575

| | |
|---|---|
| Any Senator<br>U. S. Senate<br>Washington, D. C. 20510<br>(202) 224-3121 | Jesse Helms, Chairman<br>Senate Foreign Relations<br>Committee<br>403 Dirksen Senate Office<br>Building<br>224-6342  Fax: 224-7588 |
| | Mitch McConnell, Chairman<br>Senate Appropriations Sub-<br>committee on Foreign<br>Operations<br>120 Russell Senate Office<br>Building<br>224-2541  Fax: 224-2499 |
| Any Representative<br>U. S. House of Representatives<br>Washington, D. C. 20515<br>(202) 225-3121 | Benjamin A. Gilman,<br>Chairman, House Committee<br>on International Relations<br>2449 Rayburn House Office<br>Building<br>225-3776  Fax: 225-2541 |

If we all did the things we are capable of doing, we would literally astound ourselves.

-- Thomas A. Edison

# Chapter 4

# ON RELIGION

## Is Religion A Positive or Negative Force in the World?

*Religion is the opiate of the masses.*

-- Josef Stalin
*(Historians say an estimated 30 million people were murdered or starved to death under his reign. He'd been a theology student in his youth.)*

*There exists no Arabic word for fundamentalism. No group exists in the contemporary Arab Muslim world that calls itself fundamentalist.*

-- Bruce B. Lawrence

The evolution of man in society has been slow, sporadic, and separated geographically. The peoples on the different continents had little contact with each other until much more modern times. Three of the elements of man's evolution, one natural and two acquired, played key roles in uniting the disparate groupings into larger social units and added to the sense of nation and eventually the nation state.

These elements are now major barriers to uniting man in supranational organizations. These three divisive elements are **language, race**, and **religion**. Language prevents us from communicating with each other; race tends to set us apart; and religion prevents us from understanding each other. We have briefly reviewed the strengths and weaknesses of language and race. Let us now focus on religion.

Any discussion of religion is difficult because the human emotions basic to religious feelings cannot be wholly repressed or always dealt with in a truly objective manner. One cannot render any account of religion that is acceptable to everyone; one can only try to avoid partisan distortion.

When one looks at any book on the history of civilization, two subjects stand out: wars and religions. Often they went together. Man has probably always pondered his existence, from whence he came, and where he might be going and tried to explain the human emotions and human needs. There are many religions around the world and most have subsects, denominations, branches, or other groupings of diversity within them; but three were particularly important to Western civilization: Judaism, Christianity, and Islam.

The Old Testament is the Jewish national record. The original Jewish people were a Semitic tribe that probably originated in the Arabian desert, closely related to Arab nomads of later history. They migrated to different areas including Ur and Egypt. After moving to Palestine, they established their kingdoms and flourished in trade, however they remained small and never regained the greatness of Solomon.

Historians have pondered over what held the Jewish people together. They conclude it was their beliefs. They were the first people in Western civilization to believe in one god. They developed ethical concepts of the good life and a concept of an after life with eternal happiness in heaven or eternal punishment in hell. The Egyptians were concerned with an after life as evidenced by the Pyramids, but they had many gods for different subjects.

Christianity came directly out of Judaism. Some consider that it is our greatest debt to the ancient Middle East, which also gave us the alphabet, algebra, and the domestic cat, as well as many other advances.

The Greek and Roman Empires had many gods as they tried to explain and understand the world around them. The Olympic Games were originally closely tied to religious rites. The Greek gods were transferred to Rome: Zeus became Jupiter; Poseidon, Neptune; Ares (War), Mars; Aphrodite, Venus; Athena, Minerva; etc.

The Romans also came up with "epicureanism" and "stoicism." However, they were too intellectual, too philosophical for the ordinary man who yearned for a religion of hope not of resignation. That answer was to come in Christianity. However, the Roman foundations of law, languages, and organization still are fundamental in the oldest major institution of the Western World -- the Roman Catholic Church.

An effective religion needs both theology and church organization, both spirit and letter, both faith and works. By the early medieval centuries, the church had almost a monopoly of literary culture, and therefore had moved fully into governing.

The word "clerical" referring to clerks and keeping records comes from this background. By definition, religion was involved in politics. The split between Rome and Istanbul was more political than the religious differences professed. Istanbul, which is a corruption of three Greek words which mean "to the city," was the key city on the outlet from the Black Sea to the Mediterranean and the line between Europe and Asia. Also known as Byzantium and then in the time of Constantine as Constantinople, it was the seat of Eastern Orthodox Christianity for centuries.

The newest of the religions was Islam which was born in Mecca in the 7th Century. The Muslims (followers of Islam) swept across North Africa to the Atlantic in Morocco and then north into Spain and France, through the Middle East up through the Balkans to Vienna and east to the Indian subcontinent and eventually to Central Asia, parts of China, Malaya, Indonesia, and the Philippines.

Now Jerusalem, the seat of the Kingdom of Judah of the southern Jewish tribes when they split with the northern tribes in the Kingdom of Israel in the 10th Century B. C. and the home of Christ, was under Muslim control. In time, some of the holiest places in Islam after Mecca and Medina would also be in Jerusalem, thus causing a problem til this day.

As one Muslim put it, Islam is Christianity plus law. We believe in Christianity too. Jesus and the prophets of the Old and New Testament are found in the Quran also. In a sense, a Muslim is a Jew, a Christian, and a Muslim. "Before Muhammad, we were all Christians. Before that, we were all Jews."

The Crusades were a Holy War by the Christians against the Muslims for the Holy Places. They were generally failures but they increased the power of the papacy since they were such large international endeavors. However, as more people discovered that the Muslims were not the demons Rome painted them to be, there was disillusionment with the papal concept of the Crusades. The Crusades have been referred to as a medieval colonization movement inspired by the church.

In the Dark Ages, there were two ways for upward mobility: through intelligence and administration via the clergy or through fighting and related athletic prowess and become a noble. By the time of the Renaissance (1300-1600), the church had deteriorated; priests were often illiterate and immoral. There were rumblings of discontent in the Catholic Church.

The Protestant Reformation (or more like Protestant Revolt to Catholics) became prominent on 31 October 1517 when Martin Luther nailed his 95 Theses to the door of the court church in Wittenberg in German Saxony. The word Protestant dates from 19 April 1529 when a group of German princes supporting Luther's doctrine, lodged a formal "protest" at the Diet of Spires against an annulment of an earlier imperial decree.

These reformers, such as Luther and Calvin, did not see themselves as setting up a new church but rather going back to the true old church (they might be called fundamentalists in current terminology). In practice, the Protestants were just as intolerant as the Catholics. Regardless, the Protestant Reformation was a major economic, social, and intellectual revolution.

Each new religion or church opposed the idea of Rome as the only true faith, yet each saw itself as the only true faith. Freedom of religion and separation of church and state were not normal in the 16th or even the 17th Centuries. There was considered to be only one church and everyone was supposed to follow its doctrine, except for the Jews who were outside the church but paid the price of having to live apart in ghettos.

The religious governance and the political governance were the "two swords" of power and that led to many disputes. It was not until the Enlightenment, late 17th and early 18th Centuries, that a doctrine of religious toleration appeared. Indeed there was still thought to be only one true religion which a person may one day find, but people must find their own way freely. However, there was still debate over religious variation and religious indifference.

The Catholic Church did clean its house and we had the Catholic Reformation (or Counter-Reformation in Protestant history). Many new sects appeared including the Jesuits, formed by the Spaniard Ignatius Loyola in 1540, who became the soldiers of the Catholic Church. The House of Habsburg, both its Spanish and German branches, led political Catholicism for the next several generations.

Historians try to pick a date for the beginning of modern times. There are several but one often used is 1492, particularly in Spain. In that year, Ferdinand and Isabella, who had united Aragon and Castille into Spain, recovered the last part of Spain from the Muslims. It was also the year of Columbus which would open the way to the great Spanish Empire. It was also the date of the Inquisition by which Isabella turned the Inquisition, a special ecclesiastical court first formed in the 13th Century, into a royal instead of a papal instrument for Spanish nationalism.

Thus in 1492, the Jews in Spain were given the immediate choice of baptism or exile with loss of all their property. Ten years later the Muslims were offered the choice of baptism only. She gained many converts out of fear but at a great cost because it suppressed some of the most productive elements in Spain. The torture and brutality of the Inquisition have remained a stain on the Catholic Church.

An interesting linkage was expounded by the German, Max Weber, between Protestants and Capitalism. Since the Protestant states, such as England and Germany, progressed faster than some of the Catholic ones, such as Italy, he tried to relate the philosophy to the economic success. The role of the individual, relationship with the state, and growing tendency toward democracy were key in his view.

We have discussed religion and nationalism in the previous chapter. Both the Protestant and Catholic Churches played a strong role in unifying many nations on their way to statehood. There is still a very strong relationship between religion and politics in many states: the Arab states, but particularly Saudi Arabia; some other Muslim states, such as Pakistan, the Sudan, and Iran, which was taken over by the mullahs; India; and Israel.

## ARROGANCE OF RELIGION

There are some 5.7 billion human beings living on Earth. Over 1.2 billion of those people live in China, which has been under atheistic Communism for 45 years but has a long philosophical tradition of Taoism and Confucianism. Almost another 1 billion live in India, which is predominantly Hindu. About 1 billion are Muslim. There are many different religions in the world. Yet each one professes to be the only true religion. Its people talk to "God" and they receive special compensation from their "Almighty."

In the realm of propaganda, nations like to espouse "world public opinion" or "the conscience of mankind" to assure themselves, as well as others, that their foreign policy is acceptable everywhere and beyond reproach. "The judgment of history" is similarly used by those who are more philosophical. The religious use the "will of God" to rationalize their causes and believers then see the strange event of the one and same God supporting the armies on both sides of the battlefield and leading both armies to either deserved victory or to undeserved defeat.

We have "chosen people" who deserve special treatment of some sort because their God directed it or because it is written somewhere in what they consider holy scriptures. There is "biblical land" which belongs to a people because it says so in the Bible. But there is also a Quran, the Veda, and other books that are equally important to large numbers of people.

All of the "great books" were "written" long ago and usually originated as oral history, later written down and no doubt embellished to fit the age. Each in its own way is the propaganda of that religion's political and theological history.

Religion has played a major role in history. Its good part has been as a unifying agent for peoples and nations and the betterment of mankind. Its bad part has been its divisive role and when it strayed from its humanitarian greatness and sank to torture and murder.

When religion has stood for universal man, it has been great. However, when it has stood for tribal man, or national man, or state man, or man of only its exclusive religion, it has added to the division of the world and man's misery.

When a religion considers all non-believers as infidels, we have by our earlier definition "politics" because of the conflict of values. There are three general ways such religions can go.

First, they can be so exclusive that no one not born into the faith can ever really be considered good enough to join. They would be the true royalists since they do not want converts.

Second, they can be so confident of the universal nature of their religion that they feel divinely guided to bring the light to all the "heathens" of the world. They will be the missionaries and try to convert the world.

Third, they can be content to remain in the middle ground and tend to their flocks without trying to force their views on others. They will be the quiet monks and people of peace.

Many, in addition to the Jews themselves, consider Judaism the religion with the highest morals and the most sophisticated degree of civility and character. The Jewish people are brilliant and talented, yet they have suffered contempt and mistreatment in the Diaspora. Some of the hatred of the Jews was manifested in the miserable and racial anti-Semitism.

The Jewish response was Zionism, which evolved in the last century and was catalyzed by the Dreyfus Affair in France. If they could not live peacefully with their neighbors, then they should have their own home.

The impetus for that movement came from Europe, mostly Eastern Europe. Interestingly, if one accepts the idea of "the thirteenth tribe" of Arthur Koestler, that the European Jews came from the converted Khazars, then those Jews were not Semites. (Koestler claims it was the Khazars, caught between Western pressure to become Christians and Eastern pressure to adopt Islam, who converted to Judaism about 740 AD followed by a high period of trade and learning on the Black Sea. These were the people who migrated to Poland and formed the cradle of Western Jewry.)

The European Jews prospered and were some of the most successful and productive people throughout the continent. However, the hatred that had plagued them for centuries reached its zenith under Adolph Hitler and the Holocaust. That terrible human tragedy solidified the Zionist view and the state of Israel was formed in 1948. Ironically, the Jews who migrated from Europe are known as "Ashke**nazi**" -- the last four letters being rather ironic.

The Jews from the area and across North Africa are called **Sephardic**. They tend to be poorer and disadvantaged in the political system. It is the **Ashkenazi** who have led the persecution of the Palestinians. Psychologists have made an interesting comparison with the abused child who becomes an abusing parent. The victims and their offspring from the Holocaust have inflicted terrible pain in turn on their victims, the Palestinians.

Unfortunately, the Jewish people are sometimes accused of being arrogant, as if it were a character trait. Sadly, the state of Israel is also sometimes given that same label. Under the Law of the Return, there is no Israeli nationality in Israel. Any person born of a Jewish mother or converted to

Judaism can immediately be an Israeli citizen with Jewish nationality. An Arab who was born in Jerusalem even is an Israeli citizen with Arab nationality. The difference is complete; the latter is very much a second class (or lower) citizen. The Israeli Supreme Court has legalized this process which some call Israeli racism.

Israel is a state for Jewish people and gentiles, particularly Muslims and Christians who both have strong attachments to the Holy Land, are not really welcome. Israel is not the only theocracy.

Under Islam, religion and the state are one. We saw that at its worst after the fall of the Shah of Iran and the takeover by the mullahs, led by Ayatollah Khomeini, and their brutality and incompetence in government. Pakistan and the Sudan have gone the way of the *sharia*, the Islamic law of life and government.

The role of religion in the other Muslim states varies greatly all the way to the secular state of Turkey. We have seen it within our shores; the early Calvinists established a theocracy in New England which eventually passed to middle class domination.

Saudi Arabia resulted from an alliance of the House of Saud and Wahhabi Islam. Wahhabism can probably best be compared to Puritanism in Christianity. We know it mainly for its prohibition on drinking (even though many Saudis drink when outside the kingdom), veiled women, and strict rules.

Saudi Arabia is an interesting country in that it does not want tourists. You have to have someone in the country sponsor your visit and you have to state your religion on your visa request. Most of the countries of the Arabian peninsula are tribal and Muslim. The major problem with the religion in its strictest forms is its intolerance of any other views.

Most religions are usually interested in welcoming people of other faiths into their houses of worship. Muslims often will not permit nonbelievers to enter their mosques. This is carried to great extreme in the case of Mecca. Non-Muslims are not even allowed near the city much less near the Kaabah.

There are hardly any groups more arrogant than the fundamentalists. The Islamic fundamentalists, with their warped logic, have the most unusual explanations (or excuses) for everything. They have found it easier to blame all their problems on the West rather than to look for other sources of their difficulties. But not all problems in Islam are caused by fundamentalists. Sunni and Shiite Muslims with their bitter difference over the lineage after Mohammad are often at each others' throats such as the bitter fighting between extremists of both sects in Pakistan.

Some Christian denominations are no less messianic in their actions. The history of the papacy is one of constant struggle between state and religion. The Church of England broke with Rome over such politics. The history of Christianity is replete with battles between church and state for political power. Churches played major roles in most of the countries of Europe and in South America.

The revival of religion in the former Soviet Union brought new pressure from the Orthodox Church. Old religious tensions of the Orthodox world reappeared. Serbia is Orthodox. Russian politics were always a combination of Russian imperialism and the Orthodox Church. Vice Chancellor of Austria, Erhard Busek, spoke of a pan-Orthodox power arc stretching from Russia, through Serbia, and possibly to the Adriatic. He said, "I can see Russia at the Adriatic Sea."

The Southern Baptists created quite a stir in September 1993 in Alabama when they said that 46.1% of Alabamians risk going to hell unless they were born again and accept Jesus Christ as their savior. The Baptists said the figures were only to determine where to establish new churches and find more followers, but the Catholics, Methodists, and others were not happy to hear that they were not going to heaven because they had not been "saved."

The Mormon Church (the Church of Jesus Christ of Latter-Day Saints) purports to have the "final gospel" after Judaism and Christianity. The Mormons have about 4 million members in the US, with a major role in Utah, and a total of about 8.8 million worldwide that they are diligently trying to increase.

Recent years have shown us increased activity by the Christian right in American, particularly Republican, politics with the efforts of Pat Robertson and his Christian Coalition to seize power, particularly trying to impose their views on abortion and homosexuality. They are one third of the Republican Party but half the GOP primary vote.

The evangelicals have not been able to stay out of politics. The executive director of the Christian Coalition, 33 year-old born again Ralph Reed, said: "the Christian Coalition is not and never has claimed to be a church or a ministry. It is an explicitly grass-roots lobbying organization representing people of faith and seeking family-friendly public policy."

Reed had his litmus test -- a presidential candidate who did not oppose abortion would not be acceptable to conservative Christians. This group is forcing its control over the Republican Party with its fanatic approach that only the Coalition knows the way, the truth, and the right. Their agenda is deeply divisive and a threat to the GOP, what Senator Arlen Specter calls "the intolerant right." They could easily facilitate the reelection of Bill Clinton. Opposition is growing. Numerous religious and civil rights groups urge resistance to the Christian right extremists.

Anti-religious sentiment is really quite low in the US, but you would not know it by listening to the televangelists or television preachers. Pat Robertson (under attack with charges of anti-semitism for some of his comments) calls for his viewers to send $20 every month to stop the Democrats, the liberal-biased media, and the homosexuals who want to destroy the evangelical Christians. While speaking, he shows pictures of Nazis torturing and killing Jews on the screen.

Christian bigotry was further shown in the reception given to David Wilhelm, chairman of the Democratic National Committee, when he addressed Pat Robertson's Christian Coalition in September 1993. He was booed every time he mentioned Democratic Party values, President Clinton, and tolerance and he was unable to give his entire speech. He told them he was not going to say they are bad Christians for opposing the President's budget, but "when I disagree with you, you had better not tell me that I'm a bad Christian."

That is the key. Robertson stated that the Christian Coalition had "no interest in imposing our religion on someone through government methods." However, later he said the group's goal was a government that "in its policies acknowledges its dependence on Almighty God."

Methodist Bishop James Armstrong described "The unbelievable arrogance of the Christian fundamentalists who say, 'If you do not agree with me, you are neither a patriot nor a Christian.'"

If religious groups want to be welcome in debate, they must accept dissent without calling it anti-religious prejudice. Some of these groups have not grasped that elementary principle of democracy.

Some of the most heinous crimes of history have been

committed in the name of religion, the Inquisition and Ayatollah Khomeini being merely ancient and modern examples.

Religious wars bloody the annals of our civilization. About two-thirds of today's armed conflicts have a religious base. We have not yet escaped from that cruel hoax as we watch the slaughter and rape in Bosnia, the fighting between the Armenians and the Azeris in Azerbaijan, the repeated clashes between Hindus and Muslims in India, and the occasional murder in Ireland.

It takes a great deal of faith, gall, audacity, effrontery, chutzpah, or whatever to feel that you and only you can talk to God and that same God of the universe intends for you and your people to receive special treatment and to be different from the billions of others!

As one religious educator wrote, any people on this tiny cosmic speck known as Earth who really believe that they are speaking for the power behind a million galaxies in a universe beyond human comprehension are approaching insanity.

It is that self-righteousness that has sent so many millions of people to early graves. Religion mirrors mankind itself; when it is good, it can be as magnanimous and loving as any "God" could wish; but when it is bad, it can be lower and more beastly than any animal in the jungle.

## PROSELYTING

The church often led the way as nations grew such as monks moving into the wilderness in the Russian expansion to the east. While the governments were looking for new lands and trade, the churches were in search of new converts. The Roman Empire flourished and faded, the papacy grew, the Eastern Empire grew as did the Eastern Church.

Islam went through a very martial period during its first century. By 732, just 100 years after the death of Muhammad, Islam extended from Tours (Poitiers) in France to the Indus River. In addition to part of France and Spain, the empire included the Arab World as we know it today, plus Persia, Central Asia, and western India.

The Arabian Muslims ruled their empire. Jews and Christians who retained their faith were recognized as "people of the book," monotheists who practiced a religion revealed by God through scripture, a respect that is still a part of Islamic doctrine.

The age of exploration was followed by colonization. Again while governments looked for gold, missionaries looked for converts. This was particularly true in South America where the Catholic Church is still predominant. There was more diversity in Africa because there were different colonial powers involved and the church of each took up the missionary role.

American missionaries joined the new crusade to save the "heathens" in many countries as far afield as China. The Mormons still send their young people abroad for two years to "spread the word."

The current prize to pursue is the former atheistic Communist states. The Pope visited the Baltics where there are many Catholics, but the Russian Orthodox Church watched with concern because of the flood of missionaries into the former Soviet Union.

The competition for souls is not just theological but political. In the Muslim Central Asian republics, secular Turkey is pitted against pro-Iranian fundamentalists for influence. Some of the new states are encouraging the revival of their churches to strengthen national loyalty.

The Russian legislators tried to bolster the Russian Orthodox Church and restrict other religions. President Yeltsin forced them to drop the total ban on foreign missionaries. Church attendance has swelled, services are on television, American preachers visit Moscow, Mormons have fanned out across the land, and Sun Myung Moon's Unification Church presents lectures.

Faith is important but numbers play a role in determining power. The Mormon Church is relatively small and is trying to enlarge. Judaism is small with power centers only in Israel and the US. The Catholic Church is quite large and predominant in many countries.

But numbers do not automatically equate to power. Islam is large and in many countries but it is diverse and not centrally directed. Iran and Iraq, both Muslim, fought for eight years and then Iraq invaded Muslim Kuwait.

Islam professes to regulate all aspects of life but it offers only general guidelines and principles which are always open to interpretation. There is no central source of religious authority or doctrine and there is no priesthood so divergences of interpretation of the Quran are almost guaranteed. The

Protestants are numerous but also diverse and uncoordinated.

## FUNDAMENTALISM

Fundamentalism should not be thought of as something new in religion since it refers to returning to the basic precepts or purity of a religion. Violations of human rights in the name of nationalism are often called fascism; violations in the name of ethnicity can be called tribalism; violations in the name of religion are sometimes called fundamentalism.

However, in the current world context, fundamentalism has been built by the media into a two-word, propaganda expression: Islamic fundamentalism. We will examine fundamentalism in several religions.

### Islamic Fundamentalism

There has been considerable attention given to Islamic fundamentalism in the US in recent years. It has become a caricature of radical, militant, terrorist groups in the Arab/Muslim world out to kill innocent people. They are against us and our friends and we are afraid of them. Earlier terms were Islamic resurgence, Islamic revivalism, and Islamization.

The problem is whether any of them is accurate. They resulted from events in the Middle East which raised anxieties in the US. Given American indifference to and unawareness of the region, it was only when events directly touched US interests that Americans became concerned.

The resurgence of Islam only gained public attention after the oil embargo in 1973, though there had been some attention to the 1967 war, mainly gloating over the easy Israeli victory over "those Arabs." Islamic fundamentalism only reached center stage in 1979 with the fall of the Shah in Iran and the formation of an Islamic theocracy under Ayatollah Khomeini and his mullahs.

It is usually a good rule not to apply words to describe people that they would not accept and apply to themselves. There is no word in Arabic for fundamentalism and Muslims do not call themselves fundamentalists or define others as such.

A revival of Islam has swept through the Middle East, but it is primarily a peaceful movement calling for a return to religious purity. But a small number of desperate radicals has turned to violence. It is their actions which gain attention and have made Islamic fundamentalism a current term which we must recognize. It is not as much a well-defined program as it is a mood. It is a many-sided search to reaffirm Muslim prestige in the modern world.

What then is Islamic fundamentalism? It is the advocacy of a moral ideal of Quranic purity. It is anti-intellectual and anti-modernist rejecting the achievements of the contemporary era. Muslim societies have gone "wrong" because they strayed from the righteous path due to the immoral encouragement of the West. Therefore, the only way to regain their greatness is to return to the righteous path, and that would include throwing out the West.

Fundamentalists are searching for legitimate government, a moral economy, equity, and justice for all. They feel that their leaders have not only strayed from the Quran but that they have failed to solve the chronic unemployment, corruption, and hopelessness in the Muslim World. They are activists with scriptural shibboleths.

They tout an ideology but not a theology. They may provide an enduring service by forcing people trying to understand the Muslim World to see the difference between **theology** -- related to philosophy and the comprehension of life -- and **ideology** -- related to power, which you will recall involves action programs to attain values and goals.

It is meant to be a challenge to the world in general, and the West in particular, as having been responsible for all the "problems" of the Muslim World which were caused by modern, liberal, capitalistic concepts which violate the Quran. But do not blame the Quran.

The good book states "Let there be no compulsion in religion." It is not the religion; it is the interpreters of the religion. Where it involves the US, it is aimed at punishing American support for Israel and the secular Muslim states.

It looks for mass involvement and has generated messianic ambitions by some of its leaders. The appeal is to poor, frustrated, disenfranchised Muslims living in an uncertain, overcrowded world. But on a second level, fundamentalism is a class or generational struggle. As seen in most revolutions, even the Communist, the activists are not solely disenfranchised rural rabble, but upwardly mobile transplants to urban areas attuned to social issues.

In the examples we have seen so far, the objectives of

these fundamentalists have been to remove the "modernist" government and take the country "back" to the better ideals and install an Islamic government which will rule according to the Quran.

There are several problems with that. The Quran does not tell you how to run a modern government. Many of these ideas if implemented violate the Quran which calls for toleration of the human rights of others. It tends to become a ploy to seize power using religion as a screen.

In the case of Iran, we saw a barbaric regime operate in the name of religion and commit unspeakable atrocities. They still are anxious to export their views as the Hezbollah continued to operate in Lebanon causing difficulties there and intimidating the Israelis by terrorist killings in an effort to destroy the peace agreement between the Palestinians and the Israelis. The legacy of the Ayatollah Khomeini is a blight on the world.

Much of the worst of what we call Islamic fundamentalism is really Khomeinism. We have forgotten what a sick, pathetic, despicable, evil being he was. He removed his chosen successor just days before he died because the man disagreed with his order to massacre thousands of political prisoners at the end of the Iran-Iraq War. Khomeini evidently issued orders permitting the guards to drain the blood of *mujahedin* before execution and he sanctioned the rape of *mujahedin* women on the eve of their execution. It is extremely difficult to conceive of a less pious man.

Algeria has been in turmoil since the Islamic Salvation Front nearly took power after strong showing in the elections. Pakistan and the Sudan gave in to their groups and announced that they were Islamic states and that they would be administered according to the *sharia*, a body of Islamic law.

The Islamic Salvation Group is using Germany as a base to smuggle weapons to fundamentalist fighters at home in Algeria. There are 14 Islamic fundamentalist groups organized in Germany with growing influence among the 2.5 million Muslim residents. There was evidence that Muslim militants were planning attacks in Germany.

Americans, with their brief history, tend to forget that the peoples in the Middle East, the cradle of civilization, have a glorious history of thousands of years. They have a rich culture with great traditions in science and literature. They have been humiliated by colonialism and by Israel's powerful presence in their midst. Extremism has come from alienation and social displacement in this modern world. The countries are not very democratic and there are few ways to express their concerns. The mosque and Islam are sometimes the only avenue.

Discontent runs deep because of widespread poverty, growing unemployment, and high prices. Migration to the cities has caused large slums in big cities like Cairo. There is a sense of rootlessness which can make fundamentalism attractive to poor peasants. But even young members of the middle class are frustrated when they are poor, cannot find jobs, and cannot see any prospects for a better future.

The effect of Khomeini and fundamentalism has spread across the Middle East. It was unusual to see a veil in Cairo 10-15 years ago; now many of the women wear them. Women had gained prominence in most fields in Egypt. Now the tide of fundamentalism has put the women on the defensive in many ways.

Through belief or coercion, many of the university classrooms are divided with men on one side and women on the other. The head of the women's branch of the Muslim Brotherhood calls for segregation of the schools, hospitals, and workplaces, wearing of the veil, and permitting husbands to strike their wives "lightly."

In Manshiat Nasser, one of the many slums in Cairo, 90% of the women are illiterate and fall outside any social help. Even though female circumcision is illegal in Egypt, nearly all the women there have been circumcized, their clitorises cut off with knives or razors when they were children. Domestic violence is common and rape is treated lightly. This is the legacy of fundamentalism. Educated women should not tolerate it.

The search for a scapegoat is not unusual in such circumstances. Many in the Middle East have found that scapegoat in the US rather than searching for the true sources of their problems. Many are convinced it is an American conspiracy to run the world.

They see the Middle East as the main American strategic target because it has what we want (oil) and what we do not like (Islam). Unfortunately, this is not just cranks, but the view of many politicians, academics, and journalists as well as religious leaders. **They see the New World Order as a plan for American control.**

There are three themes for why Washington is seeking world hegemony -- anti-Islam, colonialism, and lust for oil. Fundamentalists see hatred of Islam as the main motive. Radio Baghdad announces "The New World Order simply aims at crushing Islam and its people in the Islamic World." This results from a combination of the Christian "Crusades spirit" and Jewish plans for a Greater Israel.

Nationalists see colonialist motives. Libya claims the CIA is creating "a world dictatorial police system under the control of the United States" to restore colonialism. A Jordanian newspaper claimed the US Government had plans to make "Arabs and Muslims into the new Red Indians under the hegemony of the New World Order."

These people can then explain most US actions in a slanted vein. Kuwait was a "trap" for Saddam Hussein, an effort to impose American-style Islam, and to control the oil. The World Trade Center bombing was done by the CIA to discredit Islam in America, also done by Israeli intelligence to discredit Palestinians. Somalia was "genocide" and new colonialism. The Cairo Population Conference was to weaken Islam by reducing the Muslim birth rates, an attack on Islam to break the family system and weaken social values. Obviously, there are deep misperceptions of US aims in the Middle East.

President Clinton wanted to improve relations with Muslim countries. Islam, like Christianity or any other religion, has its moderates and its extremists. It is the extremists who give us difficulty, not Islam.

Clinton's task would be easier if he had less Israeli influence in his Administration and in US foreign policy. (Clinton has numerous "warm" Jews in the President's office, 7 out of 11 top staffers in the National Security Council, two cabinet officers, and a long list of officials in the State Department.)

The 14-year war in Afghanistan created an army of fanatics. Volunteers from 50 countries supported the rebel *mujahedin*. Some of them received military training and fought there. Some of these former fighters are now back home in Egypt, Algeria, and Tunisia working in the radical groups.

Interestingly, after three years of civil war by these various warlords who cannot agree on how to run Afghanistan, in 1995 an Islamic fundamentalist student militia, called the **Taliban**, was formed. The Taliban was disgusted with the power-hungry warlords and marched on Kabul hoping to throw all of them out.

If you accept that the attraction of Islamic fundamentalism is the frustration and sense of hopelessness of the Muslims with their contemporary problems, one of their largest problems has been Israel. Israel is a Western country that was forced on the Arabs by Europeans who did not want Jews in Europe. The fact that the US has become the major, and now the only, supporter of Israel has placed the US in an ambivalent position for the Muslims who now both love and hate America.

It was former Prime Minister Golda Meir who said that Palestinians "did not exist." There never had been such a people. That made serious negotiations difficult.

Since Israel refused over the years to make peace with the Arabs, it follows that perhaps the **greatest legacy** of the US ardent support of Israel has been the growth of Islamic fundamentalism.

In a similar vein, the continuation of the slaughter and rape of Bosnian Muslims only adds to their  frustration and adds legitimacy to the appeal of the activists that the Europeans (and the Americans) really hate all Muslims and the only path is the return to the true roots of Islam. **Frustration breeds despair. Desperate people take radical actions.**

We are witnessing the creation of the new bogey man, Islamic fundamentalism, to justify new policies. The Russians are increasingly using the argument that radical Islamists are a threat to ethnic Russians. In Central Asia, they used that justification to intervene to protect the local Russian population. As we have already seen, the Russians were shelling Afghanistan.

There were strong calls in Moscow for intervention not only to protect Russian interests in Tajikistan, but in all the former republics of the Soviet Union. It is not clear that the Russians in Tajikistan were in any danger; the only Russians killed were combatants on the border.

At the same time the Russians were shelling Afghanistan, the Israelis were shelling southern Lebanon, claiming a defensive act against Hezbollah. Israel for years tried to sell itself to the US as a critical ally against the Soviet Union. With the demise of the USSR, Israel needed a new justification for all that money it takes from the US. Israel worked assiduously to convince the American people that

Islam was as great a threat to Western values as the Communists were. It then painted Iraq as the great evil of the area. After the US smashed Iraq, Israel had to shop again. This time it was Iran.

Ironically, the Israelis supported Hamas while they were trying to destroy Arafat and the PLO. Now Hamas is murdering Israelis in an effort to block the Israeli agreement with Arafat.

Israel could attack Iran from the air but could not be sure of removing its nuclear development facilities without placing forces on the ground which they are unable to do. There was much discussion in the Israeli media about how Iran must start a war so that they can be dealt with like Iraq was. Of course, the US would be needed to provide the forces and they would need to "persuade the US" to take action.

The Israelis have been at least partially successful because of the new Clinton policy: keep Israel militarily strong and maintain a dual containment policy against Iran and Iraq.

Just as radical Jewish and Christian leaders are not necessarily violent, the same is true of some of the Muslims. The leader of Egypt's radical al-Gamaa al-Islamiyya (the Islamic Group) calls for dialogue and no violence. He still wants to overthrow the government and install religious rule but he states "there should be no bloodletting" according to Islam.

There has been an historic struggle between dogmatic (fundamentalist) and dynamic (modernist) Islam. Islamic fundamentalism, or radical activists who happen to be Muslims, represents an influence far greater than their numbers.

It is a handy menace to use as a new crusade. It will remain a threat to the secular Muslim governments and to the West as long as the underlying problems remain: frustration with the inability of those governments to deal with the social and economic problems and as long as Israel will not return the lands taken in 1967 and permit the formation of a Palestinian state. When better conditions prevail, there will be little attraction for the radical activists of Islamic fundamentalism.

## Jewish Fundamentalism

There has been so much propaganda generated in the American media that we have been conditioned to associate the word "fundamentalism" only with Islam much as we have been conditioned to associate the word terrorist with Arab or Muslim. This has been quite deliberate in an effort to keep the Muslim World estranged from the US. This has been so successful that we fail to associate fundamentalism with any other religions.

Like most Muslims, most Jews tend to be secular and separate religion from politics. But like most religions, there is an ultra-Orthodox fringe that takes the religion to extremes.

The Israelis have been plagued with several small religious political parties with each having a few seats in the Knesset. They have political power far out of proportion to their numbers because the Labor and Likud Parties have been about evenly split in recent years and these small parties are needed to make a parliamentary majority. Thus, they are able to force some of their religious positions on the country in order for Labor or Likud to form a government.

The ultra-Orthodox want some observances that would truly disrupt the country and violate many other peoples' rights. For example, they want a total ban on the use of vehicles during the Sabbath, including the grounding of El Al air line.

Many of the people who were attracted to settle in the occupied West Bank and Gaza are radical in their religious beliefs. They call the West Bank, Judea and Samaria, an integral part of Eretz Yisrael, the land God gave to the Jews.

Some of the settlers threatened violence in response to the agreement between the government and the Palestine Liberation Organization for autonomy in Gaza and Jericho. An example of some so-called religious figures is former Chief Rabbi Shlomo Goren who stated, "Arafat is responsible for thousands of murders. Therefore, everyone in Israel who meets him in the streets has the right to kill him." So much for brotherly love!

The *haredim*, or fervently Orthodox Jews, now constitute about 10% of Israel's Jewish population. They have a very high birth rate and one chief rabbi claims they will constitute a majority in Israeli society within 20 years.

The radical settlers, **Gush Emunim**, who were encouraged to move into the West Bank and Gaza by Begin, Shamir, and Sharon to create new history, represent an obstacle to any peace agreement since they will try to block it. These settlers are already armed and have been attacking Palestinians for years.

Shortly after the announcement of the Israel-PLO peace agreement, the Judean Police, a group (1,000 or probably many less) of Jewish vigilantes in the occupied West Bank, vowed that they would shoot on sight all members of the Palestinian police force to be created. The settlers will be a problem for any Israeli government as it tries to finally permit the formation of a Palestinian state.

There are many ultra-Orthodox Jews in the US, but Jewish extremists were not a major threat to the US even though they have caused some trouble in America. The extremist Kach organization, which the late Rabbi Meir Kahane founded, called for Israel Defense Force soldiers to disobey any orders to evacuate Jewish settlements in the occupied territories and his son stated that members of his Kahane Chai organization were undergoing military training in several camps in the US.

The Anti-Defamation League of B'nai B'rith has gotten itself into a lot of trouble since it was caught spying on American groups by illegally obtaining police files and selling some of them to South Africa. There have been numerous attacks, the worst being the assassination of Alex Odeh in California.

The main threat of Jewish fundamentalism is the restrictions it places on the freedom of operation of the Israeli government. This only compounds the frustration on the Muslim side.

## Christian Fundamentalism

The threat is most ominous from the evangelicals and the Southern Baptists, however the entire abortion dispute has been heavily tainted with religious fervor. Another of their targets has been censorship of books and other materials in American schools.

Leading the challenges are the Christian Coalition, Citizens for Excellence in Education, and the Eagle Forum which are conservative groups which want fundamentalist Christians to win seats on school boards to exercise control over curricula, employment of administrators and teachers, and school activities. They objected to certain works for promulgating Satanism, "New Age" thinking, or challenges to heavenly authority.

The group that mixes politics and religion the most is

the 40 million evangelical fundamentalists. They claim the term "evangelical" is not a synonym for fundamentalist or conservative. They claim to believe in a personal relationship to Christ, not through denomination or clergy, and are committed to spreading the gospel to nonbelievers.

Television has given them great power, both to reach people and to raise money. Their latest effort to strengthen their power base is to bring the Word of God into the courtroom.

There is a rapidly growing network of Christian legal organizations for liberal activism and the creation of their own law schools to train "Christ's attorneys." One of those is Regent University School of Law in Virginia Beach, Virginia founded by Pat Robertson in 1987 which teaches jurisprudence with "biblical underpinnings."

The Regent Law School mixes Bible study and evangelical strategy to provide "God's perspective on law." Just like Robertson, who could not pass the bar examination, these students are low on passing the bar exam, but they are ready to apply their "First Amendment fundamentalism."

Also based at Regent is the American Center for Law and Justice "To defend the rights of believers." These organizations focus on school prayer, home schooling, free speech, and to outlaw abortion. A current drive is for a religion amendment to the Constitution for freedom for religious activity in the public sphere.

"These religious-right legal groups have done a very effective job of convincing people there is war against religion in this country when there is not," according to Barry Lynn, a lawyer and clergyman, executive director of Americans United for Separation of Church and State.

Another group, Life Dynamics, Inc., founded by Mark Crutcher in Denton, Texas, is sponsoring a program for abortion malpractice. They have 500 expert witnesses to testify and will help in lawsuits to drive abortion clinics "out of business by driving up their insurance rates." Crutcher talks about a "civil war" between pro-choice and pro-life supporters.

According to Molly Ivins, a political columnist for the *The Fort Worth Star-Telegram*, these are "The most frightening people in America. And anybody who doesn't feel alarm doesn't have a lick of common sense.... I see no reason to let these blue-bellied nincompoops screw up the First Amendment." A colorful Texas description!

The evangelical belief system centers around the biblical land of Zion and the modern Zionist state of Israel, which they consider to be the same. Hal Lindsey, author of *The Late Great Planet Earth* and *There's a New World Coming* and other books, stated that God has foreordained that we fight a nuclear Armageddon. The television evangelists who have received the word from God include Pat Robertson, Jimmy Swaggart, Jim Bakker (recently released from jail), Oral Roberts, Jerry Falwell, Kenneth Copeland, Richard De Haan, Rex Humbard, etc. In their view, God has divided us into two categories: Jews and Gentiles. God has an earthly plan for the Jews and a heavenly plan for "born again" Christians. The rest of the world, Muslims, Buddhists, Hindus, etc. as well as Christians not born again, do not concern Him. Planet Earth will be destroyed and Peace is not for those not born again.

These people believe that a nuclear Armageddon is inevitable and that born again Christians should welcome that catastrophe. When the final battle begins, Christ will lift them up into the clouds. They will be saved. They will be **Raptured**. They will endure none of the torment below.

President Ronald Reagan supposedly believed this as well as some of those around him. All of this is centered around Israel which accounts for their total devotion to that country. [It is unfortunate that House Speaker Newt Gingrich's wife works for an Israeli company and that neither sees anything wrong with it.] This is a fantastic and sad view of mankind. (For the shocking details, see *Prophecy and Politics, Militant Evangelists on the Road to Nuclear War* by Grace Halsell, Lawrence Hill & Company, 1986.)

In 1988, a small but vocal group of Christian fundamentalists argued that Mikhail Gorbachev was the Antichrist, the Devil's agent on earth, Mr. 666. According to New Testament lore, the Antichrist is the Satanic dictator who will plunge the world into war and misery before Jesus Christ returns to save the faithful. They quoted scriptures to support their thesis. Obviously since Gorbachev was the Antichrist, no deal should be made with him, there should be no summits, no START talks, and no agreements.

When Israel and the PLO reached an agreement in 1993, the prophecy scholars were busy going back to the Bible to see whether the step toward peace was also a step closer to Armageddon. They argued over whether Yasser Arafat was the Antichrist and whether everything in the Middle East could be interpreted as a prelude to the end times.

Jerry Falwell was given a jet airplane by the Israelis and he repaid them with his full support. When the Israelis bombed the reactor in Iraq in 1981, the first person Menachem Begin called was not a Jewish senator or a rabbi but Falwell to get to work for him.

Likewise the Moral Majority's Cal Thomas called the bombing a brilliant military operation and termed winning in war was following the Golden Rule -- "Whoever has the gold, rules." That could be considered both unChristian and unAmerican.

During the 1982 invasion of Lebanon, both Falwell and Thomas went over and met Major Haddad, the Israeli puppet in southern Lebanon. They became publicists for the Likud government upon their return.

The demise of the Soviet Union must be devastating to these people because as one said, Armageddon cannot take place in a disarmed world.

One is tempted to write off such people as the lunatic fringe, but such as Pat Robertson and Jerry Falwell reach millions of people via television and their positions are accepted as coming from holy people. The fact that these evangelicals have ardently supported Israel in its aggressive acts only compounds the US problem in the Middle East.

The drive to seize control of the school boards across the country and the Christian Coalition's "Contract with the American Family" have led many to feel that the fundamentalists are moral busybodies who are taking the good word *family* and using it as a code for censorship. Critics of the religious right have learned their lesson: "Once people truly understand the agenda, they reject it."

GOP leaders backed the religious right's agenda: public prayer, restricting abortion support by Medicaid and Planned Parenthood and in foreign aid, eliminating the Education Department and federal programs for the arts and humanities, etc. However, opposition to the agenda drew a challenge from over 80 Christian leaders and a large ecumenical group met with leaders of both parties and informed them that "the Christian Coalition does not represent the whole evangelical community, let alone most of the churches."

Religion was in the news also after the shocking Oklahoma City bombing. Religious scholars were forced once again to look at the relationship between cult violence and Christian fundamentalism.

> The traditions of fundamentalist and orthodox Christianity give powerful support and impetus to cults of fantasies and fanaticism.
> -- Weston LaBarre, Duke University

Almost every violent right wing group employs the symbols and language of Christian fundamentalism. There are militias with names like The Christian Patriots, The Righteous, Defenders of the Pure, God's Posse, and the National Alliance of Christian Militias. They tend to idolize the Book of Revelation without a clue to its meaning.

A group in Idaho called Almost Heaven, refers to themselves as a "Christian Covenant" and proclaims that white people are the masters of the world. A Baptist preacher leads the Michigan Militia and says: "Our God is not a wimp. He's the God of righteousness and wrath." David Koresh was reading the bible to his followers up to the end in Waco.

Thus religious and biblical illiteracy can become toxic. A strong savior arrives -- a dominant, authoritarian, fatherly, charismatic figure who is usually paranoid -- and finds followers dreaming of heaven and new birth.

This savior concept is appalling to Taoist, Buddhist, and Hindu since they are self-realization religions. The savior figure is found only in Christianity and to a small degree in Islam.

> Today, our Constitution is under a severe challenge (by the political and religious right) which should stir every American.
> -- Justice Potter Stewart
> U. S. Supreme Court

The academic dean at Stanford wrote: "**The Christian Right is potentially much more dangerous to our nation than the Communist Party ever has been. This group presents the gravest crisis of this century, because of the wedding of religious slogans with the politics. They're infringing upon a precious right, that each of us inherited from those learned men of the 18th century who expressly**

**separated church and state in these United States of America."**

When Voltaire posed the question, "Which is more dangerous? Fanaticism or atheism?" His reply was that "Religious fanaticism is a thousand time more deadly."

## Frustration

The various fundamentalists have added to the frustrations of many people in power. The Islamic fundamentalists are a headache to secular Muslim leaders; they killed President Anwar Sadat and are after President Mubarak and have brought Algeria to a standstill. Their terrorist elements have been a menace to governments and organizations.

The radical elements have been a threat to conservative elements among the Muslims themselves. In addition to the Israelis trying to kill Arafat and his lieutenants, with great success, radical Muslim groups were also out to assassinate him.

Hamas in Gaza and the West Bank attracted many followers during the *intifada* and the Israeli suppression of the Palestinians. Hamas still calls for the destruction of Israel and the establishment of an Islamic Palestine leading to a greater pan-Arab union.

There is nothing that will completely remove fundamentalism from politics because it is precisely that, the use of religion as a cover for political action. That is just as true here in the US as abroad.

The Middle East could become calm with a just settlement between the Arabs and Israel, but the living conditions in the various countries must also improve if the fundamentalists are to lose their appeal.

Similar problems around the world, in Bosnia, Georgia, Azerbaijan, etc. need to improve to reduce the threat of religious fundamentalism. And we must not forget that fundamentalism spawns right wing fanaticism.

## Possible Actions

- Stress separation of church and state.

- Try to keep religion out of the political parties

starting at your local level.

•    Try to keep religious elements out of local power centers, such as school boards, book review committees, etc.

•    Ban religious organizations, groups, associations, radio, and television stations from any political activity.

•    Urge your representatives in Washington to try to apply a more balanced policy toward Israel, treating it as any other foreign country, and holding it to proper compliance with international law.

•    Urge Washington to stop pouring your hard earned tax dollars into Israel.  You  might want to stress: Fifty years are enough; stop aid by 1998.

•    If you do not feel the Christian Coalition agenda is what is good for America, let the leaders know.  (Do not count on an answer from them unless you are a constituent, but they all have hoards of young people who tally the incoming mail and calls and even if they do not have the courtesy to reply, or claim they are too busy, they do keep track of the numbers.)

House Speaker Newt Gingrich
242B Rayburn House Office Building
Washington, D. C. 20515
(202) 225-4501  Fax:  (202) 225-4656
georgia6@hr.house.gov

House Majority Leader Richard K. Armey
301 Cannon House Office Building
Washington, D. C. 20515
(202) 225-7772  Fax:  (202) 225-7614

Senate Majority Leader Robert Dole
141 Hart Senate Office Building
Washington, D. C. 20510
(202) 224-6521  Fax:  (202) 228-4569

Religion is still a powerful force in the world and two-thirds of today's armed struggles have a religious base.  Over

6,000 people attended a Parliament of the World's Religions in September 1993 in Chicago. It sometimes seemed more like a parliament of the world's conflicts. They had difficulty getting beyond dogma to ethics. They observed that too many religious and political leaders were there only for political power.

They came up with "The Declaration of a Global Ethic," one part of which stated, "We affirm that a common set of core values is found in the teachings of the religions and that these form the basis of a global ethic." It added, "there will be no better global order without a global ethic." This was the first time the world's religions joined together and proclaimed a religious counter-ethic to conflict.

Religious beliefs should be individual and personal. They are no one else's business. Religion should be private with no public sector role.

We might all do better if we would follow the simple guidance of Thomas Jefferson.

> I never told my own religion nor
> scrutinized that of another. I
> never attempted to make a
> convert, nor wished to change
> another's creed. I am satisfied
> that yours must be an excellent
> religion to have produced a life
> of such exemplary virtue and
> correctness. For it is in our lives,
> and not from our words, that our
> religion must be judged.
>
> -- Thomas Jefferson in a letter
> to Mrs. Harrison Smith, 1816

# Chapter 5

# A UNIPOLAR WORLD

## How Should the US Act?

*The Union of Soviet Socialist Republics, as a subject of international law and a geopolitical reality, is ceasing its existence.*

-- December 1991

*Do we leave [Somalia] when the job gets tough -- or when the job is done?*

-- President Bill Clinton

The rapid demise of the Union of Soviet Socialist Republics immediately changed the world order. True, there were nuclear weapons in Ukraine, Belarus, and Kazakhstan, but they were barely considered and those states were not really thought of as great powers. The new Commonwealth of Independent States was moribund and, like most confederations, was not able to establish any significant role for itself. The major remnant of the Soviet Union was Russia.

The new Russia, thrashing about with its internal problems in political disarray between its president and the old line People's Congress and economically trying to adjust to a market economy, at least for the near term, was a badly wounded bear which could barely hobble and certainly could not run. It was probably a great power in deference to its size, armaments, and international position, particularly its permanent seat on the UN Security Council, but it was no longer a superpower. The bipolar world, if not gone, was at least in recess.

The Communist World was defunct from the bipolar world perspective in that the export variety of Communism was dead. The only players left were China, North Korea, Viet-Nam, and Cuba. So the two blocs that had kept the world in the shadow of nuclear war for 45 years had dissolved.

But was it now a unipolar world? The US was the only superpower, but it was a wounded eagle which had spent so much money in the Cold War that its economy was weak and it was not necessarily up to playing a major unilateral role in the world.    Since the US was not about to use its nuclear arsenal, the world appeared less unipolar than polycentric with various power centers from Japan to Europe.

## THE WORLD'S POLICEMAN?

The end of the Cold War did not result in peace breaking out all over as hoped.    The US quickly became involved in international conflicts.    Even before the US could start withdrawing its troops from Europe, Iraq invaded Kuwait on 2 August 1990.    The US, with Russian approval since Iraq had been a Soviet client state, led a coalition to liberate Kuwait.

After six months of building up a massive force of over 500,000 troops and then six weeks of aerial attacks and 100 hours of ground assault, Saddam Hussein was ejected from Kuwait.    Since he was still in power and there were no-fly zones in the south to protect the Shiites and in the north to protect the Kurds, and sanctions were still in place four years later due to Iraqi non-compliance, there was still unfinished business with Iraq.

As the Soviet Union fell apart, the US had several concerns but did not wish to interfere with their internal affairs.    There was concern about the control of the nuclear weapons which were now in four of the former republics so the US tried to help with the assembly, control, and destruction of these weapons and to determine compliance with the arms reduction treaties that had been signed with the USSR.    There was the problem of employment of their nuclear scientists and the theft or sale of nuclear weapons to foreign countries.    On top of that, there was fighting in various parts of the former Soviet Union.

The West had a vested interest in Russian success and that it not revert to its old ways.    The West was sympathetic to President Yeltsin's problems and tried to help him.    They deferred debt payments and provided aid.    It was well recognized that it was going to be a difficult transition for the former Communist states and the world community was careful not to place any additional pressures on them.

Yugoslavia disintegrated and Slovenia and Croatia were recognized and joined the community of nations.    Bosnia represented a different problem.    The Europeans were less supportive of the Bosnian Muslim state (the other two are

Catholic) and soon Croatia and Serbia were fighting and then they joined forces to break up Bosnia and take pieces of it for incorporation into their countries. The US meekly tried to lead but the Europeans did not agree to follow and the US stood by and watched the "ethnic cleansing" as the Muslims were raped and slaughtered. President Clinton could not make up his mind what to do about it so he did nothing. More unfinished business.

Somalia went from its usual undisciplined mess to absolute chaos, so the US deployed a humanitarian force to open the way for food to reach the starving people. That went well and the US turned the operation over to the UN, but then the fighting flared again among the tribal factions and the UN and US forces became engaged in peacemaking trying to disarm the factions instead of peacekeeping. Seeing the same forces who brought those starving people food killed by their rebel forces caused many of the 28 countries supplying the UN contingent to turn against the operation. It was difficult to disengage. US troops were sent in to get the UN out. More unfinished business.

Even though the US is sometimes the only country that could effectively intervene in some of these disputes, the simple fact is that the US does not wish to be the world's policeman. President Clinton put it very succinctly when he said I do not wish to send US troops to Bosnia if they are going to come home in body bags. The US sees its preferred role as a provider of logistical support for multilateral forces, such as transportation and communications.

There are too many disputes in the world for any one state to try to be the policeman. It is time for the UN to be provided better planning personnel and facilities and better command and control plus appropriate forces assigned to the UN for contingency operations. The downside problem is that the operations in Bosnia and Somalia are destroying the UN's credibility. We will address the UN role in the next chapter.

## Possible Actions

• Unilaterally take action in some of these hot spots. That would require not only expenses but accepting casualties.

• Support regional organizations or the UN to stop international lawlessness before it sucks us into wars.

## A NEW FIRST WORLD

Early in the Cold War, there was the Free World and the Communist World and everyone else was considered either with them or against them. That faded with the non-aligned movement so a Third World evolved. That division was basically political but it then took on an economic description as it tended to be a group of poorer or less developed countries.

The Second, or Communist, World has basically disappeared. The 15 states of the former Soviet Union plus the states of Eastern Europe are now more in tune with the Free World, except that there might be some question about the states in the Caucasus and in Central Asia in the economic description.

The First World then is a fairly large group of advanced or developed countries. It is these countries which can support the UN and other regional organizations and which must provide the leadership for the world community.

## SHOULD THE CONCEPT OF THREE WORLDS BE CHANGED?

Even though the entire idea of three worlds is necessarily arbitrary, it has been useful as a tool for dealing with some aspects of world affairs in generalities. With over 180 states now, 185 presently in the UN, that makes for a very large Third World or grouping of less developed countries (LDCs). Many countries have made great advances in their economies while others like Somalia and Liberia, for example, now are places but can hardly be called states.

If such a classification of states has any value, then a new division should be devised. The First World should be the major powers based on  perhaps gross national product, size and capability of armed forces, per capita income, and population. A second  tier of advanced  states could be designated the Second World. Regardless of the system, it will still be arbitrary; that is unavoidable. It will always be difficult to categorize countries like Singapore, Belgium, and the Netherlands or Israel which are small but advanced with countries like India or Pakistan and Indonesia, which are large but not as advanced in some ways. Yet, some have nuclear weapons like Israel and probably India and Pakistan. It will be difficult to agree on the criteria for differentiation.

There should then be perhaps Third, Fourth, and Fifth Worlds to provide some differences to reflect the great diversity of states which range to very poor, very far behind, and very small down to just a few small islands in the ocean.

If there is too much of a stigma attached to any such categorization, then, for simplicity, we could establish the first two categories and leave all the rest in the Third World or LDCs. Almost all the money and many of the troops for the UN and the various world organizations are going to come from the first two groups.

## INTERNATIONAL BOUNDARIES -- SACROSANCT?

We have been taught for the past half century that international boundaries must be considered sacrosanct and that we must be extremely careful in even thinking about changing them. There are several explanations for this. The first probably is that any change would open Pandora's box and lead to an avalanche of demands for rectifications. That comes from the boundaries drawn by empires in their colonial areas. That includes almost all the boundaries in Africa, many in South America and the Middle East, and a few in Southeast Asia.

The second is the boundaries in Eastern Europe which the Soviets moved rather drastically in places and any attempt at rectification would launch irredentist claims from other states. Another area which was not considered significant at the time was the shifting of borders within the Soviet Union itself. That was rather unimportant until those areas became independent upon the breakup of the Soviet Union. Many of those borders are artificial and there are claims, some of which were being fought over.

The term "nation state" describes a state inhabited by one ethnic group. However, few such nation states exist since most contain several or numerous ethnic groups. The question of self-determination then is an on-going problem. The European states and North America agreed in 1975 in the Helsinki Final Act that frontiers should be changed only "by peaceful means and by agreement."

The 52 members of the CSCE signed the Pact of Stability in March 1995 agreeing to peacefully settle disputes. This meant that former East bloc countries would have to settle longstanding border disputes and ethnic conflicts before they could join NATO or the European Union.

## The Soviet Union

There are many, many disputed borders within the former Soviet Union that were imposed by that totalitarian regime. Now that those former republics are separate states, some of those differences are international disputes. Also, all the borders with Europe were adjusted by Stalin after the Soviet army marched west in World War II. Those are the borders with Poland, Slovakia, Hungary, and Romania.

The Polish border was moved west 200 miles. There are Polish-speaking minorities in Lithuania, Belarus, and Ukraine and a German minority in southwest Poland. What is now Moldova was part of Romania before World War II. Neither Romania nor the people in the area accepted the seizure by the USSR. Kaliningrad in the north was part of Prussia. After the war, Stalin forced the German population out and it is now entirely Russian. However, it has no land access to Russia since Lithuania became independent.

The fighting in Azerbaijan and Georgia will most likely result in some form of border adjustments. It appears likely that there will be discussions of borders within some of the former republics as well as between some of them and their neighbors despite the agreement by the leaders of the CIS that borders were inviolable.

## Reunification of Germany

One of the most stirring moments of the end of the Cold War was the removal of the Berlin Wall. It had represented everything that was evil about the Communist Empire. A wall was built not to keep foreigners out but to keep their own people in; many died trying to get through the barbed wire to cross those plowed strips to freedom. My own recollection is still vivid: free Berlin was a vibrant city living in technicolor; crossing at Check Point Charlie into East Berlin was to change to black and white; it was drab and dreary.

In this case, the number of world states was reduced as the two Germanies were reunited on 3 October 1990. There was only one divided country left from World War II: Korea. (Another peaceful reunification was the case of the two Yemens, but with subsequent difficulties.) The reunification was traumatic. The two sectors had grown far apart in their economies and even culturally. It cost West Germany an enormous amount of money to absorb the East and led to a recession in Germany. Many West Germans suffered salary cuts and reductions in their social benefits.

The East was years behind in technology so unemployment soared in the East and there was social despair as they had to make radical adjustments to catch up with the West. Germany absorbed hundreds of thousands of newcomers. With high unemployment and housing shortages, it was not surprising that there was some violence. There were riots in several European countries. Security had come to be more concerned with economic stability than with armies.

German reunification was seen as irreversible. Scandanavia moved to pull the Baltic states under its wing. There were ideas of Pan-European security and economic cooperation, but there was also potential for chaos.

## Division of Czechoslovakia

Early on it was clear that the marriage of the Czechs and Slovaks was headed for divorce. Fortunately, this turned out to be a friendly divorce and the two split peacefully. However, the two were likely to have a more difficult time separately in the economic world than if they had stayed together. With Western Europe trying to unite, they were headed in the opposite direction.

## Disintegration of Yugoslavia

We have already addressed the breakup of the former Yugoslavia in some detail. Yugoslavia was an artificial country created by the amalgamation of six republics (Slovenia, Croatia, Bosnia and Hercegovina, Serbia, Montenegro, and Macedonia) plus two provinces (Vojvodina and Kosovo). There were deep religious and historical differences among these groupings and they had been held together by the strong personality of Tito. After his death in 1980, the rather loose confederation with a rotating presidency was short lived.

The various entities were not geographically homogenous. Slovenia was the most, but Serbia, Croatia, and particularly Bosnia-Hercegovina had the various peoples mixed in their populations. In addition, there had been considerable intermarriage so that it was really impossible to align the country by the old labels.

Serbia wanted to keep the old Yugoslavia together. The others wanted out, mainly because of Serb domination. Slovenia had the makeup and the potential to go it alone, and it was not contiguous with Serbia so the Serbs were more limited in their potential to stop the Slovenes. All the rest bordered Serbia, and with the Yugoslav Army dominated by Serbia and with Serbs intermixed in the areas, it was easy for Serbia to invade to "protect" Serbs and to strive for a Greater Serbia.

The Muslim majority of Bosnia received no support from the Europeans, who were not particularly anxious to have a Muslim state in Europe. Serbia attacked and dominated most of Bosnia in a strange alliance with the Croats who they had been fighting only a short time before. Since the Europeans would not intervene, they sent a strange representative to mediate: Lord David Owen, a former foreign secretary who had split the Labor Party, divided the Liberal Social Democrat alliance and then destroyed the Social Democratic Party, who was known as Dr. Death in a British satirical magazine. Along with US former Secretary of State Cyrus Vance, he tried to get the Muslim leadership to accept the division of Bosnia. Vance finally withdrew from the plan, but Lord Owen continued to press for the dismemberment of Bosnia.

The plan offered Serbia 52% of Bosnia (they were in control of about 70% of the republic), 17% to Croatia, with 31% left to the Muslims. In addition it was a gerrymandered area that would not leave Bosnia as a viable economic entity. The Muslims refused the offers even though their military situation was desperate. They continued to fight on in hopes that someone in the world would come to their rescue. Much unfinished business there including some war crimes trials that should be held.

Also, the two provinces may have problems. There is a large Hungarian minority in Vojvodina and an Albanian majority in Kosovo. The final borders of what was Yugoslavia are not yet determined. More unfinished business.

## Israel

The entire history of Israel is a sad collection of lies, deceptions, dreams, and nightmares. The British made promises to both the Jews in Europe for a homeland in Palestine and to the Arabs in Palestine to garner their support in defeating Germany's ally Turkey in World War I. The British deceived both of them. They then joined with the French to divide up the old Ottoman Empire. The immigration of Jews into Palestine grew during the interwar years. This generated a not surprising harsh reaction from the Palestinians who were being displaced. After World War II, the British, exhausted from their war with Germany, tired of the Jewish terrorism in their Palestinian Mandate and turned it over to the UN in 1947.

There was no mention of a Jewish state in any of the negotiations prior to the UN vote in 1947 -- the promise had been for a Jewish homeland. The Israeli delegate to the UN was instructed by Ben-Gurion not to agree to boundaries specified by the UN then or subsequently. His explanation to his diplomats for accepting partition but not agreeing to the partition boundaries was that Israel should accept what it was granted, and acquire the rest when it could (as it did in 1967).

The UN General Assembly passed a non-binding resolution in November 1947 partitioning Palestine. Even though there was a large Arab majority, 56% of the land was given to the Jews and 44% to the Palestinian Arabs. Jews then were only about one-third of the population (608,000 to 1,327,000) and owned about 9% of the land. In the Jewish part of the partition, there were 498,000 Jews and 497,000 Arabs; in the Arab part there were 725,000 Arabs and only 10,000 Jews. Jerusalem, which was to be a *corpus separatum*, had 105,000 Arabs and 100,000 Jews. The Arab world protested this betrayal and the UN backed off from its partition plan and started work on a trusteeship for Palestine.

The Zionists seized the opportunity to conquer a new state. The Jewish terrorists groups, the Irgun (led by Menachem Begin) and the Stern Gang (led by Yitzhak Shamir) terrorized the civilian population, notably with the bombing of the King David Hotel and the Deir Yassin massacre. More than 750,000 Palestinians fled in fear or were driven out at gunpoint changing the Arab majority in Palestine to an Arab minority whereby David Ben-Gurion declared Israel an exclusive Jewish state on 14 May 1948.

President Harry Truman was against recognizing the new state and Secretary of State George Marshall was strongly against it as damaging to US interests, but Truman was having trouble in his bid for reelection and his special assistant, Clark Clifford, told him recognition would give him the Jewish vote. Marshall was so upset by Clifford's recommendation that he told the President, if he voted, he would not vote for him, and the General never spoke to Clifford again. Thus the US became the second state, after the USSR, to recognize the new state of Israel.

One of the key points is that no Israeli leader has ever defined the borders of the state of Israel. As was to become characteristic of Israeli diplomacy, some of their greatest land acquisitions came after ceasefires. In 1949, they seized the Huleh valley below Syria's Golan Heights. One rarely reads of the Israeli provocations that led to Syria's firing on the newly established kibbutzim below the Golan Heights.

At the end of 1948, the Israeli government moved from Tel Aviv to Jerusalem. Israel attacked Egypt and then Syria and Jordan in 1967 and seized the Sinai (returned by the Camp David Agreement in 1979), Gaza, the West Bank, East Jerusalem, and the Golan Heights. Other than stating that Jerusalem is forever the capital of Israel which has been totally rejected by the international community, the government still has never stated what it considers to be the boundaries of Israel.

The initial agreement between Israel and the PLO in September 1993 to turn over Gaza and Jericho to PLO administration left the status of the frontiers for future negotiations. Israel does not want a Palestinian state, and the US, in violation of all its heritage of support for human rights and the strong stand normally taken for the right of self-determination, still sides with Israel and against a Palestinian state. The power of an influential lobby in Washington! More unfinished business.

## Possible Actions

• Perpetuate the myth that no borders should be changed except by peaceful agreement. However, Bosnia would make it difficult to look in the mirror!

• Accept that some borders probably should be changed and create border commissions in either regional organizations or the UN.

## THE NATION STATE

The explosive growth in the number of states from about 50 at the end of World War II to nearly 200 now provokes the question of the viability of the nation state as the fundamental unit in world politics. At the same time that we observe the European Community (EC) trying to bring states together into a larger unit for better conditions, mainly economic, we see other states breaking up into smaller entities. With few exceptions, such as Singapore and Taiwan, the smaller states are having a very difficult time providing for their people.

World War I shook the stability of states in the modern sense as the two large empires, the Austro-Hungarian and the Ottoman, were destroyed and replaced with new states under the principle of national self-determination. World War II further shook that stability. The advances of technology made the territorial states obsolete. Industrialization brought economic vulnerability and modern communications radically changed the capabilities for propaganda, psychological warfare, and the exchange of information. The threat from bombers, nuclear weapons, and intercontinental ballistic missiles rendered territorial frontiers vulnerable to all states including a superpower. We are all aware of ICBMs, and some remember the missiles launched against England late in World War II, but the Gulf War emphasized it on a reduced but realistic scale when Saudi Arabia and Israel were hit by *Scud* missiles launched from Iraq.

At the same time that states lost the  impenetrability of their sovereign areas, they faced strong domestic pressures. Regardless of the regimes, all states had become very complex social organizations which had increasing difficulty in satisfying all their functions. For security and some economic purposes, they were too small; but for some domestic issues, such as the dissatisfaction of minorities, they were too large.

Also, while facing these internal pressures, there was a growth of non-state organizations. Interstate governmental organizations evolved with regional, functional, and comprehensive roles. Thus we had NATO, the EC, the OAS, the OAU, ASEAN, the Arab League. etc. which came to play significant roles. OPEC became the most famous functional organization but there were many others dealing with space, nuclear energy, aviation, etc. These organizations are merely extensions of the nation states so that they can pursue their interests. The comprehensive organization is the UN which we will address in the next chapter. It is still a grouping of individual states but it occasionally acts on behalf of the international community.

There are also interstate non-governmental organizations such as Communism (now removed from its Soviet export base), the Catholic Church, many humanitarian groups, and as we have just covered the growing Islamic fundamentalism. There are thousands of these organizations around the world. In addition, there are the multinational corporations such as British Petroleum, IBM, Ford, and General Motors. Many of them are larger economic entities than many of the small nation states.

There are even intranational players such as Greenpeace, the Jewish lobby, Communist parties, and groups trying to remove governments, such as resistance movements (for example the Palestinian resistance movement which has several factions such as the PLO, Hamas, etc.).

Another area that has grown rapidly is the international economic system. There are many unequal players in this field. International trade had been the main arena and there is still much activity there with the EC, regional groupings in Africa, South America, and Southeast Asia and now NAFTA (North America Free Trade Agreement) with more envisioned. Trade imbalances have become major problems for some countries such as the US. Other major problems have come in international finance with exchange rates and heavy indebtedness of some countries to the point where solvency has been created to prevent bankruptcies of some states.

Of the thousands of international institutions, there are some 200 that are intergovernmental and about half of them are regional. These vary from the Universal Postal Union to the World Bank, the IMF, to the UN and its many agencies.

The sovereign nation state in its traditional form is in a major crisis. It is no longer self-sufficient or really safe within its frontiers and all states are seeing their sovereignty reduced. Would the world be better off with a smaller number of states?

## IS IT TIME FOR A WORLD REALIGNMENT?

As we have seen, nationalism has been a powerful force historically and the concept of national self-determination and the nation state have played a major role in world politics. But nationalism has also shown itself to be a very divisive force such as in Bosnia and parts of the former Soviet Union. There are many "nations" which are not states and, in this modern world where many peoples have moved about, most states are multi-national.

Nationalism is psychological; it is how one considers oneself. If you consider yourself an Ibo rather than a Nigerian, the country will have trouble if many feel that way. To be an American is to feel strongly for America regardless of whether you or your ancestors came from some country in Europe, Asia, Africa, or Latin America.

The need to provide security, education, jobs, and a decent living for one's people makes the task of a modern state quite difficult. It is not clear that the small entities can succeed. There are mini-states like Andorra, Liechtenstein, Monaco, and various small island states such as Tuvalu consisting of nine small islands in the South Pacific with a population of 8,000. The mini-states survive because the larger states permit them to. (An enclave like Goa was removed in a matter of hours and Hong Kong will soon revert to China.) These mini-states are recognized as states the same as China with 1.2 billion people or India with 800 million people.

The Liechtensteins and Monacos have survived and prospered. The real concern is for the poor states that gained their independence from the old colonial empires. The worst cases are in Africa where the standard of living has suffered in all the former colonies. These are artificial states created by European empires with little regard to the ethnic makeup of a very complex continent. Boundaries often cut across tribal lines or include tribes that have been fighting each other for centuries.

Nation states are not the answer for Africa. Each state now is really multi-national (or multi-tribal to be more accurate) and they are still not viable. Smaller units would not have a chance. Their only opportunity is to coalesce into larger economic units which have a chance to survive economically. The problem with that is to establish governments that will function well economically and still protect the rights of the various minorities. Up to now, the tribes that have gained power have used that power to reduce the strength of their rivals.

Economic unions are the wave of the future. The

Common Market is growing into the European Community with an increased political role, and the EC already includes some of the advanced economies of the world. (It is difficult to comprehend the French willing to give up the franc for a European currency to keep the mark under control but they are.) Eastern Europe will want to join. There are efforts toward greater economic cooperation in other areas such as Latin America, Southeast Asia, and North America.

Realignment is always difficult. We have seen most changes come from wars or the disintegration of empires. We are currently observing the realignment after the fall of the Communist Empire. The freeing of the colonies in Africa was generally peaceful because the Europeans would not permit any realignment. With the independence of Eritrea, that precedent is now broken and it may well be time for additional changes to be made. They cannot, however, be made by outsiders. If the peoples there wish to realign peacefully, the outside world should support them.

## Possible Actions

• Strive to maintain the nation state.

• Move toward larger political entities. The economic groupings such as the EC are probably the wave of the future. The USA was the precedent in many ways except that it brought together more homogeneous units.

• Support the revamping of some of the more difficult areas such as Africa. The solution to the fragmentation of Yugoslavia will have a major impact on future efforts.

It is not really a unipolar world just as it was not really a bipolar world for the past forty years. The US is currently the most powerful nation but it too must rely on other states and cannot stand alone in isolation. Japan has grown into an economic giant despite its recent slowdown. Germany is the powerhouse of Europe along with Russia which will continue to play a major role in world affairs. China is exploding economically and will either cooperate with or threaten the Orient. There are numerous power centers so the world remains polycentric and needs an international organization.

# Chapter 6

# THE UNITED NATIONS

## Love It or Leave It Is Not Good Enough; We Need to Fix It or Replace It

*The Purposes of the United Nations are:*

*1.   To maintain international peace and security...*

-- Article 1, UN Charter

*Ad hoc approaches dominate what should be a far more efficient and regularized system of peace-keeping operations.*

-- Madeleine Albright
US Ambassador to the UN

As World War II was drawing to a close, the victorious allies assembled to replace the League of Nations with a new organization to establish a post-war world order.   Thus the United Nations was born in June 1945 with 51 members.   It represented the best that could be negotiated at the time of disintegrating empires and a nascent Cold War; politics is still the art of the possible.

The five permanent members of the Security Council were the victorious allies against Germany and Japan which are now economic superpowers.   Two of the original five have changed: Red China replaced the Republic of China and Russia has replaced the Soviet Union.

The UN was not set up as a world government because it is a body of sovereign states.   With that built-in constraint, it was bound to have limitations.

## WORLD FORUM

Despite all the complaining about the UN, it has helped,

it has stopped some fighting, and it has become the true world forum. Who will ever forget Nikita Khrushchev banging his shoe on the desk of the Soviet delegation or Adlai Stevenson showing the pictures of the Soviet missiles in Cuba? The UN was one of the major battlefields of the Cold War. And while each superpower tried to line up allies in that Cold War, the states of the Third World found that their best place to express their views and exert any influence was in the UN. Thus it came about that the General Assembly, where each small state has one vote the same as a superpower, became the forum for the Third World; and, if they banded together in blocs, they could truly be heard.

The current Secretary General, Egypt's Boutros Boutros-Ghali, was not elected because of his lifetime of experience in international affairs but because the Africans insisted that it was their turn for UN leadership. Fortunately, he was well qualified and there were hopes he would be the one to reform the bloated elephant. He started out to revamp the mess but he later demonstrated less interest and became a typical political bureaucrat.

The UN has become overstaffed, mismanaged, underfunded, wasteful, and hobbled by politics resulting from a patronage system designed to provide "geographical balance" in filling many positions. These slots are often political payoffs and are protected even if they are no longer needed. With personnel from all over the world, it is a management nightmare which is run like a club and does not know how to set priorities, but is magnificent at resisting change.

It is a slow motion bureaucracy that cannot keep up in a real time world. It has no concept of management and politicians block any efforts to streamline operations. They spent a million dollars installing a security system in New York but it did not work and had to be scrapped.

The Advisory Committee on Administrative and Budgetary Questions, which is key to monitoring financial practices, has been headed for 18 years by the same chairman, Conrad Mselle of Tanzania. He was reelected for another two years despite accusations of nepotism and his rejection of a financial disclosure code proposed by the US.

The US contributes about $2 billion annually to the UN, paying 25% of the regular budget and about 31% of the peacekeeping costs. Many in the US, including Senator Jesse Helms, chairman of the Foreign Relations Committee, think this is a terrible waste of money.

The new Republican Congress voted to not allow US troops to be placed under foreign command in UN operations and also wanted US spending for peacekeeping to be part of the regular dues, which would seriously reduce the UN peacekeeping capability.

The Security Council has done fairly well, particularly when not hampered by the veto. In the early years, it was the USSR that blocked Security Council actions with an eventual total of 115 vetoes.

The US had made a great propaganda point of that by not using the veto. That ended under President Nixon in 1970. Since then the US has used the veto 70 times, 30 of them to shield Israel from international criticism, censure, and sanctions.

The pressure to give Germany and Japan permanent seats has raised the fear that the Third World might insist on its own representation by regional seats for Brazil, India, and Nigeria.

However, the agencies of the UN have gotten out of hand sometimes fighting for control of projects. The General Assembly did appoint a coordinator who could overrule agency heads. What is needed is reductions. The Trusteeship Council does little now but still has a big staff. The Military Committee never has done much but pours out paper. A number of specialized agencies have grown up outside the control of New York.

A particular embarrassment was UNESCO (the UN Educational, Scientific, and Cultural Organization) in Paris with its unsavory director Amadow-Mahtar M'Bow of Senegal. It took two years after the US, UK, and Singapore withdrew in 1985 before M'Bow and his relatives were forced out.

Another case is the Food and Agriculture Organization (FAO) in Rome which has been run by Edouard Saouma of Lebanon for 16 years. The UN Secretariat itself has become bloated with 69 top level officials.

With the end of the Cold War, there was even more interest in UN mediators, technocrats, and the UN's blue beret soldiers. The UN became involved from Bosnia to Somalia to Cambodia. There is much for the UN to do around the world and an internal housecleaning would add to its capability and flexibility.

## Possible Actions

•   Continue to muddle along with a bloated monster that is drifting with no clear future.

•   Send in a brutal team of administrators, probably mostly American, and revamp the UN.    Terminate **all** employees, clean out the deadwood, and hire back only those who are competent and needed.    Institute good management procedures, particularly concerning personnel controls starting with top officials.

•   Call for a world conference, but dominated by the major powers because nearly 200 delegations cannot agree on anything, to restructure (or replace) the UN with more authority.

## SANCTIONS

One of the means available to the UN after attempts at peaceful settlement of disputes and before committing armed forces is the imposition of sanctions (they used to be called boycotts).    Under Article 41 of the UN charter, "These may include complete or partial interruption of economic relations and of rail, sea, air, postal, telegraphic, radio, and other means of communication, and the severance of diplomatic relations." They can be effective in the near term, but over the longer term defections usually appear.    Their effectiveness tends to gradually erode due to some countries searching for profits, or others more concerned about balance of trade, or general skepticism about the effectiveness of sanctions.

Sanctions on South Africa, which were imposed for many years in protest of apartheid, were lifted in October 1993; but it was not clear that they had any significant effect. Actually, they forced South Africa to become more independent and they developed a very sophisticated indigenous arms industry to replace their lost sources.

Economic sanctions were imposed on Iraq after it invaded Kuwait.    There was considerable debate about the necessity for the Gulf War if more time had been permitted for sanctions to force Saddam Hussein to withdraw.    Sanctions continued after the war and they clearly weakened the country and made life difficult, but it was quite clear, since they were continued for years, that they would not have forced an Iraqi withdrawal. The sanctions were still in place four years after the war, but France and Russia were pushing to have them lifted despite American objections.

The sanctions against the former Yugoslav republics have worked against the objective of stopping the slaughter and rewarded Serb aggression. Serbia controlled the Yugoslav Army and therefore had access to all its equipment. The only ones hurt were the Bosnian Muslims who were prevented from obtaining arms thereby making them even more vulnerable to Serb aggression. In that case, the sanctions were imposed on the victim rather than the aggressor.

The US imposed economic sanctions on the Sudan in August 1993 due to its support of international terrorism. That made Sudan ineligible for all US aid except humanitarian and that the US would oppose any Sudanese requests for aid from international institutions such as the World Bank or the International Monetary Fund.

The US also imposed limited trade sanctions against China and Pakistan for two years because China sold missile technology to Pakistan in violation of an international arms control agreement. Sanctions had been lifted against Haiti but were reimposed in October 1993 when the military leader failed to step down in accordance with an agreement to permit the return of President Aristide.

President Clinton imposed sweeping sanctions on Iran in May 1995 to preclude even harsher measures proposed by the Congress, both concerned about Iran's nuclear program and its support for terrorism. There was concern that only US companies would suffer the economic loss but that there might be retaliation against some of America's friends in the Gulf, such as Saudi Arabia, Bahrain, and the UAE.

The UN imposed sweeping economic sanctions on Libya for its alleged role in the 1988 bombing of Pan Am Flight 103 which killed 270, including 180 Americans. The problem was that the sanctions were full of loopholes. Also, it took so long to gain approval in the Security Council that Qadhafi had time to buy and ship all the sophisticated oil equipment he needed and to move and hide his assets.

The sanctions froze Libyan assets as of 1 December 1993, but do not apply to oil revenues generated after 1 December. Qadhafi has thus thumbed his nose at the sanctions and at the world community.

Sanctions have not been particularly successful in forcing compliance and are of limited value as a deterrent. They can be useful as international symbols of political opposition, and since they are less risky or provocative than the commitment of armed force, they can give the image of doing something.

## Possible Actions

Since the UN is not a world government, any improvements in the authority of the UN will yield improved effectiveness in its actions. As with any organization, its pronouncements or threats are only as good as their enforcement.

• Sanctions need to be enforced. If a country violates the sanctions, such as Iran supposedly buying oil from Iraq, then sanctions should be slapped on that country also.

• Use sanctions sparingly. We have seen that they have been generally ineffective for very difficult problems such as South Africa and Iraq.

## UN FORCES

In the summer of 1993, the UN had 80,000 troops deployed in 13 countries with requests pending for an additional 14 peacekeeping missions in states from Liberia to the Solomon Islands. Peacekeeping cost nearly $4 billion in 1993, nearly five times the 1991 expenditures.

The original peacekeeping role was to stand between hostile forces, mainly in a police role. The missions the UN has undertaken have expanded to include maintaining security within a wider area, such as southern Lebanon; disarming insurgents, as in Nicaragua and Cambodia; providing humanitarian assistance, as in Cyprus and Somalia; and monitoring elections, as in Namibia, Nicaragua, Haiti, and Cambodia. The UN has become more involved in managing conflicts within a single country rather than between countries.

The large UN-authorized **peacemaking** operations envisioned by the UN Charter were made impossible by the Cold War. The UN designated North Korea an aggressor in 1950, only because the Soviets were boycotting the Security

Council. The next UN-authorized peacemaking force did not come until 1990 when the Soviets agreed to the action against Iraq in Kuwait. Peacemaking is badly needed, and the UN needs its own force.

Boutros-Ghali has called for the UN to have its own rapid deployment force under a strong Secretariat so that the UN can move quickly in times of crisis. Under the present system, it is a slow process of soliciting (begging for) troops and money from member states. Each commitment is an ad hoc arrangement, often pulled together on very short notice.

Money and logistics are constant problems. The first Pakistani UN battalion deployed to Somalia initially sat at Mogadishu airport doing nothing while subsisting on rice ordered from Karachi by their commander and paid for with his Visa card.

Not surprisingly, the US-led operations have been more successful since the US forces are fully integrated with transport, logistics, support, and maneuver elements. However, the US Congress under its new Republican leadership was anti-UN, wanted less UN peacekeeping actions, and was against US troops being placed under foreign command. President Clinton stated that any US troops committed to Bosnia would be under NATO, not UN, command.

The UN took over the Haiti operation on 31 March 1995 with about 6,000 peacekeepers and 900 civilian police. About 2,400 US troops remained with the peacekeeping force which was commanded by a US general.

## Kuwait

The massive commitment of forces into the Gulf to evict Iraq from Kuwait was authorized by the UN but was generally under US command (with close cooperation with the Saudi military leadership) and involved some 700,000 troops, 500,000 of which were American.

Operation DESERT STORM had a precise mandate from the UN, which did **not** include removing Saddam Hussein from power. When that mission was accomplished and Kuwait was liberated, the multi-lateral force was promptly withdrawn.

After the departure of the multi-lateral forces, the UN had on-going talks with Iraq concerning the long term monitoring of Iraq's weapons programs and attempts at an arrangement to sell $1.6 billion in oil to finance food and medicine purchases and to provide money for reparations for the Gulf War. Iraq was difficult and recalcitrant at every step of the talks, inspections, and negotiations and Saddam preferred to let his people suffer to show his contempt.

There was considerable consternation over the survival of Saddam Hussein and the fact that he was not captured and removed from power.  In October 1993, former President George Bush stated that

> "If we had gone beyond the UN mandate and marched on Baghdad ..., I'm convinced that we would be there still in a never-ending guerrilla war chasing Saddam from hiding place to hiding place, our sons and daughters engaged in urban street fights. And then in a show of unity the Arab World probably would have turned against the United States and its allies.  This heterogeneous, historic coalition that we forged together would have instantly shattered."

(He also stated that without that Arab support, there would have been no peace agreement between Israel and the PLO.)

The intervention in Kuwait was very important for several reasons:

First, when the international community decides that aggression is not to be tolerated, it must act quickly and forcefully.  One of the major lessons from Viet-Nam was applied by General Colin Powell, Chairman of the Joint Chiefs of Staff: if you are going to commit US troops, commit them in overwhelming force so that you are sure to succeed.

Second, an international consensus must be developed for the proposed operation.  That was done and a solid coalition was developed, forces were provided, and their troops were committed to the fight.  Our so-called "strategic ally" in the Middle East, Israel, was specifically told to stay out of the fight in order to preserve the Arab alliance.  Of course, that cost us additional money.

Third, a domestic consensus must also be developed. The American people strongly supported President Bush's actions.

Fourth, commit an appropriate force for the requirement, develop a comprehensive plan for the operation, execute it forcefully, then withdraw.

That was a **peacemaking** or combat operation, not

peacekeeping. Small UN forces which are ad hoc combinations from diverse countries are not prepared, armed, or trained for peacemaking operations which are actual fighting. Those UN contingents have been most successful in peacekeeping involving lightly armed forces in a police-like mission to stand between parties that have already agreed to a ceasefire in a dispute and keep them apart.

## Somalia

About 350,000 Somalis died in 1992 from famine, disease, and warfare. A US operation, launched in December 1992, successfully stopped the famine and opened the routes for food relief. With US forces committed in strength, about 30,000 US troops in Somalia, the warlords remained fairly quiet.

In March 1993, Somalia's 15 major political factions agreed to a ceasefire and to mediate their disputes. Most of the US forces were withdrawn and the operation was turned over to the UN in May 1993. The peacekeepers soon found themselves under attack.

The problem in Somalia was that it was initiated as a humanitarian mission to clear the way for food relief to the starving population. That was accomplished, a ceasefire between the clans was agreed, and the operation was turned over to the UN for **peacekeeping**. As the fighting flared again, the UN force was caught in a **peacemaking** operation for which it was not prepared, and it needed US combat troops.

This was a crisis for the UN because the prestige of the UN was at stake. These petty warlords, such as Mohammed Farrah Aidid of the Habr Gedir clan, demonstrated their contempt for the world body. When 24 Pakistani soldiers were ambushed, the UN was placed in a dilemma. If the UN did not retaliate, that could invite more attacks; if they did retaliate, it would likely draw the peacekeepers into Somalia's clan warfare.

Attacks against Aidid were launched, particularly with the US forces including Rangers. When the US took additional casualties, the stakes went up again. The UN was back in a peacemaking operation and needed additional US forces to conduct combat operations.

Somalia represented the worst type of problem for the UN. The country had totally collapsed: there was no government at all, full anarchy reigned with various clans fighting for their turf and potentially for the country.

The requirements were enormous: stop the clan fighting, disarm them, rebuild the limited infrastructure that was there, install some form of police force, establish a government, train new leaders, then turn the country over to them. That was a case for total **nation building**. The small contingents from 24 countries in the UN force were not prepared to undertake such a task.

The US was in the position of grabbing another sticky tar baby. We had made our humanitarian commitment successfully to help the people. Now we were having our troops killed there. The dilemma was whether to cut our losses and get out as the Congress and many of the people were demanding or to hunker down and fight it out and stay the course. That was a tough call, because it could mean years of US troops fighting and dying in a place where we were initially greeted with open arms and now were looked upon as new colonialists. The beginning of a quagmire!

President Clinton responded by dispatching another 5,300 US troops and setting a deadline of 31 March 1994 for US withdrawal. He spelled out a four-task mission for the US forces: the first was to protect the entire US contingent and its bases. He added the key statement: "Those who attack our soldiers must know they will pay a very heavy price."

---

**The UN needs a motto:    "Attack a Blue Beret and you will have to pay!"**

---

The other missions dealt with keeping the roads open, pressure on the warlords, and making it possible for the Somalis to solve their problems and survive after we departed.

The UN declared failure in February 1995 and withdrew. It took more US troops to cover the UN withdrawal. Thus ended a sad adventure of over two years, that cost $1.66 billion and 42 American and over 100 other UN lives.

As was discussed earlier, Somalia, a semi-desert scrubland, is not a nation. It has a feudal, nomadic, anticolonial past with no democratic traditions. Its 6.5 million people are still mostly nomadic, and they are divided by tribes or clans, six major clans and many sub-clans. The clans have fought for centuries over the scarce resources, mainly water rights and grazing. More recently, they have fought over who would rule the country.

Its history, for hundreds of years, has been one of egalitarian clans. That makes the task of nation building that much more difficult. There is no solid base or consensus on which to rebuild Somalia

## Possible Actions

• The major clan families should consider reorganizing the country as a federation. The present 18 regions should be reduced to less than half that number. Borders could be redrawn along clan-family lines into semi-autonomous provinces. The provinces could then jointly develop articles of federation clearly delimiting the powers of the national level.

• This would have been a natural for the UN International Trusteeship System, whereby the UN would take over the area, place it under another country or international organization as a trust territory to rebuild it and prepare it for self-government under the supervision of the Trusteeship Council. The UN does not have the ability, force, or expertise to undertake such enormous tasks itself.

This problem needed UN and OAU (Organization of African Unity) leadership with as little participation as possible by the US. Unfortunately, it was Americans with their firepower, particularly the helicopter gunships, who were called on to do most of the shooting, which meant Somali civilians being killed.

## Bosnia

The challenge of the aggression in the former Yugoslavia grew into a supreme crisis for the UN. It was not an easy task for the UN because, with fighting still in progress, it remained a combat situation, not peacekeeping.

The Europeans refused to act except for sending mediators who were amenable to rewarding aggression by dividing up Bosnia. Because there had been some terribly brutal and criminal actions committed, the UN finally agreed to send in some troops to protect some of the people and try to get food to them. The US was even parachuting food in to the

124 You and the New World Order

starving people.

However, the commitment of UN peacekeeping (not peacemaking) troops on the ground prior to a stabilized ceasefire, in violation of the normal UN policy, only complicated the chances for a solution. First, the Serbs and the Croats challenged the UN forces by blocking their convoys, demanding payment of bribes, even looting them and killing the truck drivers, preventing them from moving freely, and in effect holding UN soldiers as hostages. UN helicopters were forced to land for Serb or Croat "inspections."

Those are the types of **totally unacceptable actions** that the UN must absolutely stop if it is ever going to be a respected organization. When there was no reaction from the UN or the West, the Serbs and Croats were only emboldened in their conviction that the West was not going to do anything and that they could do as they pleased.

The second result was that with the UN troops on the ground, which included British and French contingents, the western Europeans, particularly Britain and France, resisted any serious military measures against the Serbs. They were concerned about **reprisals** against their troops. The UN forces had become **hostages**.

It was sad that Britain and France did not have the guts to tell the Serbs that if you touch one of our soldiers, we will destroy your army! Serbia could have been stopped quickly. So could Hitler in 1936!

NATO talked about air strikes against the Serb artillery positions ravaging Sarajevo but could not obtain full agreement to conduct them. The UN let the Serbs "get away with murder" hoping it would eventually lead to peace. Some 85 peacekeepers were killed in Bosnia. Boutros-Ghali finally permitted his beleaguered peacekeepers to shoot to kill to protect themselves.

The situation worsened in May 1995 when the Bosnian Serbs attacked and killed UN troops. After US pressure, there were some air strikes against Serb positions and ammunition dumps. The Serbs retaliated by seizing over 300 UN troops and handcuffing them to bridges and dumps.

It was a world class embarrassment to see a British officer in a blue beret handcuffed to a pole. This should have been the last straw to cause NATO to call for the UN withdrawal and then go in and clean out that mess, bringing Bosnian Serb leader Radovan Karadzic and his military chief

Ratko Mladic to trial as war criminals and, if guilty, execute them. (More below under war criminals.)

The US talked but had only sent a company of troops to Macedonia. Talk was cheap.

One of the nagging problems was the disappointment in the Muslim World. It was obvious that if oil had been at stake or the victims were Christians, there would have been action. But the slaughter of Muslims did not evoke much sympathy in Europe or the US. That attitude only fed Islamic fundamentalism. That may be one of the major nightmares that comes back to haunt the West in the years ahead.

The UN, or probably NATO, was ready to commit 50,000 troops to the area after a peace was agreed upon. President Clinton had promised up to 25,000 Americans (at an estimated cost of $4 billion for the first year). The ceasefires had been numerous but ephemeral. The peace was being decided on the battlefield not by negotiations.

The Muslims were at a distinct disadvantage, with an embargo on arms sales to them, and with the full strength of the Yugoslav Army available to Serbia. The Muslims were slowly being slaughtered and driven out of their areas.

On 12 January 1995, Croatian President Franjo Tudjman ordered the 12,000 UN peacekeepers out of Croatia by 30 June. Once again, US troops may have to be committed to cover the withdrawal of the UN force.

A monstrous new term had entered our vocabularies: **"ethnic cleansing."** The Bosnian Muslims were raped, tortured, slaughtered, and forcibly relocated. Centuries old mosques were dynamited (for example the ornately decorated Ferhad-Pasha Mosque north of the town of Banja Luka, dating from 1583, one of the most beautiful in the Balkans; and Arnaudija, 1587; and five mosques in Bijeljina).

As was covered earlier, these people are the same ethnically; they were divided historically and came under different religions. The West, including the US, stood by and did nothing while Slobodan Milosevic, the Serbian President, the Butcher of the Balkans, showed his contempt and continued his pursuit of a Greater Serbia. We will address that further below under war crimes.

### Possible Actions

- Continue to meekly follow the European

appeasement.

•    Call for a UN peacemaking force.

•    Send a NATO Corps (with at least one armored division [probably US] but preferably with British, French, and German units also) into Bosnia. The first roadblock that tried to stop it should be obliterated. Inform Serbia to withdraw and desist or else all of Serbia would be at risk.

•    Provide air cover to the Corps and announce to Serbia and Croatia that any hostile movement against any UN or NATO force would be destroyed and their support system would be at risk.

•    As one of the Youngbloods, Newt Gingrich's political roundtable show, answered as to how he would handle Bosnia, "We bomb the Serbs into oblivion until they start acting like a civilized community instead of the Nazi genocidal maniacs they've acted like before."

The UN could do little as long as Europe and the US were unwilling to act. That terrible drama was left to play out on the ground. It was a sad day for so-called Western civilization.

## Cambodia

The commitment of the UN Transitional Authority in Cambodia (UNTAC) was the largest, most ambitious, most complicated, and most expensive in UN history. A peacekeeping force of nearly 22,000 soldiers, police, and other officials was committed for 20 months at a cost of $2 billion to implement a peace agreement signed by the four factions in Paris to end a 13-year civil war. They were to disarm most of the 250,000 fighters of the factions and supervise the rest in special cantonments around the country, repatriate 360,000 refugees in Thailand, monitor the ceasefire, and organize democratic elections.

The Khmer Rouge violated almost every provision of the agreement, refused to disarm, and boycotted the elections. UNTAC reported that Thai troops stood by and videotaped as Khmer Rouge guerrillas attacked and detained UN members in

Thailand. The Thai military was evidently supporting the Khmer Rouge.

UNTAC reported that 400 Khmer Rouge guerrillas, fleeing from the Cambodian Army, were evacuated by Thai army trucks to a Khmer Rouge base in Thailand. UN headquarters in New York overruled a request by UNTAC to announce the action because they wanted to avoid an open dispute with Thailand.

The Cambodian government, which had originally been installed by Viet-Nam, also refused to place its troops under UN control and resumed its attacks on the Khmer Rouge. UNTAC had no mandate to impose punishment. There were continued human rights abuses and the government refused to punish violators and the UN would not force them to. The UN bureaucrats sent from New York did not know how to run the daily operations of a collapsed government.

The elections, however, were a bright spot in the operation. Under quite perilous conditions, over 90% of the registered voters turned out. Unfortunately, the Phnom Penh government rejected the results leading to renewed confrontation with the opposition factions, including the Khmer Rouge. It was a collapsed state and it needed more than elections.

The UN started its scheduled pullout in August 1993 leaving a country without a working civil service, a judicial system, a police force, or a real economy. Norodom Sihanouk was named king again on 24 September 1993 after 23 years. His task will not be easy with the Khmer Rouge holding 20% of the country.

## El Salvador

Not all UN commitments have been failures. UN Blue Berets stand guard at numerous posts around the world successfully keeping antagonists apart. One of the success stories was the peace mission in El Salvador.

A civil war there claimed 70,000 lives and probably would still be going on without the UN. The mission mediated between the two sides and then oversaw peace negotiations. A peace accord was signed in Mexico City on 16 January 1992.

The UN dispatched military observers to verify the ceasefire and rebel disarmament and also human rights observers. There were no violations during 20 months of ceasefire. With the country quiet, UN police envoys assisted in building a new police force.

The UN observers served as election supervisors for presidential and legislative elections, which included candidates who were former rebels. The active role of the UN Secretary General and his aides built confidence and trust among the parties.

The peace agreement was quite complex, fundamentally changing Salvadoran society and would probably have been impossible without the UN role. Problems still remain but the UN was phasing out its presence in 1995 after a job well done.

## Possible Actions

The deployments of UN forces have caused the most damage to the prestige of the UN. Much of this is our fault as we have tolerated the insults and contempt. For example, we do nothing but talk about the UN problems in Bosnia and we permitted Israel to show its constant contempt for the UN and then protected it against sanctions by our veto.

The commitment of UN forces has become a threat to the UN and to the innocent troops being sent out. We must either demand and enforce the respect for UN forces accorded to police or else stop sending them. This can only happen with American leadership which is totally lacking.

• Stop all UN commitments until the UN is reorganized.

• Establish as a principle that any action against a UN soldier will bring instant retribution. But it must be done! This nonsense of killing UN troops or holding UN troops as hostages, UN convoys being stopped, or UN helicopters being inspected must stop. A tank division should be sent into Bosnia and if any checkpoint tries to stop a convoy, it should be destroyed immediately.

• Create a permanent UN force. Since America has joined the Europeans in running away from responsibility, the UN (or any replacement organization) needs its own force. See Chapter 10.

## INTERNATIONAL CRIMES AND PUNISHMENT

One of the inherent weaknesses of the nation state system is that there is no judicial system above the state level. Yes, there is an International Court of Justice (**ICJ**) under the UN, but it deals only with states and they have to agree to accept its jurisdiction. There is no court to try individuals accused of major crimes.

The Nuremberg and Tokyo war crimes trials were conducted by special tribunals established by the victorious allies. The world needs an international tribunal which could be created by the UN, or the UN Charter for the ICJ could be amended to give it jurisdiction over individuals as well.

The world was appalled by the Holocaust whereby some six million Jews, Gypsies, and others were exterminated in a most brutal example of genocide. The cry was Never Again! A great museum was built in Washington to honor their memory (and to keep pressure on Washington).

Yet Washington, the Jews, the Europeans, the whole world stood by and did nothing while "ethnic cleansing" took place in Bosnia. The Jews can probably be excused because if they spoke out, it would open Israel to criticism for its suppression of the Palestinians. But there was no excuse for the rest of the world.

The history of the problem in Yugoslavia was covered earlier. In the summer of 1992, Serb troops started rounding up Bosnians, checking to see if they were Muslims by stripping them to see if they were circumcised. They were forced to renounce their property and then shipped to Austria or Hungary in sealed freight cars. If they refused to go they were killed.

The "ethnic cleansing" of Bosnia was under way by means of theft, rape, torture, and murder. Muslim towns and villages were wiped out. The hatred of these so-called civilized Europeans was unbelievable.

Probably over 2 million people were on the move, with thousands dead and the rest as refugees in neighboring countries or in various parts of the former Yugoslavia. Perhaps a quarter of the 4.3 million people in Bosnia have fled spreading out across the world. Some 500,000 refugees are in Croatia and Serbia, but over 670,000 refugees are in Western Europe, which already has severe ethnic problems and economic shortages.

If Bosnia is partitioned as proposed, it would require

the resettlement of 1.5 to 2 million people. Bosnia, with its centuries-old heritage of being home to Muslims, Croats, Serbs, and others, has fought for the ideal of a multi-cultural society. This is reflected by the fact that 27 percent of all Bosnian marriages are mixed; mixed families may constitute as much as 20% of the population. A humanitarian problem of the magnitude of Bosnia has not been seen in Europe since World War II.

The fanatical perpetrators of these atrocities are destroying their own countries at the same time. Slobodan Milosevic has taken Serbia into ruin. Agriculture is subsistence, industry has stopped, and barter is the main mode of economic exchange as the dinar has become worthless with hyper-inflation calculated at 10 billion percent a year in July 1993. President Franjo Tudjman of Croatia has shown similar indifference for his country.

The UN announced some strong charges against Croatia in October 1993. In one report, the UN said that Croatian army troops gunned down at least 70 Serbian civilians and torched every building in 11 villages. The report suggested that the Croat leadership condoned the civilian slaughter and scorched earth tactics because it was too "systematic, thorough and well planned" to have been the work of renegades.

According to the report, Croatian soldiers looted houses, slaughtered livestock, poisoned wells, and razed more than 500 buildings. In a separate report by a UN refugee official, Croat nationalist gunmen rounded up 530 Muslims in the divided city of Mostar and expelled them across a dangerous no-man's land riddled with mines and corpses.

Enough crimes have been committed in Bosnia to keep a tribunal busy for years but there is one special aspect of the Bosnian disaster that is particularly heinous. **Rape** reached a sophisticated new level as an instrument of war. Rape is not specifically listed as a war crime according to the Fourth Geneva Convention, but the Convention does recognize rape as a "crime against humanity." Grace Halsell and other key women have visited Bosnia and talked to victims. (See *The Washington Report on Middle East Affairs,* Grace Halsell, April/May 1993, p. 8.; Representative Susan Molinari, September/October 1993, p. 19.)

An European Commission report of January 1993 estimated that 20,000 Slavic Muslim women had been raped in

Bosnia alone, mainly females 10 to 30 years old, but the *New York Times* put the number at 50,000.

Catharine MacKinnon, a law professor at Michigan who represents the Bosnian women *pro bono*, claims the total is 50,000 or higher plus another 100,000 women and children killed. There are documented cases of Serbs raping 3-year old girls on up to an 82-year old woman.

A "**rape strategy**" was part of the overall plan for ethnic cleansing. Representative Susan Molinari, from New York and chair of a Republican task force on the Balkan crisis, met rape survivors in Bosnia. They were pregnant by Serb soldiers. They were permitted to leave the camp only after they became pregnant (raped about 10 times a day until accomplished) and when they were beyond being able to abort; they wanted them to give birth to "little Chetniks." They were in Zagreb waiting to give birth, abandon the babies, and return to their villages to try to find their families. However, if their families or others learn they had been touched by a Serb soldier, they would be thrown out, ostracized, or even killed, because they had been disgraced. Their lives were destroyed.

Ethnic cleansing is not a new idea. We remember Hitler. Stalin was brutal not only killing millions but forcibly scattering hundreds of thousands around the Soviet Union and sending Russian immigrants to colonize the republics leaving the legacy which now haunts Russia and its neighbors. The Rape of Nanking was part of the Japanese invasion of China. The danger is that if this genocide is not punished, it may well incite others to imitate it.

Cowardice in the West has unleashed religious intolerance and militant nationalism on a scale unseen in Europe since Hitler. Without restraint, which has been totally absent so far, violence is almost sure to spread in the former Yugoslavia. Milosevic and his henchmen are likely to turn to other groups for "cleansing."

There are 300-400,000 Hungarians in Vojvodina. Radical Serb nationalists would like to expel them. Sandzak is a predominantly Muslim area on both sides of the Serb border with Montenegro. Cleansing has already started there as Serb gangs terrorize the Muslims.

The Albanian Muslim majority in Kosovo lives under terrible conditions and is denied basic human rights. Since Milosevic is ridding his Orthodox Serb state of Muslims and since he feels sure the West will not do anything about it, violence in Kosovo seems only a matter of time.

However, unlike Bosnia, these peoples have millions of brethren just across the border. Thus any large scale cleansing of the Hungarians or the Kosovo Albanians could force a reaction by Budapest or Tirana.

There are millions of Russians outside of Russia now that the empire has crumbled and high level officials have already called for their "protection." All across the states of the old Soviet empire, there are intermixed populations, nagging grievances, and illogical borders. They provide strong ammunition for the new nationalist demagogues, who have turned the concept of a nation's right to self-determination into justification for tyranny by the majority. The threat is that there may be more Bosnias.

In May 1993, the UN Security Council passed Resolution 808, creating a war crimes tribunal which was set up six months later as the Yugoslav War Crimes Tribunal based in The Hague.

Richard Goldstone, the tribunal's chief prosecutor, went to work. Several indictments were issued but the prospects for trials were hampered in that few of the accused were in custody and the fighting was still going on. The tribunal has no right to arrest suspects and the Bosnian Serb authorities have refused to turn over anyone.

The tribunal was able to extradite a Bosnian Serb, Dusan Tadic, from Germany accused of atrocities at the Omarska detention camp in northwest Bosnia. Also, it named as war crimes suspects Bosnian Serb leader Radovan Karadzic, his army chief Ratko Mladic, and his police director Mico Stanisic.

The tribunal also announced that it was investigating genocide charges against Bosnian Croats for their actions in a Muslim village in the Lasva River Valley.

However, even though the tribunal cannot try suspects in absentia, it has held public hearings and collected evidence. But as time goes by, it will be more difficult to collect evidence. Fortunately, however, Helsinki Watch and the Conference on Security and Cooperation in Europe (CSCE) also started investigating camps and collecting evidence.

The Security Council also set up a Rwanda War Crimes Tribunal to deal with the 1994 ethnic slaughter. The General Assembly will select the six judge panel to be based in Arusha, Tanzania. The tribunal had identified 400 suspects and hoped to issue its first indictments in the summer of 1995.

---

It is true I killed 900 people, and I expect to be executed.

-- Musoro Ndura, one of the first
suspects tried for genocide in Rwanda

---

Unfortunately, the human rights mission in Rwanda was criticized for focusing more on violations by the current government than on the massacres. The UN was accused of overly protecting the rights of those accused of genocide. Nothing is easy for the UN!

## War Criminals

We have many candidates for war crimes, crimes against humanity, or international crimes. There are hundreds if not thousands of candidates in the former Yugoslavia. But there are also many high ranking officials who should be brought to justice.

The list is long: Pol Pot and his henchmen in the Khmer Rouge for killing a large percentage of the Cambodian people, estimates range from one to two million slaughtered during his brutal reign over Cambodia.

Saddam Hussein for his rape of Kuwait.

Slobodan Milosevic, the Butcher of the Balkans; Bosnian Serb leader Radovan Karadzic; Franjo Tudjman of Croatia and many of their assistants and military commanders.

Theoneste Bagosora, chief of cabinet of the Ministry of Defense, and many others for the slaughter in Rwanda.

There have been many reports of atrocities among the seven warring factions in the civil war which has been going on in Liberia for five years.

Possibly Mohammed Aidid in Somalia. Old timers such as Idi Amin of Uganda and Jean-Bedel Bokassa of the Central African Republic (Empire while he was the self-proclaimed emperor) and many more who were never brought to any kind of justice.

Man has organized society fairly well within the nation state so that there are generally acceptable modes of behavior, deviations from which should be punished. The sovereignty of the nation state and the resulting near anarchy on the international level leave a vacuum for dealing with international crimes or actions that are clearly crimes against humanity.

States differ from individuals in that they are not subject to law. International law is a law **among** states and **not above them.** However, monstrous crimes have been committed in the name of states. We clearly need a system of law to deal with individuals who commit crimes on a state level where they will not be tried by their state.

## Possible Actions

• Create a World Court under the United Nations.

• Amend the charter of the International Court of Justice to include crimes committed by individuals.

• Create a World Court separate from the UN, perhaps at The Hague.

• There have been repeated reports of violations of human rights, rape, torture, and murder. Names of the accused should be announced so that it is clear to all that anyone following the illegal orders of such criminals risks trial also. No one can hide behind the "I was just following orders." excuse.

• If the UN is unable to proceed with its tribunal, there are other avenues available if the members want to act. The EC, NATO, or OECD or other groupings of major states could establish a tribunal to deal with these major crimes. Action is required if man is ever going to rise up out of the gutter of tribalism, militant nationalism, and religious intolerance.

## WHERE DO WE GO?

Our **options** are fairly limited. We either have to stick with the UN we have and try to improve it or else create something else.

In sum, the UN plays a major role in the world order. Its problems are in organization, funding, and respect. Since it is a creation of nation states, it can only assert the power directly delegated to it by its creators. In terms of respect, if the UN is ever to play an effective role, it must have respect. Too many countries over the years have held the UN in contempt.

The UN must be given the means to enforce its directives. Until the world community feels that one does not dare cross the UN, the UN will not be able to function up to its potential.

## Possible Actions

• Disband the UN and create a new world entity. Call a world conference to form the new entity which would probably need taxing authority and its own military force, then dissolve the UN.

• Force the drastic reorganization of the UN. The US would have to act like a superpower and lead.

• Grant the UN some revenue base, such as perhaps from anything taken from international waters (fish, minerals, oil), licensing all shipping, international air, space, or give it some international land, perhaps even a percentage of all oil and gas.

• Stop tolerating rogue countries. Place them under the UN Trusteeship Council until rehabilitated. See Chapter 10.

• Stop the childish noise in the US Congress and do something constructive about the UN. Fix it or replace it!

## Citizen militias fear the UN will rule the world.

One of the fallouts of the Oklahoma City bombing was the increased awareness due to the publicity concerning the militias. A major theme of one segment of the militia movement is fear of One World Government, a New World Order that threatens constitutional liberties.

They suspect that some federal officials are plotting to eliminate the US Government and replace it with the United Nations as a global authority. This new world government through the UN would by its agents, including the US president, impose martial law, suspend the Constitution, install totalitarian rule, and seize all weapons from individuals. These poor misguided souls and some members of our Congress refuse to face the real world and work for solutions.

If we do not wish to be the world's policeman, then the UN or something like it is absolutely required. It is needed for the many other jobs it performs. It is time for the US and the rest of the world to stop acting like spoiled children under the protection of the anarchic nation state system and do something for the good of mankind. The world badly needs leadership and the US is the only candidate. We must act before it is too late as the world continues in strife.

| | |
|---|---|
| Boutros Boutros-Ghali<br>Secretary General<br>The United Nations<br>United Nations Plaza<br>New York NY 10017 | Tel. (212) 963-5012<br>Fax: (212) 963-4879 |
| Ambassador Madeleine Albright<br>US Mission to the United Nations<br>799 United Nations Plaza<br>New York NY 10017 | Tel. (212) 415-4444<br>Fax: (212) 415-4443 |

# Chapter 7

# ARE THERE TOO MANY PEOPLE IN THE WORLD?

## What Can Be Done About the Uncontrolled Population Growth and Resulting Problems?

> *Population tends to grow faster than the means of subsistence.*
>
> -- Thomas Malthus, 1798
>
> *California's foreign-born population increased from 15% in 1980 to nearly 22% 10 years later.*
>
> -- *U.S. News & World Report*
> 4 October 1993

There is growing strife around the world, some of which we have already covered in considerable detail. There are many causes for the ailments of mankind. In this chapter, we will look at some other problems facing the community of nations. These are overpopulation, famine, unemployment, disease, and migration. They tend to be closely linked and it will be difficult to keep them separated.

## OVERPOPULATION

Thomas Malthus inspired society to think about the problems of unbridled population growth. Our understanding of this problem has been minimal. In 1944 before the end of World War II, the *Encyclopaedia Britannica* figured the world population at 1.9 billion and projected that it would increase to 4 billion by the year 2031. The present population is 5.7 billion and at current growth rates, it will double by 2030. That would be an error of almost 200% -- not very good!

Probably the greatest disservice ever done to much of the world was to provide them advanced medicine without tying it to the cultural problems it generated. Agricultural societies have traditionally had large families to add hands for the fields and because many of the babies never survived to adulthood. As societies became more urban, industrialized, and educated, their birth rates declined.

In a humanitarian zeal to do good, many diseases were reduced and babies were helped to survive resulting in the extension of lives of many millions of people, yet unwittingly creating a new problem of burgeoning population that governments could not easily feed, clothe, house, educate, and provide jobs.

According to the UN, life expectancy in the poorest countries in 1960 was 53 years; now it is 62. Infant mortality per thousand in 1960 was 110; now it is 73. Of the 5.7 billion people in the world, 1.3 billion live in abject poverty and 1.1 billion live on $1 or less per day. There has been progress but it is an uphill battle. Poverty has been reduced from 70 percent in 1960 to 32 percent now. India has the most poor with 350 million and South Asia is the poorest region with 50 percent in poverty. Access to clean, safe water has doubled from 33 percent in 1960 to 68 percent now.

In addition to more babies and adults surviving, people everywhere are living longer. The life span is 28 years longer now than at the beginning of this century.

> **Two-thirds of all people who ever lived past 65 are alive today!**

There are major problems with the large population in the world now. What will they be if it really does double before the middle of the 21st Century? There are some interesting scenarios as to how the world could grow. If high fertility rates continue in some regions, offsetting lower trends elsewhere, the world population could go to 11 or 12 billion in 2050 and to 28 billion in 2150. If fertility were to fall to a level where couples replace themselves, the world would have about 10 billion in 2050 and 11.6 billion in 2150. If low fertility were to become a worldwide trend, we might have a world with under 9 billion in 2050 and 8.5 billion in 2150. If we think we are going to have a problem in the 21st Century, there will be real problems in the 22nd Century.

The largest growing sector of the population is the poor. It becomes quite clear that what is needed is elimination of poverty, increased access to schooling and jobs, and the adoption of population policies.    Funding for population assistance had doubled since 1988 to $200 million.    But no aid has been provided by the US because the family planning assistance to China includes abortions.    Unfortunately the Reagan and Bush administrations took exception with abortion and the US withdrew much financial support from this effort.

| Man's greatest pollution of Earth is the flood of additional human beings. |
| --- |

It is clear that population control must be an integral part of any development strategy.    Unfortunately, the abortion issue has been taken over by radicals on both sides, yet polls have repeatedly shown that a majority of Americans support a woman's right to choose an abortion.    The abortion opponents in their micro view fail to realize the disastrous impact of their views at the macro level in the world.

Birth control is a major requirement in the world and the US must support it.    It is a vital issue for the West as well as for the Third World.    The monumental change, at least in perception, is that the women in the Third World want to practice birth control.

There are an estimated 50 million abortions worldwide each year, more than a third are illegal and nearly half take place outside any health system.    As many as 200,000 women die each year from unsafe, illegal abortions, mostly in the developing world.

A survey showed sharp birth-rate declines in Asia, Latin America, and the Caribbean, and in three African nations. There was also an increased demand among women for birth control.    In the developing world, about one-third of the women are using modern family planning methods.    This is the result of the great efforts by the UN and other agencies.

The Catholic Church, unfortunately, has never been helpful in this need with its prohibition on contraception.    Pope John Paul II, in his encyclical "The Splendor of Truth," again singles out as evil artificial birth control and abortion, and forcefully restated the church's opposition to contraception and embryo research.    The church, with its archaic view of compassion and intelligence, has brought additional misery to the world.    The Hispanic world is heavily Catholic so it has only aggravated the problem.

> Abortion stinks, but the church (and the government) should keep their noses out of our private business.
>
> -- *Talkers Magazine* on papal encyclical

In addition to religious and cultural mores and a general ignorance about reproduction or a reluctance to discuss it, there is always the underlying concern that birth control is a plan by the whites to reduce the number of "coloreds." That is hard to argue simplistically even with the burgeoning numbers, but most of the countries are beginning to see that it is not a "white man's plot" but the only way they are going to make it into the next century.

A lower birth rate in the Third World would yield dramatic results. The enormous strain on resources which adds to political and social chaos would be lessened. Poverty would be reduced and living standards should rise. Consequently, the Third World would likely be more stable and less dangerous for its people and for the rest of the world.

India has a relatively low growth rate among Third World countries but it still adds an average of 17 million new mouths to feed each year. Two-thirds of the population live in rural areas and with 350 million poor, some 196 million fall way below the poverty level. The remaining third live in 23 cities with over a million each and three cities have over 8 million. The population is expected to pass one billion by 2001.

India is one of the countries where a woman is often less than a slave, her purpose being to produce a treasured son. It is ironic that 1993 was the "Year of the Woman" in India, but they are trying to improve their lot. Out of 880 million people, 325 million are illiterate; 200 million are female. Such illiteracy makes progress an uphill battle for India.

Hillary Rodham Clinton seems to have taken up this mission. Mrs. Clinton's visit to the subcontinent in 1995 brought attention to the plight of women there. Such high level attention could force reforms to help women.

One of the toughest population control programs in the world is in China with its 1.2 billion people, but even with its authoritarian government which can impose its edicts, it has had troubles. Its population is growing at 1.1% but 21 million births last year were offset by only 13 million deaths. Despite much opposition, particularly in the rural areas, the government has renewed its program of only one child per family in an effort to hold the growth rate to 1 percent and the population to 1.3 billion by the turn of the century.

The Chinese Government position of permitting only one child per family raises some interesting questions. In the hunting, nomadic, and agrarian phases of man's evolution, there was never any consideration of limiting the number of children. But now in the post-Industrial Age, perhaps the question should be asked. Does every person have the **right** to have as many children as he or she wishes?

There has been mention of restricting the insane and carriers of certain diseases or genetic defects from reproducing. Fortunately, we did not reach the age of Big Brother in 1984. But we do control almost every aspect of your lives now: you have to have a Social Security card even if you are a baby, you have to have certain shots to go to school, you have to have a license to drive a car or fly an airplane, you need a license to get married, you cannot drink or vote until a certain age, you may even have to pass a drug test to get a job.

Yet a teenage girl can have a baby if she wants to and a poor woman can keep having more babies and there is no license required!   There is no test to determine if she is mentally capable, whether she is on drugs or has AIDS, whether there will be a father for this child, whether she has the money to have the baby, the money to raise the baby for the next 20 years.   In other words, she does not have to have anyone's permission to bring a new person onto this planet who will cost several hundred thousand dollars to support, require a complete infrastructure to support including hospitals, day care if she ever works, schools, food service, clothing, housing, utilities, entertainment, courts, jails, transportation, roads, and hopefully a job for this new soul who may live over 70 years.

> **Perhaps there is a myth that hard working, tax paying people  — who often cannot afford to have children of their own  --  will continue to permit their money to be used to subsidize children or poor women having babies.**

This is a monumental decision that impacts on every taxpayer. Perhaps it is time to reconsider whether she has that **right.** This is certainly more significant than driving a car.

Yes, she could kill someone with a car, so we make her get a license.    But offspring from poor mothers have a high probability of killing someone too.    These are some of the punks who walk up to a car and shoot a 65 year old woman and steal her Honda.  **Perhaps it is now time to require a license to have a baby!**

We treat animals with more logic.  We cull herds of wildlife so they do not exceed their habitat and starve to death. We have programs to neuter our cats and dogs.  But we still have too many and put millions to sleep each year.  We cannot start putting our excess humans to sleep, so we had better get to work now to stop having too many born before we destroy our own world due to our stupidity and lack of discipline!

Freedom and individual rights have always needed to be balanced by responsibilities and their impact on other people's rights.  We agree on freedom of speech but still agree that one cannot falsely yell "Fire" in a crowded theater.

The question is does government have to protect you from yourself?  The people of the world in general and the US in particular seen to think they have a God-given right to act like idiots.  The problem comes when that act affects you or me.

Cory Farley, a Reno columnist, put it quite well even though, in this case, he was referring to mandatory use of helmets when riding bicycles.

> "My interest is financial.  If the wrecker can toss you on the landfill with your crumpled bike, I have no right to complain.  But, if you expect medical care, so your decisions raise my taxes and insurance costs, then I'm vested in the argument.  And **if it's going to cost me money, I don't give a damn about your freedom.**"

I contend that we are all vested in the population issue, both in our country and around the world, and therefore it dramatically **impinges** my freedom and **your freedom. There is no "right" to pollute the world with unneeded, and often unwanted, babies.**

Many studies over the years have shown that improvements in the level of education in a country result in lower birth rates.  A recent study by the World Bank showed that educating girls as well as boys may be the best investment for the future for developing countries. Providing women with even an elementary education raises the living standard in poor countries. The changes are that they have fewer children, take better care of the ones they have, work better at home, and earn more on jobs or when they market their own crops.

There are many obstacles to educating girls in many countries. Some have to go to extremely poor quality schools with little or no facilities. Some cultures think that school encourages promiscuity because they see it as Western liberal education which encourages sexuality. Cost is a problem for some and in other countries, even the smallest girls are expected to help their mothers. In Benin, where average income has been dropping all through the 1980s, one adult in four can read and write, but only one woman in six. The study concludes that investment in education of girls may well yield the highest return available in the developing world.

A large percentage of the world's population is young. As these billions of young people enter their reproductive years, there will be the threat of worsening economic distress in developing countries and even greater immigration. According to Werner Fornos, president of the Population Institute, "Failure to address the population problem may be the ultimate global blunder."

Historically, the population of mankind has been kept in check by disease, war, and famine. Modern medicine has put a brake on disease except that AIDS may set us back. We have tried to reduce war and the breadbasket of the US has slowed famine. But the consequences of overpopulation are more than famine and possibly migration. The economic pressures can lead to political upheaval and potentially to violence either internally or spilling over internationally.

The increasing pressures of populations in less developed countries will leave us with **few options**, particularly if their effects spread over into our spheres of economic interest or draw us into wars. We will be forced to abandon our pious policies and lead a world effort to reduce populations, starting with our own population.

## Possible Actions

• Help educate the women of the world. This is a slow process but it has a very high return.

•  Lead the world in asserting the rights of women.

•  Support family planning around the world. Despite the objections of the anti-abortion and some overly pious foes, there are many aspects of family planning that can be taught to people. There are numerous forms of contraception: pills, tying tubes, condoms, implanted patches, and shots. Stringent measures will be needed most likely including abortion.

•  Urge your government to take some of your tax money being wasted on foreign aid, such as in the Middle East, and use it specifically for population control.

•  Impose sanctions on governments that do not make significant efforts to restrain undue population growth.

•  Urge governments, including our own, to ban all children born out of wedlock; they would be taken over by the state.

•  Urge governments, including our own, to place a limit on the number of children a couple may have (1 or 2) and require a license to have a child.

•  The most radical action probably would be to have the international community depose governments that do not make adequate efforts to control population growth.

If we do not take some of these actions, we may well fine ourselves reacting to dire situations created by these circumstances. This will be a long, slow process, and we need to get started. We need to act before the disasters strike us. In the meantime, as the world's population continues to grow, will there be enough food to feed them?

## FAMINE

At the same time that the world is faced with ever growing population, the sad truth is that we are finding that even now there is less food. The supply of fish, meat, and grain is lower than it was five years ago according to Worldwatch Institute.   This was the first clear sign that population growth was outpacing the food available for humans.

There has been a slowdown in what had been decades of increasing food supplies. The main sources of food, which are farms, livestock ranches, and oceanic fisheries, appear to be approaching or have reached their maximum per-capita output. World meat production per person has started falling after 40 years of increases. Beef is at its lowest per-capita level in 30 years. For the third year in a row, 97 million tons of fish were taken from the oceans. Some scientists feel we may never again see the peak harvest of 100 million tons in 1989 and the costs of seafood are increasing around the world.

Grain production per person increased 40 percent between 1950 and 1984, but it has fallen 8 percent since then. Growth in cropland area, water supplies, and fertilizer use are not keeping up. According to the FAO, the world is losing about 17.5 million acres of cultivable land annually. That is almost the size of Ireland.

David Pimentel and others at Cornell present an even darker picture claiming that erosion is destroying about 29 million acres of farm land annually. They claim it takes about 1.2 acres to feed one person a varied diet for one year. However, with about 3.7 billion acres available worldwide for crops, there is only about 0.6 acre per person available now worldwide and in 40 years, it will be down to 0.34 acre per person. Topsoil cannot be replaced quickly and it is being lost 17 times faster that nature replaces it.

The additional result is that erosion has also significantly reduced crop yields. Erosion can be dealt with to some extent by better farming techniques such as contour plowing and proper grass coverages at proper times to reduce losses.

Some land is being lost due to man's actions. The Sahara Desert continues to advance relentlessly forward. Part of the reason is that the people along the edges cut the bushes and trees for firewood for cooking. Without the ground cover the desert quickly advances.

"Land degradation is now proceeding so rapidly that few African countries can hope to achieve sustainable agriculture in the near future, while serious food consequences could eventually be felt as well in Latin America and Asia," according to FAO Director General Edouard Saouma. "This raises a fundamental question: Are we going to have enough good land to feed the extra 2.6 billion people who will be on this planet by the year 2025?" What will that do to the new world order?

In addition to reduced production, the FAO also reported falling prices for agriculture, fishery, and forestry products, including sharp declines for coffee and cocoa. This only compounds the problems for the developing world. Lower prices will mean less jobs for poorer countries, which over the past dozen or more years have seen slow growth in demand, increased protectionism, and rising productivity in wealthy countries all contributing to loss of markets for their commodities which are their lifeblood. The slow down of trade growth is expected to last through the end of the century.

As usual, there are differences in statistics. As noted above, the Worldwatch Institute said seafood prices were rising while the FAO said they were falling. Also, there was a group in Iowa that said the planet could feed 10 billion people; of course, we would have to cut down the forests and all become vegetarians.

The declining production of food could lead to famine in some areas. Mankind has known famine across the centuries. In the 1930s, it was the poor, starving children in China. In recent years, it has been famine in the Sahel in Africa. We have been called upon to repeatedly send relief to famines in Africa.

However, there have been different aspects to those famines. Some were truly the sad situation of no rain and poor crops resulting in not enough food for the people in a particular region. The more dastardly version though was the deliberate blocking of food to people for political purposes. The latter was the case in Ethiopia where Menghistu Haile Mariam deliberately blocked food from reaching his rivals in a bitter civil war.

The repeated famines in the Sudan come from two causes: one as part of the ongoing civil war, and second because of a lack of infrastructure whereby crops regularly rot in one part of the country because of the shortage of transportation means to move them to another part. The UN sent food regularly into southern Sudan by relief flights. Relief workers often had to be evacuated when towns came under attack as part of tribal rivalry. Thousands of people would be forced to flee to the countryside where there was no food, or to other villages which hopefully were receiving relief supplies.

Similarly, the famine that was killing so many people in

Somalia that prompted the commitment of US troops in December 1992 was exacerbated by warlords who were stealing, extorting, or blocking the shipments of food. Thousands were starving in Angola due to the renewal of that war. War brought a similar fate to Europe where the Bosnian Muslims were cut off from food and the US even parachuted food to them. There were reports of food riots and domestic insurrection in North Korea as people grew ever more hungry and desperate.

Lenita Powers, a columnist in Reno, Nevada, had some perceptive comments on Somalia. After seeing the photo of a dead US soldier being dragged through the streets of Mogadishu, her angry reaction, like most Americans, was,

> *"The hell with all of them. Let's pull our troops out and let 'em starve."* However, she had pangs of guilt since she recalled other photos that showed "stick-figure women with stick-figure babies at their dry breasts and more starving stick-figure children at their bony feet. *Damn! If you can't feed the children you have, why have more? If we're going to send flour and milk, toss in some birth control pills, for Pete's sake."*

When we were concerned about the limit to the food supply in the 1950s, we came up with a **"green revolution"** that greatly increased food productivity. It does not appear that we will be able to repeat that miracle even though the US and China signed an agreement to develop a genetically altered strain of rice by the end of the century. It is hoped the **"super rice"** can increase yields by 20% without chemicals or irrigation and also be pest and disease resistant.

Starvation is a terrible fate. Who can forget the horrible photograph in *Time* (23 August 1993) of a naked Sudanese man walking on all fours with a totally emaciated body reminiscent of the pictures of the survivors of Auschwitz. We do not treat animals like that. No human being should suffer that fate.

World leaders must address the problem of overpopulation and the inability to feed their peoples. There are only **limited options:** migration out of the areas, population reduction, or agricultural improvements. All cost money, require education, and are difficult to implement.

## Possible Actions

• Continue to provide training in better farming techniques.

• Assist with better food creating equipment. "Give a man a fish and he has food for a day. Give him a fishing pole and he will have food for the rest of his life."

• Encourage other developed countries to send people like our Peace Corps to help the less advantaged countries.

## UNEMPLOYMENT

Another product of overpopulation is unemployment. We are observing around the globe that the world cannot provide productive work for its young, and many of the older population as well. Unemployment figures stay in double digits throughout the Third World. In times of recession, even industrialized countries like France run unemployment over 10%.

According to the UN, there were 2.8 billion workers in 1994, but there were 120 million looking for jobs and 700 million who lacked enough work to live on. That is **over 800 million people** who cannot find a job or find enough work to make ends meet.

Teenage boys and young men stand idly on street corners from Cairo to Colombo, from Oslo to Capetown, from Havana to Buenos Aires, and from New York to Los Angeles. They are candidates for the gangs and radical movements of the world who will have them if no one else will. As young disasters waiting to happen, they can become key to questions of war or peace. We have already seen their indifference to life by the way they are ready to kill anyone at anytime for little or no reason.

The UN in its studies has found large amounts of unemployment worldwide, but particularly bad in many of the less developed countries. Much of the Third World has not industrialized. It has not been able to create jobs for its millions of new people. In many ways, the major crop of some of these countries has been people, but as more of them have left the land and moved to the cities, there is nothing for them to do. Many went to the industrialized countries to work when there was a shortage there.   But now, in the so-called post-industrial era, those jobs are disappearing as those states cut back their work forces.

Social values have been weakening on every level.   The threat is that wars of the future may not be so much soldiers' wars on borders, but people's wars involving migration or internal ethnic conflicts.   There does not appear to be any likelihood that enough jobs will be created to keep pace with the flood of population.

## Possible Actions

Any actions which reduce population will eventually reduce pressure on food production and on unemployment but not in the short run.

• Help countries to create jobs.   One interim project could be to help them form groups like our Civilian Conservation Corps of the 1930s and send young people out in the countryside to build roads, reforest areas, or other useful infrastructure building or environmental efforts.

• Encourage countries to set up something like a Job Corps which would train young people in needed skills.

## DISEASE

Disease was a constant threat to early man and it served as a brake on runaway population growth.   There were many different diseases that were chronic keeping the average life span rather short.   There were also devastating plagues that struck from time to time such as the Black Death, or bubonic plague, which swept eastward across Europe starting in 1347. It killed more than half the population in some places in just a few months.   This went on for about 50 years.

In addition to the rather common diseases that were around, we remember from the history books the outbreaks of cholera, yellow fever, and tuberculosis.   Advances in medicine slowly put an end to them to the point where now cases of such diseases are news.   However, there is a new flu virus every couple years and about every 20 years a super-virus appears such as ebola in Zaire.   The flu epidemic of 1918 killed 30 million people, several times as many as World War I.

The World Health Organization reports that half the world's people are sick at any one time and many die from easily preventable diseases. "Poverty is the world's deadliest disease." Poverty, poor sanitation, and lack of medical facilities in the Third World still leave many people exposed to diseases but not to the extent of population control.

However, it appears that we now have a disease that may, at least until the doctors can devise a cure, actually kill millions. That is AIDS (Acquired Immune Deficiency Syndrome). AIDS first appeared in Africa in the 1970s. It spread across Africa and with the modern mobile world of aviation, it soon spread around the world.

As an example, one out of every eight Ugandans is infected with the virus and most of the population is at risk of dying from AIDS. Some 2 million of the 17 million people in Uganda carry the HIV (Human Immunodeficiency Virus) that causes AIDS, and another 300,000 have already developed the disease. They do not know how many thousands have died from AIDS since it was first diagnosed in Uganda in 1983. Despite a major campaign by the government, youths still engage in indiscriminate sexual practices.

When AIDS struck in the US, it first hit the homosexual and drug community. However, it has since spread to the heterosexuals. Another controversy about the UN peacekeepers is the presence of AIDS among the peacekeeping forces. The militaries of some of the countries in sub-Saharan Africa have HIV infection rates as high as 80% and many of those countries send troops to UN missions.

AIDS has generated much controversy and stands to cost untold billions of dollars for research and the medical support for the millions of victims. It does not appear that there will be a cure or vaccine soon.

Traditionally, public health officials have used proven methods while they developed a cure. They tested the population, treated those infected as best they could, and isolated the irresponsible people who spread the disease. With the AIDS epidemic, those methods were attacked as witch hunts and violations of civil rights.

In 1993, AIDS passed accidents as the No. 1 killer of US men from 25 to 44. Cases among women are increasing about 17% a year compared to only about 3% among all US citizens. By the turn of the century, 72,000 to 125,000 US children and teens will lose their mothers plus another 60,000 young adults 18 and older.

It appears that AIDS will be with us for some time, however the rate at which it is spreading has levelled off and the number of new cases reported each year is declining. In the US, there is a National Commission on AIDS and an AIDS czar. This may prove to be what reduces some of the population pressure in Africa, albeit a terribly sad solution. For the pious, it may be God's punishment for immoral behavior; for others, it may be another cycle of nature.

Assuming that AIDS was "destined" to remove hundreds of millions of our population to relieve that pressure, an interesting "moral" question arises as to whether it is "right" to save all those people by medicine, assuming a cure is found, unless complementary policies are also executed to reduce population growth.

---

That **tough moral question** becomes: **Is it moral to save a person from AIDS so that he can starve to death?** Maybe contraception measures should be as important as those against AIDS.

---

## Possible Actions

•    Link all medical assistance with family planning progress.

•    Continue to educate people on sanitation, hygiene, but add family planning.

---

**MORAL DILEMMA: A life saved by medicine is one less baby needed in that society.**

---

## MIGRATION

Another product of overpopulation or a result of its pressure is migration.    It is estimated that between 1820 and 1925, over 33,000,000 people left Europe and settled in the United States. People can migrate voluntarily or they can be forced as refugees as we saw millions displaced as a result of World War II and most other wars, including the current refugees from the former Yugoslavia and the Palestinian refugees of the last half century. The UN reported there were

**125 million refugees**, emigrants, in 1995. In 1976, there were 2.8 million refugees under UN care, now there are 23 million.

In the early years of the US, immigrants were welcomed to build and expand the country. Now they are not as welcome. The subject of **immigration** has become white hot in the US. In addition to the costs to state governments to support illegal immigrants, there is pressure to reduce the overall number of immigrants entering the US. With over one million immigrants entering the US annually, there has appeared a group that wants immigration held to 100,000 per year and also a reduction in the birth rate to slow the population growth.

---

**Negative Population Growth, Inc., 210 The Plaza, P.O. Box 1206, Teaneck, New Jersey 07666** was formed in 1972. It wants the government to halt illegal immigration and to cut legal immigration from 900,000 to 100,000 per year.

---

In the boom years of Europe after the war, labor was imported to support the rebuilding economies. Now the boom is over, but illegal immigration is increasing. From 1980 to 1992, 15 million people migrated to Western European countries. There are estimates that 5 to 10 million people plan to leave Eastern Europe and the former Soviet Union; half of them want to go to Germany. This has generated many problems, including racist violence, and riots broke out in Belgium, France, Germany, and Italy.

As should be expected, **one country's solution may become another country's problem.** Thus, when millions of people leave a country, that government may be relieved of the burden of housing, feeding, clothing, educating, caring for, and providing jobs for them. But those requirements devolve on the receiving country and if its economy is weak, then it may not look favorably on all those immigrants, particularly if they are poor, illiterate, or unskilled and do not assimilate easily due to cultural, racial, religious, or language differences.

Costs to Western Europe of millions of immigrants run into many billions of dollars. It is difficult to determine the similar costs in the US, but a new study for the state of California alone reported that undocumented immigrants cost their state and local governments $5 billion annually. That is not helpful to California which was in a difficult financial condition with the business cutbacks.

Small numbers can almost always be absorbed easily and quickly, but an influx of very large numbers strains all the infrastructure and facilities of an economy. If that economy is already fragile, then there is the possibility of serious backlash against the newcomers leading to xenophobia.

Many refugees fled for their lives with few or no possessions. Life is tenuous in refugee camps like in Gaza and Lebanon and the many camps around Rwanda. They are often preyed upon by others and killed. Radical xenophobes often feel threatened by these "foreigners" and resort to bombings or worse as we saw in the killings of Gypsies and attacks against Croatians in Austria.

Trying to get to another country whether one is fleeing or just looking for a better life can be harrowing. Mexico has a reputation for rapes, beatings, and betrayals for migrants trying to pass through Mexico to the US. If captured, illegals are deported to Guatemala or Belize regardless of their country of origin.

An additional problem is the emigration of the educated or skilled, often called "**brain drain.**" This often results from those who go to other countries for education and then decide that there is little future or life is not too good at home so they emigrate to that country. Of course, that robs the home country of one of the key ingredients it needs for progress, more educated people.

In August 1993, a young Angolan jumped to his death in the Seine River in Paris when stopped by the police for interrogation under tough new anti-immigration laws intended to reduce the flow of clandestine immigrants into France, estimated to be about 100,000 per year. The French blame immigrants for joblessness, drug trafficking, and rising crime. In Germany, there was an increase in neo-Nazi gangs and racist violence with a number of people, such as Turks, killed which could be attributed to the unchecked flood of economic refugees and the worsening recession. Uncontrolled immigration threatened economic stability.

With so many people from the East trying to move to the West, Western European governments clamped down with new regulations, deportations, gunboats, and stronger border controls. Germany, which had to absorb as many as 600,000 newcomers in one year, was flying people from Germany back to the East and even paying cash to help the countries absorb the returnees. From Sweden to Greece, the doors were slammed shut as the governments were trying to establish zero-immigration policies.

The world's longest fence is currently being built in India to block immigrants from Bangladesh. "People who are impoverished are going to find a way to make a new life for themselves," according to the president of the Population Institute.

The sad situation is that because of the size of the world population now, there is no suitable place for refugees or migrants to go. The two big magnets are Germany and the US and neither needs more people. Germany has undertaken an enormous burden with the absorption of East Germany and the American economy is fragile.

Once again, the concept of freedom can be overstretched. The "right" of one person to move and live where he desires is possible to accommodate. However, movement of millions of people can destabilize governments. Infrastructure, food, schools, hospitals, housing, and jobs cannot be instantly created. These are long term problems. People cannot be put on shelves to wait for new construction and they cannot be slaughtered like a herd of cattle with hoof and mouth disease.

## Possible Actions

• Work with governments to alleviate the problems that lead their people to want to emigrate. It is preferable to keep these people in their native land than to export their problems.

• Work with the UN or some form of world government to bring order out of the chaos of the nation state system. This problem is too large for any one state to handle. There are too many countries now where government is ineffectual, nonexistent, or tyrannical.

Migration will not end but it is not a solution to overpopulation. There are no more great empty spaces for people to go to for a new life. Any large movement of people only shifts the problem from one government to another and may result in conflict.

# Chapter 8

# GROWING CONFLICT IN THE WORLD

*The mind of a nation in dispute is its mob-mind, credulous and savage.... Whenever the mob-mind rules, mankind shudders. Its voice is the evil banshee of nations.*

-- Homer Lea

*If you wish for peace, understand war.*

-- B. H. Liddell Hart

The problems in the world are many from too many people to feed, to not enough food to feed them, not enough jobs for them, to weak economies, to racial, ethnic, and religious differences. Differences can result in disputes that vary across a spectrum of conflict from tension to strife to riots to terrorism and to wars from small and limited to much larger.

## THE SPECTRUM OF CONFLICT

We consider peaceful competition as normal. But tension can enter these relations, particularly in international economics. World trade can go from competitive to cutthroat. Economic warfare can grow into psychological warfare and propaganda. Threats from North Korea and occasionally from China could be labelled tension.

As we proceed along the spectrum to actual conflict, there can be strife. Strife or forms of unrest may be manifested in different ways but it usually leads to demonstrations or marches against government policies which accidentally or deliberately can turn into riots. We have seen these in many cities around the world from Paris to Seoul, from Washington to Los Angeles.

If enough people are dissatisfied, they can carry their protests farther to guerrilla operations or terrorist acts. These groups can also operate across international boundaries and in effect become non-state actors on the international stage. These are not new forms of international violence; each has a long history. What has changed is the nature of international conflict.

Before World War II, most wars were waged by the armies of two or more states.  However in the post-war period, there is little agreement about what actually is a "war" in a period with no declarations of war and where 80% of the violent conflicts have been on the territory of only one state and were internal.

There are many levels of disputes across the spectrum of conflict as we move up to limited and conventional war. The fighting in Cambodia was really low level but still bloody. The war in Bosnia was a little higher with lots of artillery being used but little air.  Most of the fighting in Latin America and Africa was relatively unsophisticated with some artillery and air but mostly guerrilla warfare, with the exception of Angola which had extensive Soviet equipment including jet aircraft. The flareups in the Middle East were much more sophisticated in that they employed the latest in electronic warfare and precision guided missiles.

## TERRORISM AND GUERRILLA WARFARE

Terrorism is a revolutionary action challenging the authority of government.   Now the labels become more difficult, because one person's **"terrorist"** is someone else's **"freedom fighter."**   An insurgent guerrilla may be a fighter for liberation.   Those who are freedom fighters or independence fighters to the supporters of change become terrorists to the defenders of the status quo.

A guerrilla operation may include terrorism, but not necessarily.  In both cases, the opposition groups start from a weak military position.  A great part of the guerrilla operations of the last half century around the world were Communist insurgencies as part of the Soviet doctrine of Wars of National Liberation.

One of the lessons of the Korean War was that direct aggression met with strong resistance.   So when the Communists in Hanoi started an insurgency in South Viet-Nam, they were very careful to keep it concealed and led the world to believe it was an internal affair led by the Viet Cong. They were not successful and by early 1965, Hanoi committed regular army units to the South even though they scrupulously preserved the facade of an internal insurgency until the end in 1975 when 17 North Vietnamese divisions invaded and seized the country.

Terrorism is usually a small operation and may be compared to public relations.  It is a flexible and multi-purpose instrument of influence that can be used by nonstate actors or states.  The destruction or deaths produced by terrorists are not the main purpose, which is the dramatic and psychological effects those acts have on governments and people.

Terrorist attacks can take many different forms.  The most common that we have seen are car bombs; bombs on airplanes; assassinations; small attacks on individuals, crowds, buses, or buildings; hijackings; and occasional larger bombings.

The use of nerve gas in Tokyo emphasized the potential of mass destruction weapons in terrorists' hands.  The great potential threat comes from biological agents surreptitiously placed in water supplies or such and the possible nuclear blackmail if a nuclear device were secreted in a large city.

As we saw so often with the hostages in Beirut, the terrorist's greatest ally is television.  It is publicity; it is theater, designed to gain the attention of and to convince or frighten the target audience through shocking actions.  It is the use of violence for political ends to weaken governments.

Recent terrorist activity by dissident groups against governments includes: Islamic fundamentalists in Egypt and Algeria, black factions in South Africa, the IRA in Northern Ireland, Palestinians against Israel, several different dissident groups including Sikhs, Hindus, and Muslims in India, the bombings of the World Trade Center in New York and the federal building in Oklahoma City, the murders near the CIA entrance and of diplomats in Pakistan, the gas attacks in Tokyo, and many others.

> *There's been an informal bond between terrorists and their victims not to exceed certain constraints -- chemical, radiological, nuclear and biological weapons.... Now the terrorists have begun to exceed this contract.*
>
> -- Robert Kupperman, terrorism expert, on the nerve gas attack in the Tokyo subway

President Clinton moved against terrorist organizations by freezing the assets of 12 groups in the US.  Included were Kach, founded by Rabbi Meir Kahane, which had operated in both the US and Israel where Baruch Goldstein killed 30

Palestinians in a mosque in 1994, and Hamas which opposed the peace agreement between Israel and the PLO.

In early 1995, the US Government displayed excellent intelligence work and captured Ramzi Ahmed Yousef, the accused mastermind of the World Trade Center bombing and also of bombing a US airliner in the Pacific. His capture evidently thwarted an amazing plan, called Project Bojinka, to blow up 11 US jumbo jet airliners at the same time over the Pacific in a day of rage at the US. Yousef's group appeared to be part of those who were trained during the fighting in Afghanistan and who were unhappy with US aid to Israel.

There was an interesting reaction by the Party of Islam, a small anti-American fundamentalist group in Pakistan, where Yousef was captured. They demanded that Madonna and Michael Jackson should be brought to Pakistan for trial because they are terrorists as much as people who set off bombs. "Michael Jackson and Madonna are the torch bearers of American society, their cultural and social values... that are destroying humanity. They are ruining the lives of thousands of Muslims and leading them to destruction, away from their religion, ethics and morality. Terrorists are not just those who set off bombs; they are also those who hurt others feelings."

More of America as the Great Satan! However, this is further evidence of what Professor Samuel Huntington calls the clash of civilizations, the inevitable clash of Islam with Western liberal civilization.

Terrorism has become linked with Islamic fundamentalism, a particularly radical and vengeful interpretation of Islam. However, their brutal acts have been condemned by the Islamic Conference Organization (50 countries) as "a clear deviation from the teachings of the righteous Islamic religion and blatant violation of our values, norms and heritage."

## U. S. Veto Infuriates Arabs

The above headline showed the Arab outrage when Clinton blocked the UN Security Council from calling on Israel to return 140 acres of Arab land it confiscated outside Jerusalem to build more Jewish housing in direct violation of international law. Syria immediately refused a US proposal for ending the Syrian dispute with Israel and America's role as a mediator was challenged due to US support for Israel.

By such blind support for Israel and in violation of our own principles, the President probably unwittingly sentenced some Americans to death. Frustrated Muslims will likely kill some Americans, usually innocent civilians, such as tourists, businessmen, or academics who teach in the Middle East.

The Rabin Government ignored all outside pressure but had to relent to the power in the Knesset where the Arabs, the Likud, and the religious parties threatened to bring down his government.

It is interesting that the accused mastermind of the World Trade Center bombing released a statement that US aid to Israel gives Palestinians and Lebanese "the right to attack U.S. targets."

In April 1995, Americans were shocked by home grown terrorists and the bloody killing of 168 people, including 19 children, in Oklahoma City. This enormous blast, some 4,800 pounds of easily obtained fertilizer and fuel oil, showed how vulnerable we are. This group seemed to be associated with "militias" that are unhappy with the US Government concerning various issues from taxes to gun control to the handling of the Branch Davidians at Waco, Texas. However, good police work brought the culprits to jail, but justice is slow. This is an example where a public hanging might be appropriate.

The use of the nerve gas, sarin, by a doomsday cult in Tokyo further showed terrorism with mysterious agendas. The Aum Shinri Kyo (or Supreme Truth) cult is a radical group predicting apocalypse in 1997. They had enough chemicals to kill millions of people.

Hardly a day goes by without a report in the media of a terrorist incident somewhere. There were about 300 incidents annually in the 1970s compared to 2,517 in the first six months of 1993, but they have been declining. The FBI thwarted over 75 plots in recent years including one to blow up the UN headquarters and New York commuter tunnels.

Terrorism can be conducted by a small group or by parts of large organizations, but dissident terrorism should be distinguished from state terrorism. States can support groups in their terrorist acts against other states. In the past, the US has claimed that Iran, Libya, and Syria sponsored international terrorist groups, and Sudan was recently added to the list. States can employ terror either against their own people or against other states or groups.

To control through fear, states have used arbitrary arrests, beatings, kidnappings (disappearances), torture, exile, and murder. There is a long history of such terrorism, such as in the Soviet Union, Chile, Haiti, Israel, and many other countries.

We remember the KGB, the Gulag, and the horror stories in the USSR. There were many "disappearances" in Chile. The *Tontons Macoute* wreaked terror on the people of Haiti. Israel (Prime Minister Yitzhak Rabin, when he was Defense Minister) established a policy of "breaking bones" in the occupied territories, exiled many people including 400 in 1992, and Israeli law sanctions torture. Middle East Watch published a 180-page report, *A License To Kill*, which painstakingly documents 20 killings by Israeli undercover units, soldiers dressed as Arabs, sometimes wearing brassieres to look like women, executing young Palestinians. (In another such attack, the Israeli soldiers accidentally executed one of their own soldiers.)

The Soviet Union conducted terror outside its borders by occasionally killing certain people. Libya's Qadhafi boasted that his enemies were not safe anywhere in the world, and a number of corpses substantiated his claim. Also, "The Tehran Connection" hunted down its enemies abroad. Former Prime Minister Shahpour Bakhtiar was brutally butchered in Paris by three Iranians. The Iranian head of intelligence, Fallahian, an ardent follower of Khomeini with a reputation as a "hanging judge," boasted of his bloody record in tracking opposition figures abroad.

Likewise, Israel has killed directly such as Palestinian leaders in Tunis and Europe and Arab scientists in Europe. Israeli Mossad agents regularly assassinated or bombed Palestinians or other Arabs in Paris and other cities. On 21 July 1973, Israeli agents gunned down Ahmed Bouchiki, a Moroccan waiter in Oslo, Norway. It came out in the trial that he was killed when they mistook him for a Palestinian they were after.

With Hamas killing Israelis, the Israeli Government lifted any restrictions it had on its security forces and authorized "shoot on sight" of any wanted terrorists. Maj. Gen. Ilan Biran, commander over the West Bank, confirmed the policy of killing fugitives rather than arresting them when he told a newspaper, "We assume that there are still four or five squads that we have to kill."

Former Prime Minister Yitzhak Shamir explained his philosophy: "There are those who say to kill (an individual) is terrorism, but an attack on an army camp is guerrilla warfare and to bomb civilians is professional warfare. But I think it is the same from the moral point of view.... It was more efficient and more moral to go for selected targets." (He was a leader of the Stern Gang which assassinated UN mediator Count Folke Bernadotte in West Jerusalem in 1948.)

There are probably many other terrorist incidents in the world which we do not hear about. That means if the target audience did not hear about them, they failed, because the terrorist relies on publicity to provide the exposure to give his incident the desired effect. But remember who the target audience is. If it is a group, then they will know when one of their group is shot in the street or blown up in their apartment.

## Possible Actions

• Try to remove the causes of unrest or terrorism in the world. All terrorism stems from some frustrations or wrongs, real or imagined. It is to our advantage to remove them or help others to remove them if possible within our national interests.

• Try to have the world media be more restrained in their coverage of terrorist acts. Publicity is the backbone of most terrorist acts. Without the television and media coverage, most of it would be ineffective. That places a terrible burden on the media. We saw the power of television in Viet-Nam. Henry Kissinger recognized it when, during the early days of the *intifada* and the Israelis were breaking kids' bones, he recommended to the Israelis to stop the television coverage because it was hurting them in the US. I doubt that you have seen Palestinians being beaten since on your evening news.

• Continue to work with agencies around the world to block terrorist acts since we cannot tolerate such attacks on Americans. Swift retribution where possible is appropriate since much can be gained by establishing that it does not pay to mess with Uncle Sam! Key areas are intelligence, border controls, and the flow of financial support including preferential loans to states that support terrorism.

•    Support states, including moderate Arab states, which are attempting to contain extremists.

•    Study the roots of the unrest or terrorism. Few people will kill or blow themselves up without a strong reason. Why would sane people blow up a PanAm flight or the World Trade Center? What is there about America that makes Islamic fundamentalists call us the Great Satan? Why does our special relationship with Israel generate such hatred among some Muslims?

Professor Huntington is right when he talks about the clash between Islam and Western liberal civilization, but many of the Islamic fundamentalists who turn to terrorism are upset by what they consider America's blind and unswerving support for Israel, particularly when it violates the human rights of Muslims.    Since these are the people killing American diplomats and American civilians such as in the World Trade Center, we should consider their position.

One group that is working to combat the threat of terrorism is The American Jewish Committee.    For further information and how you can help, write them or call them at:

The American Jewish Committee
1156 15th Street, N. W.
Washington, D. C. 20005     Tel. (212) 751-4000 ext. 210

If you agree with America's ardent support for Israel and that they are worth $6.3 billion of our tax money each year, then you have no problem finding them. There is a multitude of organizations raising funds for Israel. No doubt they are in contact with you, led by AIPAC, the lobby in Washington.

American Israel Public Affairs Committee
440 I Street, N. W.
Washington, D.C. 20001     Tel. (202) 639-5200

If you do not agree with the support provided by the President and the Congress (Patrick Buchanan has described Capitol Hill as "Israeli-occupied territory"), then let them know. They condone the seizure of more Palestinian land and the building of more settlements and **you,** the taxpayers, will have to pay even more for each part of any peace agreement Israel accepts.

President Bill Clinton
The White House
1600 Pennsylvania Avenue, N. W.
Washington, D. C. 20500
White House Comment Line:
(202) 456-1111
Fax: (202) 456-2461

Secretary of State Warren Christopher
Department of State
Washington, D. C. 20520
State Department Public Information
Line: (202) 647-6675

Any Senator
U. S. Senate
Washington, D. C. 20510
(202) 224-3121

Any Representative
U. S. House of Representatives
Washington, D. C. 20515
(202) 225-3121

There are several organizations that might be of interest to you. Since you do not receive balanced reporting in the US media (there is actually more balanced coverage in Israel than in the US), you should read the *Washington Report on Middle East Affairs* published by the American Educational Trust.

*Washington Report on Middle East Affairs*
P. O. Box 53062
Washington, D. C. 20009
Tel. (202) 939-6050        Fax: (202) 265-4574
E-Mail wrmea@aol.com.

Another organization that advocates Middle East policies that serve the United States national interest is the Council for the National Interest. Since the US has been providing support since 1948, they have an effort called the Citizens' Amendment to reduce current funding of aid to Israel and to "END AID TO ISRAEL BY '98  Fifty Years Is Long Enough" including bumper stickers.

Council for the National Interest
1511 K Street, N. W., Suite #1043
Washington, D. C. 20005
Tel. (202) 628-6962        Fax: (202) 628-6958
E-Mail count@igc.apc.org.

Also working to educate the American public to the issues in the Middle East is:

Partners for Peace
3133 Connecticut Avenue, N. W., #702
Washington, D. C. 20008
Tel. (202) 745-0701        Fax: (202) 328-0315

The NACC is an umbrella organization for more than 150 NGOs (non-governmental organizations) based in the US and Canada working on Israeli-Palestinian peace and justice issues.

North American Coordinating Committee
1747 Connecticut Avenue, N. W.
Washington, D. C. 20009
Tel. (202) 319-0757          Fax: (202) 319-0746

The fact that there are so many terrorist incidents indicates that there is a large amount of discontent in the various nation states. Our American cities have become war zones with urban terrorists (thugs or punks) stalking the streets. Gangs and tribes control many areas in the world. Gangsterism is on the rise and threatens the future of Russia. It appears that terrorism will only increase. That seems to be one of the characteristics of the new world order.

## WARS

In addition to the ongoing terrorist incidents and some guerrilla warfare such as the renewal of fighting in **Cambodia,** the **Shining Path** in **Peru,** and the occasional attack in **Colombia,** there are other disputes that are more highly organized, more overt, and more continuous so that they can be regarded as wars.

There are **29** such conflicts around the world now, compared to 24 in 1992, according to the Center for Defense Information in Washington. Most of them are ethnic or religious conflicts, again part of what Samuel Huntington of Harvard calls "the clash of civilizations." European imperial power and then the Cold War buried these historic and cultural affinities which have now resurfaced.

It is a basic concept of military evaluations to differentiate between **capabilities** and **intentions.** Intentions can be good or bad, peaceful or bellicose, and they can change rapidly by a change of government or circumstances.

Capabilities on the other hand are more concrete and measurable and cannot change as rapidly. If a country has bellicose intentions and little capability, it is not a major threat. On the other hand, if a country has significant military capability, it has to be considered in contingency planning regardless of its intentions. Therefore, we must first look at the military capabilities in the world today.

Military capability must be assessed in terms of the potential area of conflict and the capability to project military power within that area or outside that area.

Since the Soviet Union was the major threat to peace for some 45 years, we cannot ignore the capabilities of those powerful forces in their new circumstances in the **Commonwealth of Independent States.** The USSR at the time of its collapse was a superpower with the largest military forces in the world, 3.7 million soldiers, sailors and air force personnel down from 5 million, and a vast array of modern weaponry including a monstrous arsenal of small, medium, and very large nuclear weapons. While peace is the theme in the CIS, the massive military capability, mainly of **Russia**, must be considered because of the instability and uncertainty of the future of those forces. Times are difficult in Russia and we must be concerned about Yeltsin's threat of a "Cold Peace."

The buildup in **China** has been awesome. The 1993 defense budget was supposedly $7.3 billion but the actual figure for all military type spending could be two or three times as much. Also a dollar goes a lot farther in China than elsewhere such as in Japan.

China was shopping to buy an aircraft carrier and was looking in the Ukraine and Russia, but may have found the cost a little rich for its budget when the full cost of a carrier task force ($4 to 6 billion) was considered. China was also reportedly interested in developing an aerial refueling capability which would permit it to operate its conventional forces well beyond its own borders.

The Russians were reported to be trying to sell supersonic Tu-22M *Backfire* bombers to China. The massive conventional capability, without even considering the large nuclear arsenal, of China was beginning to increase anxiety in the region. (You might want to check the Resource Directory for my book, *World War IV, China's Quest for Power in the 21st Century.*)

**Japan** has the third largest defense budget in the world, after the US and Russia, but it is somewhat exaggerated by the high operational costs in Japan. The US protective umbrella has shielded Japan since World War II, permitting the "economic miracle" and the Self-Defense Forces, while modern and well trained, lack the aircraft and ships to project their military power beyond the islands.

The enmity between **North** and **South Korea** has not abated despite talks attempting to end the half century of division. North Korea's enormous conventional capability is made even more unsettling to the region by the possible threat of North Korea developing nuclear weapons. In June 1993, Japan announced that North Korea successfully fired an extended range *Scud* missile. The significance was that it could reach all of western Japan. North Korea retains the capability to invade South Korea again at any time and tie up the South and the US in a long bloody war.

After long negotiations, the US and North Korea signed an agreement whereby the North would cut back its nuclear program in return for new reactors. However, the planned reactors were to come from South Korea and the North objected placing the entire agreement in jeopardy.

Territorial claims in the South China Sea, particularly over the potentially oil-rich **Spratly Islands**, by China, Viet-Nam, the Philippines, Malaysia, Taiwan, and Brunei along with other disputes in the area keep **Southeast Asia** in tension.

The long war in **Ethiopia** ended and **Eritrea** gained its independence, but the civil war in the **Sudan** has not abated in over a decade. It is a north-south civil war between the Arab Muslim North which wishes to impose its religion on the mostly animist and Christian black South. Even former President Jimmy Carter visited the Sudan in 1993 trying to mediate between the two sides.

The Sudan is a very poor country and it is sinking farther into poverty. It is sad because when we were still trying to do business there in the early 1980s and I sat on the Sudan-US Business Council, oil had been discovered (surprise -- in the south) and Chevron was beginning to make some progress which could have greatly aided that economy.

There has been civil war in **Liberia** since December 1989 when Charles Taylor's forces invaded from Ivory Coast and overthrew and executed Samuel Doe. That popular rebellion degenerated into tribal warfare with an estimated 150,000 people killed. Half of the 3.2 million people in Liberia, which was founded by freed American slaves, are now refugees. Seven of the West African states, led by Nigeria, sent peacekeeping troops into Liberia in 1991.

The UN brokered a truce in July 1993. However, it was broken six weeks later by renewed fighting which spread into Ivory Coast, which had been accused of supporting Taylor.

Interestingly, Ivory Coast is one of only a few African countries that has never had a rebellion or even a coup attempt. In December 1994, Nigeria started withdrawing its contingent, crippling the peacekeeping force and causing a major setback to regional peacekeeping operations.    However, the UN extended its observers' mandate in early 1995.

Africa's forgotten conflict, the 20-year civil war in **Angola** that has killed 500,000 people and devastated the oil- and diamond-rich country, was stopped in 1991 after 16 years and elections were held; however, UNITA refused to accept defeat in the elections and war broke out again 18 months later. Another ceasefire was  negotiated in 1993 and the rebels who were in control of much of the country were slapped with sanctions by the UN.

However, fighting resumed and the country was being ravaged with 1,000 dying daily from war, disease, and hunger according to the UN.    Another ceasefire agreement was reached in November 1994 and was still in abeyance in early 1995, but President Jose Eduardo dos Santos and rebel leader Jonas Savimbi finally met for the first time in four years. They were trying to secure deployment of 7,100 peacekeepers that the  UN Security Council approved for Angola at an initial cost of $380 million.

The fighting in **Somalia** cannot be called a war.  It is not even guerrilla warfare because it is not against a central government, because there is none.  It is tribal warfare between the various clans.  After overthrowing the dictatorship of Siad Barre on 28 January 1992, the clans could not agree on how to run the country.  The US went in to feed the starving people but got scared and ran away.  The UN took over but was caught between the warring clans and finally gave up and had to call for the US to come back to cover their retreat.  The tribes were left to carve up the carcass.

The wars in Africa, though tragic for those involved and an affront to our sense of civilization, do not present a threat outside the continent.

The war in the former **Yugoslavia** continued and threatened to draw other states in if it spread to other regions and involved the Hungarians and the Albanians.  The UN tried to separate the factions but was constantly humiliated by the Serbs.  The war was causing unrest in NATO and splitting the allies.    There was American concern that France was deliberately trying to split the US and Britain since France would like to see NATO ended and replaced by a European security alliance. UN, European, and American prestige were all badly damaged. **Bosnia was wreaking havoc with the new world order.**

The former Soviet Union had a bloody civil war which broke out in **Tajikistan** after the collapse of the Soviet Union, war in **Azerbaijan** with the **Armenians** in control of Nagorno-Karabakh and some additional area, plus the war in **Georgia.** The fighting in Abkhazia, Georgia's northwestern province along the Black Sea, went badly. Then a second rebel front was opened against the strategic port of Poti by fighters loyal to ex-President Zviad Gamsakhurdia, Georgia's first popularly elected president who was ousted in January 1992 and eventually replaced by Eduard Shevardnadze, the former Soviet foreign minister.

Shevardnadze accused **Russia** of helping the rebels. However, he went to Moscow to meet with President Boris Yeltsin and received some Russian peacekeeping troops and even agreed to bring Georgia into the Commonwealth of Independent States which Georgia had shunned.

In December 1994, President Boris Yeltsin sent troops into the rebellious province of **Chechnya.** The Russian Army suffered a bloody nose and terrible world press which threatened the still blossoming democracy in Russia.

Cross border raids by Islamic guerrillas continue almost daily in **Tajikistan.** Elections were held in February 1995 but there was extensive boycotting due to election irregularities. The European Union even refused to send observers because they did not expect fair elections.

**Afghanistan** could be called Asia's forgotten war. It received attention after the Soviets invaded on 27 December 1979 and withdrew in 1989 leaving 2 million Afghans dead and 6 million chased away. Three years later the *mujahedin,* which Washington once supported as anti-Communist freedom fighters, drove out the Communist government but nine separate Islamic factions fought for control of Kabul and laid it to waste. The casualty levels were running four times the level in Bosnia.

Closer to home, we even had a small frontier war between **Peru** and **Ecuador** plus **Mexico** faced a rebellion in the south in **Chiapas** state. The tyranny in **Haiti** abated with the introduction of US troops and an effort to rebuild that shattered government.

The large conventional military capabilities present in **Asia**, coupled with the many disputes and growing economic competition in the region, made  Asia a very tense area in the post-Cold War world.  America fought there in World War II and the two major wars it fought since were both in Asia: Korea and Viet-Nam.  America as a Pacific power would certainly pay close attention to Asia.

The 45 years of Cold War had truly turned the world into an armed camp.  Never had so much military equipment been available in the hands of standing armies.  Even though some areas were poorer and had less sophisticated hardware and fought with rather simple arms, other regions had the most advanced technology of modern electronic and missile warfare.

The world was really quite a dangerous place.  But what made it really dangerous was the number of nuclear weapons, some in uncertain hands, and the proliferation of nuclear technology and weapons production.

## NUCLEAR WAR CAPABILITIES

Man has long been capable of large scale destruction, from the days of Genghis Khan when he wiped out entire cities and slaughtered the people to the advent of strategic bombing which could also destroy cities as we did more damage with the fire bombing of Tokyo than with the atomic bombs.  The difference in the nuclear age was time in that enormous destruction could be wreaked in seconds.

At the end of the war, the Americans knew they had opened Pandora's box and tried to close it by offering to put atomic weapons under UN control.  Stalin saw it differently for the Soviet Union and rushed to develop his own. Unfortunately for mankind, there followed the most bizarre arms race of history -- **the mass destruction derby!**  We started out with kilotons of destruction; when thermonuclear weapons or H-bombs were developed, we changed to megatons.  Khrushchev could hardly hide his glee when he announced his 100 megaton weapon.  Finally, we spoke of kilomegatons equivalence of destructive capability.

We should review that age because the human mind has the wonderful capacity to forget pain and many have already forgotten the nuclear age as if it were a bad dream.

For decades, there were nuclear weapons on station nearly all over the world (and thousands of them are still there),

170 You and the New World Order

in ballistic missiles in underground silos, bombs, air-to-air missiles, mines, torpedoes, depth charges, artillery, cruise missiles, and many forms of shortrange surface-to-surface missiles. There were air-to-ground missiles to help bombers penetrate defenses, ground-to-air missiles to attack bombers, anti-ballistic missile missiles, and missiles that could be launched from submarines under the sea.

This plethora of destruction and deterrence became complicated with MIRV (multiple independently-targeted reentry vehicles) warheads, LOBS (limited orbit ballistic system) coming from space even though there was a treaty precluding nuclear weapons in space, submarine launched ballistic missiles, and cruise missiles that could be launched from ground, ships (as against Iraq), or from aircraft.

The greatest concentration of those warheads was in Europe where the NATO forces were on constant alert in the face of the Red Army. Missile units in the US were kept on alert and part of our B-52 bomber fleet was always in the air so that it could not be destroyed on the ground. Submarines were at sea for six months or more at a time and cruised submerged off the shores of the US and seas where launches could reach the Soviet Union. The early warning times were terribly short: perhaps 30 minutes for an intercontinental missile and only a few minutes for a submarine launched missile. There were enough warheads to destroy every major city in the US and the Soviet Union with thousands left over. That was the **balance of terror!**

There has been only limited exposure to nuclear radioactivity. The Japanese have experience from the very limited radioactivity of the two A-bombs, both of which were air bursts. The Russians have experience from some of their accidents and contamination, such as in Chernobyl and Chelyabinsk in the Urals where a 1957 explosion of a waste storage area contaminated a large area which is **still** contaminated.

In the early years, the Soviets dumped their nuclear waste into rivers and lakes, many of which are still contaminated and off limits. Lake Karachay is still so contaminated that it is possible at one spot on the lake to receive a lethal dose of radiation by merely standing near the site for an hour. (They were still dumping waste in the Sea of Japan in 1993.) A terrorist nuke is a terrible threat since it would be a surface blast with high radioactivity.

## The Commonwealth of Independent States

When the Soviet Union collapsed, there were strategic nuclear weapons located in four of the republics: Russia, Belarus, Ukraine, and Kazakhstan, and the leaders agreed that Russia should keep control of those weapons. That changed later, particularly when Ukraine announced that it would control weapons on its soil. Belarus announced it intended to be a nuclear-free state by 1997 and moved some of the weapons to Russia for destruction. Kazakhstan followed Russian leadership closely and made no moves against the systems.

There were estimated to be about 27,000 nuclear warheads in the Soviet arsenal, about half of which were for long range weapons. Most of the warheads were in Russia: 12 of 16 ICBM silo fields, 10 of 12 mobile missile bases, 11 of 26 medium and heavy bomber bases, and all six ports for submarines which carried nuclear missiles (63 subs with 930 missiles). There were some 17,000 tactical or short range Soviet nuclear weapons, including some 1,700 surface-to-surface missile launchers, in almost every Soviet republic but they were withdrawn into Russia.

The precise numbers are not important for our review; new items come from production and older items are retired. There is also the difference between the carrying vehicle and the number of nuclear warheads. For instance, a bomber may carry several bombs, missile launchers and artillery fire nuclear missiles and shells, which are ammunition. Reserve supplies are kept in storage.

Larger missiles were configured to carry multiple warheads (MIRVs); for instance, the very large Soviet SS-18, appropriately called *Satan*, could carry over 10 MIRVs to a range of nearly 7,000 miles. Also, reductions had started under START 1 and 2 and the INF Treaty and weapons had been destroyed by both the US and the USSR under joint supervision.

All of the 174 SS-20 IRBMs were to be destroyed under the INF Treaty. There were nearly 1,400 ICBMs, mostly in Russia, but there were two fields of SS-25s in Belarus, over 100 SS-19s and SS-24s in Ukraine, and about 100 SS-18s in Kazakhstan. Ukraine has not ratified START 1 and the experts believe that when all the parties have ratified the treaties, the three republics will have to turn over their weapons to Russia or destroy them.

However, Ukraine declared ownership of the missiles on its land in July 1993 and announced it wanted to keep 46 of the SS-24s unless a new agreement could be reached with the US. Ukraine was using its nukes for bargaining chips to be treated as an equal partner in the nuclear world, its prime concern being encroachment by Russia. They later made a deal with Russia to relinquish the weapons in exchange for debt relief.

The threat is obviously enormous. What was the Soviet nuclear arsenal is still basically intact with ICBMs capable of reaching the US, though supposedly they are no longer aimed at us. The good news is that Gorbachev and then Yeltsin have been meticulous in assuring the West, and the US in particular, that the nuclear weapons are under tight control and that they do not pose a threat.

The bad news is that Russia is turning back to nuclear weapons as the basis of its military force and strategy according to Senator Sam Nunn. The deterioration of the Russian military led Yeltsin to adopt a new military doctrine in November 1993 calling for the use of nuclear weapons if Russia or its allies were attacked.

There are several other concerns. The US worked closely with Gorbachev, then Yeltsin and the presidents of the former republics, to try to help them during their difficult transition. In addition to food and aid, the US provided hundreds of millions of dollars to pay for destruction of some of the nuclear systems. The main concern there was if Russia or one of the others should fall back under a radical regime with a return to the Cold War.

The second concern was theft or sale of nuclear weapons. Parts of the former Soviet military were in such dire straits that they were selling some of their equipment. There were reports throughout 1992 that several nuclear warheads were missing. They were supposedly from the Semipalatinsk nuclear test site in Kazakhstan which was closed in early 1992. In March, a high-ranking Russian officer confirmed the US intelligence report that three tactical nuclear weapons were missing. They suspected they had been sold to Iran possibly with the cooperation of several Kazakh nuclear specialists who had been seen in Tehran.

There was a report in November that Iran had obtained four nukes, including two 40KT missile warheads. Some newspapers claimed that two warheads were in Iran and a third, according to supposed Russian intelligence reports, had not been traced but was thought to be in the Middle East. The threat is not from any war use but if the devices were to fall into the hands of terrorists, which abound in Iran and Libya.

The third concern pertains to the nuclear scientists in the former Soviet Union. This was an elite group with high living standards and great prestige. The economic upheaval reduced them to paupers. There were probably 3,000 to 5,000 scientists with knowledge that would be vital to a fledgling weapons program. They could well be tempted to accept large cash offers to work for some foreign governments.

There are several countries that could pay large sums for that expertise adding additional headaches for US policy and further threat of nuclear proliferation. Another 100,000 scientists had high enough security access to obtain important information plus there are all the people who served in the Soviet armed forces who worked with the nuclear weapons. There is a lot of nuclear knowledge in the former Soviet Union. Some are selling their expertise via computer modems.

Finally, there is the problem of the spread of nuclear technology. Russia formally agreed in September 1993 to join the US and over 20 other nations in abiding by the Missile Control Technology Regime, which was an agreement in 1987 to limit commerce in missiles, a key element for nuclear delivery, but still insists on selling reactors to Iran.

## China

The country that we tend to ignore in the nuclear arena because it does not currently have the means to project its conventional power across the oceans, is China. It has tested and deployed two different ICBMs, including MIRVs plus at least some 60 IRBMs. Even though the Chinese could probably strike the US, their main threat is in Asia and the Pacific rim.

China maintained an ambiguous position on nuclear testing by telling President Clinton that they would give "positive consideration" to the moratorium which was agreed to by the US, Russia, France, and Britain. However, they went ahead with an underground test on 4 October 1993 and another in May 1995.

The US was irritated but decided not to resume testing

yet. China also got at odds with the US by selling missiles to Pakistan which have a range of 300 miles and can carry nuclear warheads. This was a breach of the Missile Control Technology Regime of 1987 and the US imposed sanctions on China for two years.

## The West

The US nuclear force of about 20,000 weapons (nearly half are short range) was being redeployed and reduced in accordance with various treaties plus unilateral reductions due to the reduced Soviet threat. President Bush removed all tactical nuclear weapons from Navy ships (400 *Tomahawk* cruise missiles and about 100 bombs on each aircraft carrier) and the artillery shells (about 1,470 with range to 20 miles) and short range missiles (about 690 *Lances* with range to 80 miles) from Europe.

The US still had about 450 *Minuteman* II, 500 *Minuteman* III, and 50 *Peacekeeper* ICBMs, 34 nuclear submarines with 624 *Poseidon* and *Trident* missiles, and about 300 B-1B, B-52, and FB-111 bombers. The 99 *Pershing* II launchers were destroyed but there were still about 65 *Lance* launchers, plus 350-400 *Tomahawks* and other systems throughout the armed forces.

The French *Force de frappe* had 6 submarines with 96 missiles, 18 IRBMs, over 130 strike aircraft, and 40 *Pluton* launchers. The United Kingdom had 4 submarines with 64 missiles and they received their first *Trident* submarine in August 1993. They also had 14 *Lance* launchers. In addition, there were 6 *Lance* launchers in Italy and 7 in the Netherlands.

## The Nuclear Powers

The five main nuclear powers are **China, France, Russia**, the **UK**, and the **US**, which also happen to be the permanent members of the UN Security Council. In addition, at least technically for the time being, there are **Belarus, Kazakhstan**, and **Ukraine**.

The significant, but unannounced, member of the elite club was **Israel**. Playing a cute game of never admitting to having them but still threatening neighbors with them was the Israeli game for many years. With French and American collusion, French help on reactors, testing, and *Mirage* aircraft and illegal US diversions (some 380 pounds of highly enriched uranium "disappeared" from a facility in Apollo, Pennsylvania in 1965 and the FBI declined to investigate), Israel developed its nuclear weapons at Dimona in the Negev Desert.

Israel has *Mirage* and other aircraft, *Jericho* 1 missiles (450 km range), *Jericho* 2 missiles (1,500 km range), and *Lance* launchers. Estimates range from 100 to 300 warheads. It is interesting to recall that Henry Kissinger gave Israel the *Lance* launchers during his "shuttle diplomacy" after the 1973 War as he had to keep giving Israel more. He refused to listen to anyone when told that the US Army did **not** have a conventional warhead for the *Lance* at that time. Perhaps he did not care!

Also, it was reported that Israel "blackmailed" Kissinger to airlift replacement equipment to Israel during the war or they "would go nuclear." The airlift started four days later!

Even though Israel continually lied to the US about its nuclear program, the CIA was aware of it. President Johnson was briefed in 1968 but he ordered the CIA not to inform anyone else in his Administration including Defense Secretary Robert McNamara and Secretary of State Dean Rusk. It was Johnson who had changed the US policy from balance to total support of Israel in the 1967 War and it was Johnson who covered up the deliberate Israeli attack on the USS *Liberty* which killed 34 US sailors.

The public exposure came on 5 October 1986 when the *Sunday Times* of London reported testimony from a former Israeli nuclear technician, Mordechai Vanunu, who had worked at Dimona for 10 years. Yitzhak Shamir reportedly wanted him assassinated but Prime Minister Shimon Peres objected seeing disclosure as a forceful deterrent to the Arabs without admitting possession. Vanunu was kidnapped in Rome and taken back to Israel where he was sentenced to 18 years in prison in a closed trial.

It was an open secret in Washington even though the US Government continued to play the game and not face up to the situation. Israel continued to insist the Dimona plant was for peaceful research. David Ben-Gurion solemnly claimed it was a textile mill in 1960, later that was changed  to a pumping station. Then in 1961, he announced that it was neither but was "a scientific institute for research in problems of arid zones and desert flora and fauna." John Kennedy was not amused. In January 1963, Shimon Peres, then Deputy Defense Minister, said it was a desalinization plant to irrigate the Negev Desert.

The Dimona reactor went critical in 1964. Israelis observed (? participated in) French nuclear tests in the Sahara. A US team was finally permitted to visit Dimona in 1964 and indicated they were "reassured" about the Israeli nuclear program. The Israelis had built a phony control room for the American visitors to inspect.

Israel refused repeated urgings by the US to sign the Nonproliferation Treaty or accept IAEA (International Atomic Energy Agency) safeguards. And they still have not. (In 1995, Egypt unsuccessfully pushed for Israel to sign or Egypt and other Arab countries would not renew the NPT.)

Two Democratic Representatives from New York, Stephen J. Solarz and Jonathan B. Bingham, dropped their amendment to ban US aid to countries manufacturing nuclear weapons because, after they were briefed by the State Department, they were afraid they might inadvertently cause a cutoff of aid to Israel.

**South Africa** conducted extensive nuclear weapons research and had enough fissile material on hand in the 1970s to build an atomic bomb. CIA documents stated that South Africa evidently suspended preparations to test a nuclear device in 1977 because of strong US pressure and other international reactions.

The CIA reports from 1979 and 1980 substantiated the longstanding reports of collaboration between Israel and South Africa in military matters including Israeli participation in South African nuclear research activities. The declassified portions of the CIA documents do not reveal the South African and Israeli responsibility for a mysterious "flash" over the South Atlantic on 22 September 1979. The US surveillance satellite indicated it was a 3 kiloton nuclear explosion.

South Africa announced in 1991 that it would conduct no new research and would not pursue a nuclear capability.

**India** detonated a nuclear device in 1974, but then announced that it was not going to build nuclear weapons. Regardless, India has the capability and probably substantial amounts of fissile material available should it change its policy.

The newest member of the nuclear club is **Pakistan**. The US had been in discussions for years with Pakistan trying to persuade them not to develop nuclear weapons. The

Pakistani Foreign Secretary, Shahryar Khan, admitted in Washington in February 1992 that Pakistan had the components and technology to assemble a nuclear "device."

Pakistan refused to sign the NPT but pledged not to explode such a device or transfer nuclear technology to other Islamic or Third World countries. There were two major concerns with this development. First, it might cause India to change its no-nuke policy and second, it represented the first nuclear capability in the Muslim World, which has long wanted it to offset Israel's.

## Wannabes

There were still several countries that wanted to be in the nuclear club. Pakistan, as we just noted, evidently already had crossed over the Rubicon. The next candidate was **North Korea**, the Communist hermit nation still clinging to its old ways. It threatened to withdraw from the NPT and had avoided international inspections of its nuclear facilities.

The CIA believed Pyongyang probably already had enough plutonium in 1993 to build a weapon. The regime agreed to resume talks with the IAEA about inspections and won some concessions of aid from the US. Then in September 1993, North Korea refused to resume the talks.

The US and North Korea eventually signed an agreement but it was soon in trouble. It was not clear whether North Korea was serious about acquiring nuclear weapons or merely attempting to gain political and economic concessions, but they did launch the *Scud* missile as noted earlier, a key element of a nuclear program.

**Iraq** had made significant progress toward developing a nuclear capability before it invaded Kuwait. After the ceasefire, the UN insisted on destroying all of Iraq's mass destruction capability, which included chemical and its nuclear program. There were many disputes with the UN inspectors but the Iraqi program was set back for many years again.

It had been delayed before when Israel bombed companies and assassinated Arab scientists in Europe and then bombed the Osirak reactor in June 1981 (right after Sadat's visit and 3 weeks before Begin faced elections!).

This time even the Israelis were caught short. The intelligence communities thought that Iraq was 5 to 10 years away from producing a weapon. The UN inspectors were shocked when they discovered the enormity and the sophistication of the Iraqi project and estimated they were only 12 to 18 months from their first bomb.

The equipment can be destroyed but the know-how is there and now the people have to be monitored. Iraq still wants to join the club. Saddam Hussein's objective was to produce an Arab nuclear bomb in order to confront Israel's existing bombs.

**Iran** has already been mentioned in terms of suspected purchases of nuclear warheads and the proposal to buy reactors from the former Soviet Union. Iran announced plans to build 10 nuclear power plants but denied a weapons program. They already signed a contract with China for two reactors. Again, this is a fanatical regime with a driven desire to deal with certain "satans." Iran is greatly rebuilding its military strength and nuclear weapons would add to its importance in the region.

The other country that has tried to join the elite is **Libya**. Qadhafi does not have the technological base or the trained personnel to build a nuclear device but he has money. He has been trying to buy one for years. He would represent the textbook case of the terrorist with a nuke.

## ON NUCLEAR WAR NOW

With eight countries with operational nuclear inventories and six more with unknown capabilities or dreams, there are enough nuclear warheads in the world to do unimaginable damage to the planet. What is the outlook for such a catastrophe?

The good news is that during the nearly 50 years since the birth of the atomic age, there has not been another one of these awesome weapons fired in anger. The Americans maintained very tight controls over their nuclear systems with central control from the President and two-key systems in the field so that no one person could actually fire a nuclear weapon. The Soviets claimed that their controls were even more stringent than the American's.

The bad news is that with the demise of the Soviet Union, a degree of uncertainty has entered the equation. President Yeltsin, since he took over the launch codes from Gorbachev, has tried to keep all the former Soviet weapons under one control -- Moscow. He has been generally successful but the independent thinking in Ukraine has clouded the procedures. There were no indications that Ukraine had any aggressive intentions, on the contrary, every signal was only that they were trying to protect their independence.

Nevertheless, with the former Soviet arsenal in four different states now and with dire economic problems leading to the concern that some control might be lost by theft or sale, there was obvious nervousness about the massive capability in the CIS even if there was no expressed intention of any hostility. For those reasons, the US made a major effort to assist the CIS in economic ways as well as providing funding and assistance in destroying some of the nuclear weapons.

The unknown in the club is Israel which, with its siege mentality of Armageddon or Masada complex, is more likely to initiate a nuclear launch than any of the others. Therefore, it is very important for Israel and the Arabs to reach some accommodations so that Israel might finally join the legitimate world of nations and support international law, sign the Nonproliferation Treaty, and permit IAEA inspections of the Israeli nuclear facilities.

The second part of the bad news is that several of the Wannabes are still pushing forward trying to break into the club. Iraq has been slowed but the knowledge that has been accumulated is still there. We greatly underestimated their advanced efforts letting Western egos rule in thinking that Arabs could not accomplish such modern achievements. We forgot where algebra and some of our science came from!

The radical Arab drive for nuclear weapons has been fed by their frustration in dealing with Israel which was thrust upon them by Europeans and then totally supported by the US. It will be difficult to remove the Arab desire for nukes until there is some rational arrangement with Israel and a more even-handed policy out of Washington.

If North Korea goes nuclear, it will have a major impact in the region. Japan will have to rethink its security. Then China will react to Japan. A similar problem exists with the Pakistani program. If it appears to threaten India, it may force India to reverse its policy and go nuclear. In both cases, a new member would be added to the proliferation club.

Reviewing the various nuclear powers, the CIS has the greatest capability but also the lowest intentions for the moment. The concern there is the stability of the governments so that tyrannical regimes do not come to power. Israel is more precarious but, as long as American leaders can summon some of their rare courage and make Israel toe the line, it can be kept under control.

The more difficult problem is Pakistan and the Wannabes. They cannot pose a major threat to the US, but the world has not yet seen a nuclear terrorist incident. If one of those missing Soviet nukes had been in the World Trade Center and outrageous demands had been made, it is difficult to imagine the outcome.

The NPT came up for renewal in 1995. Many Third World countries wanted it extended for only a limited period contingent on progress toward the promised general nuclear disarmament. The Arab states tried to block renewal until Israel agreed to join the 178 signatories. However, the NPT was extended indefinitely in May 1995, but that still left Israel, India, and Pakistan refusing to sign and Iraq and North Korea circumventing inspections.

In sum then, the prospects for nuclear war are still extremely low at this time. The massive nuclear exchange is hopefully a nightmare from which we are now awake. However, the possibility of nuclear blackmail or a terrorist incident has increased.

## THREATS

Having briefly reviewed the prospects for nuclear war, we should now review the prospects for conventional war. The importance will vary according to different states and their national interests.

There will continue to be fighting in Africa. There have been repeated droughts and famines and the West has rushed in to feed the starving masses often to be shot at by the warring factions who were letting their people starve. Help cannot reach the starving in the south of the Sudan and the US has declared Sudan a terrorist state. Somalia fell completely apart in tribal (clan) warfare. We rushed in humanitarian aid and ended up fighting with some of these same warlords.

We managed to get Angola and UNITA to stop the fighting in 1991. However, after what we called fair elections, UNITA went back to fighting and thousands were dying again. The West was basically fed up with Africa and will do only the minimum amount for humanitarian efforts. The frustration of dealing with Africa is summed up by the comment of a former ambassador who said, "Africa should be tied up in a plastic bag and left to rot!" There is little likelihood of any of the major powers becoming deeply involved in Africa.

There will continue to be strife, particularly in the Third World, and with little or no interest from the outside; one exception is support for anti-drug activities. The areas of strife in the former Soviet Union may attract Russian involvement, but they are unlikely to pull in other countries, except that Turkey and Iran are interested in Azerbaijan which is Muslim and has oil. Both have been courting the Muslim government there and threatening the Christian Armenians. Both move cautiously so as not to excite a Russian reaction, but in September 1993, both had massed additional troops on the frontier and Iran may have pushed some troops across into Azerbaijan.

Other disputes in the former Soviet Union will continue as many old accounts are settled. Except for possibly some problems with some of the nonsensical frontiers with Eastern Europe and the rebels crossing into Afghanistan (which will also be left to fester internally), there is little likelihood of outside direct involvement.

Since the fighting between Armenia and Azerbaijan had been going on for over five years, and the rebellion in Georgia for over a year, and then the mess in Chechnya, it appeared that the Caucasus would remain a hot spot for the indefinite future. The fighting should remain limited though in that Western Europe and the US are unlikely to choose to take any direct role and will only either indirectly support local governments or support Russia or Turkey. Iran will probably try to exert influence but with no outside help.

There are three areas which have the highest potential for causing serious international difficulties in the decade ahead. They are in priority the former Yugoslavia, North Korea, and the Middle East. There are significant national interests of major powers that could be endangered.

## Yugoslavia

The disintegration of Yugoslavia and the outbreak of some of the most bestial fighting has been a source of shame and embarrassment for the West. The supposedly civilized West had seen part of its area return to tribalism, religious internecine slaughter and rape, and nationalism at its xenophobic worst.

We should not have been surprised because Yugoslavia

was not a nation state.  The region was for centuries the battleground between the Austro-Hungarian and Ottoman Empires.  Croatia and Slovenia were influenced by Western culture and are Roman Catholic.  Serbia, Macedonia, and Montenegro belonged to the Turks and are Eastern Orthodox while Bosnia and Hercegovina was also under the Turks but has a large Muslim population.

World War I was precipitated by the assassination of Austrian Archduke Ferdinand in Sarajevo by a member of a secret nationalist movement.  After the war, the south Slavs formed a single state, but during World War II, Croatia sided with Hitler and over a million people died in the ensuing civil war.  Tito and the Communists took over in 1945 and kept ethnic tensions under control, but after Tito's death in 1980, the old enmities erupted again.

Yugoslavia was a federation with strong local governments and a weak central government with a rotating presidency.  Slovenia and Croatia declared their independence in 1991 followed by Bosnia and Hercegovina and Macedonia. Only Montenegro and the two provinces of Kosovo (Albanian dominated) and Vojvodina (large Hungarian minority) remained with Serbia in the old Yugoslavia.  Slovenia was ethnically homogeneous and economically viable.  The other republics had mixed populations of Croats, Serbs, and Muslims.  Thus the scene was set for religious and ethnic (tribal) confrontation.

The catalyst was the ruthless Serbian President Slobodan Milosevic, the Communist *apparatchik* who rose to the top in Serbia.  He claimed to want to preserve Yugoslavia, but his goal was a Greater Serbia.  He declared in August 1991 that he wanted to bring all Serbs in the various parts of Yugoslavia under his control.

He orchestrated aggression in Croatia and then Bosnia. Milosevic was the power behind Radovan Karadzic, the leader of Bosnia's Serbs, and he effectively controlled the Yugoslav Army.  He played on generations of ethnic hatreds and turned Yugoslavia into a slaughterhouse.  Even a new term was coined for his barbarism as he pursued "ethnic cleansing" of Serbian regions in Bosnia and Croatia.  He had earned the title of the Butcher of the Balkans.

The fighting was brutal.  There was sheer horror in Bosnia while Serbs proceeded with their ethnic cleansing with theft, rape, torture, and murder of Muslims.  We were observing barbarism and genocide. Modern European cities were turned into chaotic places with no water, heat, or food. There were numerous ceasefires, then quickly broken by the Serbs. The US made threats and did nothing. Sarajevo was surrounded and cut off. The hotels and ski lodges from the 1984 Winter Olympics were burned or blown up. As a Serb soldier said, "We don't want the Turks to use them ever again." Turk is the derogatory reference to Bosnian Muslims.

Shades of the 1930s. Appeasement. The failure to act in the Balkans was the most disgraceful mistake by the West since World War II. The West Europeans were baffled and sat on their hands. In the years before World War I, the Balkans played a key role in balance of power politics, but this time there were no such treaties, so they did nothing.

The US was not much better. President Clinton made threats but did not act. He would not commit any troops to Bosnia but sent 300 troops under the UN to Macedonia. It was perhaps understandable in that he said he would not commit troops if they were going to come home in boxes.

He finally got UN approval to use air strikes against Serb positions, but still did not act. The US Government could not make up its mind. In April 1993, Clinton said we had a national interest to limit ethnic cleansing. In May, Secretary of State Warren Christopher said the use of air strikes was based on our strategic interests. In June, he said we had humanitarian concerns, but Bosnia did not involve our vital interests. In July as Sarajevo was threatened with falling, he said the US was doing all it could consistent with our national interest.

Small UN contingents were deployed in Bosnia but they became hostages. The Europeans objected to the air strikes because they feared reprisals against their lightly armed UN troops. One of the stupidest errors of all was the arms embargo on all the area. Since the Bosnian Serbs had access to arms from the Yugoslav army, that was an embargo on the victims. Aggression was being rewarded.

Serbia's actions were clear violations of the UN Charter yet the West was going along with the partition of Bosnia. The US even agreed to provide 20,000 of the 40,000 troops to come from NATO to enforce the partition.

The Bosnians were appalled by the weakness of the democracies. Milosevic was contemptuous of US policy and of Clinton in particular. The whole miserable episode was characterized in the West by weak leadership and incompetent diplomacy.

As a French politician noted, the mess in Bosnia came about due to an absence of European political courage. "In the heart of Europe we have let Bosnian Muslims die. We will be reproached eternally for that."

There are several potential repercussions from the Yugoslav fiasco that bid ill for the future.

First, the powerlessness of the international community in Bosnia will leave it powerless elsewhere.

Second, the UN has suffered another setback to its prestige. Until it or its members go in and kick the hell out of some of these gangster governments or regimes, it will have no significant place in world peacekeeping.

Third, Bosnia was an American failure. As the only superpower, the world looked to the US at least for moral leadership and for more if necessary. Clinton's indecisiveness in Bosnia stirred fears of how he might react to other crises. Clinton, who ran a campaign on domestic economic issues and attacked Bush for spending too much time on foreign affairs, was not the man for the job. He talked tough but did nothing. In spite of his campaign rhetoric, the president of the US is the most important person in the world in international affairs.

Fourth, there is growing frustration and anger in the Muslim world with the lack of action by the international community over the slaughter of a Muslim population. Karadzic liked to portray the Bosnian Muslims as fundamentalists threatening the West. This was not true. The Muslims were being raped and killed and their mosques destroyed. The danger was not that Muslim fundamentalism was there but that it might be imported.

Fifth, was the threat of the spread of ethnic violence into Russia and other areas of Eastern Europe.

It is not clear yet that we have learned our lesson in shame. Europe and the US will be involved if there is a treacherous partition of the country. We are committed to sending troops to police the accords. That too can be a quagmire! The Bosnia mess is a black spot in history and is not over yet.

Such aggression usually begets more aggression. After Bosnia could easily come Macedonia which historically from the time of Alexander the Great extended into Greece. A butcher like Milosevic must be stopped. So far the West has only appeased him. Just like Hitler!

---

**Europe, 1993:  Another low, dishonest age**

**Serbian Conquest: Just as in the 1930s, democracies cower before the conqueror's boots**

The stench of the 1930s pervades.  What did the poet call it -- a low, dishonest age?  The Nazi boot crunching Europe while the democracies quailed amid their hollow excuses.  Rewarding one conquest after another, toasting the slaughtered with endless communiques.  Cowering in the light, while the dark grew all around.

And now, unenlightened by history, Europe watches the Serbian boot crunch Muslims while democratic leaders puff up like frogs, their portentious lungs croaking endlessly into the dusk.  Conquest is rewarded with peace plans based on murder.  The slaughtered are honored with a new map giving Serbia all the territory it has so brutally seized, and the Muslims only enough land to die upon.  Western Europe cowers in the light, while the dark spills out like blood.

The stench of the 1930s pervades in another low, dishonest age.

Editorial
*Reno Gazette Journal*
30 August 1993

---

## Northeast Asia

The second potential hotspot is Northeast Asia; fortunately there is no fighting there and, with some competent leadership and diplomacy, there need not be.  We have already discussed the North Korean nuclear production program and its problems.    Seoul, Washington, and Tokyo have applied diplomatic pressure on Pyongyang.

China, North Korea's principal source of oil, opposed public threats of punitive sanctions instead recommending patience and negotiations and Washington did negotiate. China did apply pressure quietly by placing trade with North Korea on a cash basis; several ships returned to China when Pyongyang could not pay for the cargoes.  The North Korean economy was faltering with residential electricity cut to a few hours per day and only four hours a year for fighter pilot training.

China permitted a UN resolution condemning North Korea without using its veto.  Seoul and Washington hope that China will permit passage of a UN resolution for sanctions if Pyongyang withdraws from the nonproliferation treaty. However, Kim was an old friend of China's elderly leaders but now that he is gone, the relationship may change.

The impact is wider that just North Korea. What happens in North Korea will affect the entire region. Japan will have to rethink its security program and China will react to Japan. The military buildup in China is already alarming its neighbors.

China's military spending is a vast amount, and with a booming economy sporting an astounding double-digit growth rate while the rest of the world is in the doldrums, the Chinese military potential is truly awesome. Lee Kuan Yew, Singapore's wily former prime minister, said of China, "This is the biggest player in the history of man."

A Southeast Asian diplomat stated it rather succinctly, "China's defense spending feeds people's anxieties." One such concern among China's neighbors is Beijing's shopping for an aircraft carrier, which obviously would be useful to support her claims to the Spratly Islands and other areas in the South China Sea.

China has said it will settle the Spratly dispute peacefully, but the Chinese have installed underwater cables to the islands and improved an airfield there according to US officials. In November 1992, a Chinese Army general was quoted in a Beijing paper, "If we had an aircraft carrier, warfare in the South China Sea would be more lively, and many situations would be easier to handle."

China supposedly expressed interest in the *Varag* from Ukraine and the Russian carriers *Novorossiysk* and *Minsk.* The high cost of a complete carrier group may be a stumbling block for China, but do not count on that. (A US carrier group costs about $20 billion, but that is a supercarrier with extremely advanced ships, munitions, aircraft, and electronics. A smaller group might cost $4-6 billion. However, a carrier in a limited war or strife mode would not need as much protection.)

The concern is clear as a Japanese diplomat bluntly stated, "If China actually buys an aircraft carrier, then we have to rethink our strategy for the entire region." That concern about Korea, the military buildup in China, and lack of US resolve could very well force Japan to rethink its security policy.

The US cannot ignore Asia. One third of our foreign trade is with the Pacific Rim, nearly double that with the European Community. The reason East Asia had such phenomenal growth was the US security umbrella, a *pax*

*Americana.*

The fear of Soviet influence blocked multilateral discussions for years. Now the US has changed its policy and in May 1993 joined security talks under the auspices of ASEAN (Association of Southeast Asian Nations -- Brunei, Indonesia, Malaysia, the Philippines, Singapore, and Thailand.) A consensus was evolving for mutual security and some arms reductions. Also, it was decided to bring China and Russia into future discussions.

The US bases in the Philippines are gone but new agreements have been established with Singapore and Thailand and talks are underway with Indonesia and Malaysia. The *pax Americana* may be over, but Asia is mistrustful of its neighbors and may need America as much as ever. The US has major interests in the area and still has treaty obligations with Japan and South Korea.

## The Middle East

There are many jokes about the Middle East. In one, various leaders ask God (or Allah) if a particular problem in their country will ever be solved. To each leader, God answers, "Yes, but not in your time." Finally, God is asked if there will be peace in the Middle East, and he replies, "Yes, but not in my time."

The Middle East has been the tinder box for the current world ever since Israel was formed in 1948. Israel fought four wars with its Arab neighbors: 1948, 1956, 1967, and 1973. It occupied southern Lebanon, invaded Lebanon all the way to Beirut in 1982, and has generally kept tensions high in the occupied territories it took in 1967 and refused to grant independence to the Palestinians.

The Egyptians agreed to peace with Israel at Camp David in 1979. The Israelis and the Palestinians took a first step in 1993 but the radicals have slowed the implementation phase, and Jordan has made peace.

The Middle East has been terribly expensive for the US over the past 45 years. The "special relationship" with Israel will be studied in history as one of the most unusual cases where a small nation was able to so strongly influence the foreign policy of a world power.

It is debatable whether Israel ever was a strategic asset to the US; in many ways, it appeared to be a liability. Yet for purely domestic political reasons (we do not help Bosnians when they are threatened with genocide), the US persisted in spite of rejection by the rest of the world to protect this small theocracy which violated all types of international law and human rights.

We deny our own democratic concepts of separation of church and state by embracing the Jewish state where everyone else is a second class person, not even a citizen. We violate our concept of the right of self determination by denying that right to the Palestinians.

We prided ourselves on never using our veto in the UN during the years when the Soviets cast so many. In recent years, we are the leader, and many were to protect Israel as we stood alone before the whole world. The fact that the US is the only country that supports Israel should make us pause and ponder why.

Nevertheless, since Lyndon Johnson made the US Israel's main arms supplier and Henry Kissinger and Jimmy Carter paid an enormous price for the Camp David peace agreement (which Menachem Begin immediately reneged on), the US has supported Israel. The 1973 War also cost us the oil embargo when Richard Nixon gave Israel $2.2 billion in special aid. That embargo and long gas lines took $100-300 billion out of our GNP. We are now up to the rate of $6.3 billion per year to Israel, for total economic costs over the years of between $650 and $850 billion. How much is enough?

American politicians want to homeport a US aircraft carrier at Haifa, because Israeli politicians want the money. That would make our sailors targets for terrorism and totally destroy our credibility in the Arab World (long an Israeli objective). Our politicians react to the lobby and push for moving the US Embassy from Tel Aviv to Jerusalem in spite of the world agreement that Jerusalem should be an open city.

Hopefully, the Israelis will seriously negotiate with the Arabs and reach an honest settlement so that those countries can live in peace. Without such a settlement or a change in US domestic politics, the US will remain the backer of that little country.

We continue to pour out our treasury to it when we need it badly at home and if another war comes, we will pay the bills. The US could impose peace in the Middle East but we do not have the political courage to do it. That will not read well in history either.

The US maintained a policy of keeping Israel militarily stronger than the Arabs and with the capability to defeat any combination of Arab countries. The Arabs, in turn, for years sought arms from the Soviet Union to try to balance that threat. Even though the Soviet Union is gone, the Middle East remains a heavily armed region with bitter disputes that can erupt anew.

The other part of the Middle East equation, which is more important than the Arab-Israel dispute, is the Persian Gulf. We have a true interest there in oil, not political donations. Iraq is still a rogue state and will have to be monitored until Saddam Hussein is gone and some kind of decent government is installed.

The other key player is also a rogue state, Iran. With its major military buildup and evidently a crash program to develop nuclear weapons, it is positioning itself to be the dominant power in the Gulf. With its present regime, that will be unacceptable.

The good part is that both Iran and Iraq are so weak internally that hopefully they will be incapable of causing any serious disruption for the immediate future, thus permitting time hopefully for better regimes to come to power. If not, there will be good probabilities of war in the Gulf again before the end of the century.

The major threat areas in the world are in Asia, Europe, and the Middle East.

## Possible Actions

• Support selected governments or peoples in their plights.

• Support regional organizations and urge them to help settle local disputes.

• Support the UN in its efforts to settle disputes. See Chapter 10.

• Intervene unilaterally to settle disputes. Be the world's policeman.

• Join organizations in your area that focus on international affairs, such as World Affairs Councils or

Forums.

- Make your views known.

Clearly, the post-Cold War world was not exactly a peaceful or trouble free place. There was obviously a multitude of grievances around the world. The community of nations had a lot of problems that extended beyond the old nation states. They urgently needed attention and they were clearly beyond the capability of any one state or even several states to handle.

It was time for the world community to pass more authority to world government. There was some nostalgia for the good old days of relative stability during the Cold War, and some of the disputes had surfaced when the tight control from Moscow was removed in the former Soviet Union. However, on second thought, not many people wanted to return to the dangerous confrontation between the superpowers.

As we knew, the Cold War was only one of the wars that raged in the world. Its end did not bring the end of fighting. It only changed the lineup of the major players. The stability that we enjoyed during the Balance of Terror faded as some other rivalries were able to erupt without the intrusion of one of the major powers which was trying to keep the peace so as not to be drawn into a superpower confrontation not of its choosing. Man continued to be as inhuman as usual to his fellow man and war as the ultimate political act was still with the world.

This has been only a brief review of the conflicts and the possibilities for conflict in the world. More details, including the military capabilities of countries around the world, are provided in my Special Study 105 (see Resource Directory).

The world was clearly a turbulent place, but where was America headed in this turbulent new world order?

---

The Pentagon calls its new weapon the Civil Servant. Reason: it won't work and can't be fired.

# Chapter 9

# WHITHER AMERICA?

## Where Are We Going?
## Where Do We Want to Go?

*Ethnic pride could tear America apart.*

-- Ernest W. Lefever

*The single biggest cause of urban decline is the decimation of the American family.*

-- George Bush

There is an old saying, Be careful when you make a wish, it might come true. That has happened to America. The Cold War is over. America has no major enemy. The US is the only superpower. America should be ecstatic.

Yet, as you see it in reality, it is a confused and unsure giant. It hesitates to lead when the meek refuse to follow. It hesitates to intervene lest it be considered the world's policeman. And it has a myriad of problems at home.

The flush of victory faded rapidly, if indeed it ever really appeared. The rather stable world seemed to tumble into turmoil. The booming economy of the 1980s crashed into recession. The economic problems were only magnified by the cutbacks in that magnificent defense establishment that won the Cold War.

Americans threw out the most experienced president in foreign affairs they ever had and elected a man with absolutely no international experience who promised to deal with the "domestic" problems. Yet he had to deal immediately with Somalia, Bosnia, and the former Soviet Union.

The recession continued, crime was rampant with senseless killings, more people were laid off from jobs, and California's recession seemed to slide almost into depression.

America has been able to cope best when its interests were bound to idealism and ideology. The intervention in the First World War was to "make the world safe for democracy."

The tyranny of Hitler and Tojo drove America in its great crusade toward Unconditional Surrender in World War II. And Russia and its people were not the enemy in the Cold War, it was the ideological enemy of Communism.

However, this new era was not a good time for crusades. There was no other superpower in view, so the US did not need allies for security. Once again, isolationism tugged at the American psyche. It seemed to be time to come home. Americans wanted to look inward.

## THE MELTING POT IS BOILING

In a period of less than 400 years (brief in comparison to some of the world's great cultures), what is now the United States of America grew from open spaces where a number of Indian tribes and 20,000,000 buffalo roamed, to the only superpower in the world. From the earliest settlers to the millions of immigrants who followed, their objective was to live in this new land and build it as their new home. For most of those who made the treacherous journey to the New World, they had no plans to return from whence they came. This was to be their new destiny and they planned to become citizens of this new country.

They came from many lands, spoke many different languages, followed many different religions, were different colors, some were poor, some rich, had different political views -- half-jokingly said they came from the best prisons in Europe, but all with a commitment to their new land. From this melting pot of people, a new nation was forged. The first generations spoke the old languages, of course, but the following generations learned American (there is a difference from English) and most importantly, they thought of themselves as Americans. That was the basis of the nation.

Our philosophy was expressed in Emma Lazarus' words on the Statue of Liberty: "Give me your tired, your poor, your huddled masses yearning to breathe free." There were about 60 million people in the US when that statue was dedicated over 100 years ago. Our frontier was still open and immigration was useful.

Now our population is over four times larger, the frontier gone, and population growth adds to the pressures on our society, economy, and the environment. Since 1950, nearly 22 million people have immigrated legally; under current legislation, about 1 million enter annually. The number of illegals is unknown but estimates range from 6 to 10 million. The US has accepted during the past 40 years many more immigrants than any other advanced country. Even though we were way ahead after World War II, the average performance of our economy has been among the lowest of the developed nations. The decline of US competitiveness has several sources but large-scale immigration of the unskilled is one reason.

The original ingredients of the melting pot were predominantly European, with a sprinkling of Chinese, and a heavy dose of Africans from our unfortunate slave history. The more recent additions included many more Asians, Hispanics, and blacks who came as immigrants. The country has always been diverse with the Irish, the Swedes, the Germans, the Chinese; but diversity seems to have become more pronounced with less commitment to the nation. Even though there was some tradition of lawlessness in our romanticized "wild west" history, the current levels of violence and crime along with racial discord have brought the pot to a boil.

We have extremists such as white supremacists and now skinheads who are neo-Nazis and would like to instigate a race war. A plot was aborted in Los Angeles of three groups that wanted to attack a black church and kill well known blacks and Jews. These punk skinheads have murdered in every part of the country. In Houston, two skinheads held a "boot party" with a 15-year-old Vietnamese immigrant named Huong Truong. Before they stomped him to death, he pleaded, "Please stop. I'm sorry I ever came to your country. God forgive me." This was one of the results of youthful embitterment at the recession economy, violent young animals full of violence and hatred against blacks, gays, and Jews.

## Guns

The skinheads were only a small group with guns; it seemed like every teenager in the US had to have a gun to prove he (or she) was cool. America has always had a love affair with guns, starting with our frontier tradition, but they were for hunting and for protection. These teenagers looked upon them as new toys to show their power, because they were too stupid to comprehend yet that death is a permanent condition. These children explained that, "Guns are just a part of growing up these days."

The drive-by shootings, "rumbles" of the gangs, and constant shootings were a growing national tragedy. Teenagers' search for thrills and their undeveloped sense of mortality mean that 1 of every 4 teenage deaths is caused by gunshots. In 1990, 4,200 were killed, and an estimated 100,000 students carry a gun to school.

Firearm death rates for black males tripled from 1984 to 1993. Death from guns have been increasing to where they are worse than the gangster days of 1932 and are passing deaths from car crashes, exceeding 40,000 per year. Young men are safer in the 82nd Airborne Division where they only might get shot at!

Matters grew worse when the gangs from Los Angeles moved eastward in 1986 to colonize smaller cities. We have created a monster generation of kids with absolutely no value for human life. Carjackings have become epidemic as these punks steal cars with people in them; they are either too stupid to know how to get into locked cars or they relish the thrill of taking one directly from the driver. It is safer in the jungle with the real animals than being on the streets with these beasts.

This is not just in the black urban ghettos; it is in the white suburbs too. It is a problem in Omaha where the unemployment rate is only 3.3%! Some of these people have turned into cold-blooded killers. Their idea of robbing someone is not, "Stick 'em up. Give me your wallet." It's shoot 'em first and then take it. And if they did not do it right with the first shot, put the gun to his head and finish it off -- cold, calculating, with no remorse.

James Fox, Dean of the College of Criminal Justice at Northeastern University, pointed out that we have the potential for a bloodbath within the next decade from a relentless pattern of drugs, guns, and murder. From 1985 to 1993, murders by adults over 25 declined by 20%. But for those 18 to 24, homicides increased 65% and for teenagers 14 to 17, murders by 165%. The entire increase was murder with guns.

That impact has been moderated by the fact that our adolescent population is unusually low due to a slow decline in the birth rate after the baby boomers. But births have risen again in the last decade. There are some 40 million children who will become teenagers in the next decade and half of them live in single parent or dual career homes.

There is a double problem: those already violent teenagers will grow up into violent adults. The sudden rise in murders by teenagers can be traced to 1985, the year of the rapid growth of the "crack" market. Crack is usually sold by the hit so it requires a large distribution network. Therefore, the drug organizations recruited teenagers as distributors, with big money.

When you see young punks on the Metro in Washington wearing their brand new Adidas and with several gold chains around their necks, and you know they never worked a day in their lives, guess where they got that money? But in the drug business, you have to have a gun, so the teenagers were provided with guns.

Colorado had a bad summer of violence so the governor called a special session of the legislature which passed a law banning guns for those under 18.   Other states were considering similar action and trying other measures such as searches without warrants.

There is a major drive on in the states to permit legitimate citizens to carry guns.   Only 11 states and the District of Columbia outright prohibit carrying a concealed weapon.   Some 37 states have passed pre-emption legislation prohibiting localities from regulating guns.   Some 13 states have bills pending that would allow virtually anyone, not a felon, to carry a concealed handgun.   Of the 23 states that are now less restrictive, Florida is a good example where, since their new law in 1987, the homicide rate has dropped 22% and gun killings are down 29%.

It is pretty sad when we say school can be hazardous to teens' health.   "Violence in the school is a major health problem for teens," -- over 10% of high school students said they carried a gun on school property, 25% said they were offered, sold, or given drugs at school, 16% had been in a fight, and over 7% were threatened or injured with a weapon at school.

Our cities have become war zones with urban warriors roaming the streets, better armed than the police.  Gangs and tribes will control some of our suburbs.   Terrorism will increase. Is this what you want for the future? If not, **you** need to act.

President Clinton complained in his health care reform speech about the "outrageous cost of violence." It ranks 12th in the causes of death and first as the cause of death and disability for those between the ages of 15 and 34. The costs of violence are staggering in both human and economic terms.

Death is cheap. But those who survive drive up the costs, often spending weeks or months in expensive intensive care units and rehabilitation centers. Victims can rarely pay their own way or have insurance so the costs fall on taxpayers like **you** because hospitals jack up the prices of other services.

*Time* (11 October 1993, p. 59) reported that the average cost for a gunshot victim in New York was $9,646 without follow-up. If intensive care was required, it was as much as $150,000. A San Francisco hospital noted that 86% of gunshot expenses were paid out of taxes. It was estimated that the cost of firearm injuries exceeds **$4 billion annually** in the US. **You** do have a vested interest; **you** are paying for them!

### Options

Banning guns does not seem to be viable since there are already so many millions present and most Americans feel it is their right to own guns. But the right to own a gun is not the right to use it illegally. Simplistic solution of boot camps and "three strikes" are not necessarily the answer. We need to remove the illegal drugs and guns.

What must be addressed is **who** has guns, **where** they have them, and **from whom** they were obtained. Let your officials know what you think.

### Possible Actions

**WHO.** As long as we have a free country, the average person should not have to feel a need to carry a gun in public.

• Criminals and people under 21 (or 18 or 19) could not be allowed to own, possess, or carry guns. Or people under 18 could be prohibited from handling or carrying guns without adult supervision (possible exception for those between 14 and 17 engaged in hunting or target practice). Penalty could be 100 hours of community service and loss of driver's license for one year for first offense. Second offense could be 250 hours of community service and suspension of license for two years. For those without a license, the age when they become eligible to obtain a license could be extended one or two years.

•    Stiffer penalties for carrying concealed weapons.

•    Register all weapons. (Disliked by those who fear a possible police state which could confiscate those weapons.)

•    Ban private ownership of all pistols and automatic weapons. (Criminals already have their weapons illegally and the argument goes that this would only take away the guns from the honest citizens leaving them even more outgunned by the criminals.)

**WHERE.** The question of guns in the home has not been a major problem except for the ongoing argument as to whether they cause more grief than good. Our home is our castle and we claim the right to protect it.

However, guns on the streets and in the schools are different. Crime has gotten so bad in some areas that citizens have pushed for the right to carry concealed firearms for self-defense. Florida has one of the most liberal laws and has issued over 270,000 permits. About 25 states have taken a liberal approach and it is a current issue in several states.

•    No guns permitted outside the home, except for legitimate hunting and target practice. Continue strict limitations on permits to carry a concealed weapon.

•    More relaxed policies for "good" citizens to carry concealed weapons. For example, Florida approves permits for citizens over 21, not a felon, passed a firearms test, not convicted on a drug charge or confined for alcohol abuse in past three years or committed to a mental hospital in past five years.

**FROM WHOM.** There is no difficulty for any good citizen to purchase almost any type of weapon from a legitimate source. The problem is the people who are illegally selling weapons. The gun runners driving a trunk load of automatic weapons from the Carolinas up to Washington or New York are the ones who need to be put out of business.

• Major crime for importing weapons illegally.

• Major crime for possession or selling weapons illegally.

The problem with most of these options is that they are laws now; enforcement is the difficulty. With much of the gun activity being related to drugs, some of the special drug laws can be used to put teeth into the gun restrictions, such as confiscation of cars, houses, and other property. Penalties can range from fines to execution.

Obviously the threat of prison has not served as a deterrent and our court system is so slow that it is a joke. We must determine what is important to these people and deprive them of that. The key is **effective** and **timely** enforcement. Some more stringent possible measures will be mentioned below.

Racism plays a part in some of the shootings. The blacks and Hispanics have become so numerous now that when they stay in ghettos, these are very large areas. Miami is Cuba north now. Southern California now has a majority of blacks and Hispanics. In the Los Angeles riots, blacks pulled a white truck driver out of his truck and smashed him (and were acquitted), but they also turned on their Korean neighbors and burned their stores. Tourists are apprehensive about visiting Florida now (which relies on a $30 billion tourist industry) because of random killings of tourists. A Japanese-American group office was firebombed in Sacramento, California. The melting pot has remained quite segregated.

## ASSIMILATION

Segregation was basically a black-white problem. The civil rights movement went far to break down those old barriers. However, in many cases the flight of the whites to the suburbs left the inner cities more segregated than they were before. (Now the middle and upper class blacks have also fled to the suburbs.) The immigration of Hispanics has brought a new group to prominence and they are projected to pass the black community in numbers in less than 20 years.

The people who built this country learned the language and became "Americans." It is not clear that that is true for many of the recent newcomers. Some 2.1 million Mexicans, a quarter of the newcomers, entered the US between 1980 and 1990 doubling their numbers to 4.3 million.  They skew all the immigration figures because of their predominantly low education and income levels.  On 2 July 1993, 75 Mexican immigrants and one Peruvian were sworn in as naturalized citizens.  That is not unusual except that the ceremony was conducted in Spanish at the request of US District Judge Alfredo Marquez.  This should have bothered earlier immigrants who took pride in learning the language of their adopted country.  To top that off, the Department of Education has issued a guide, "Preparing Your Child for University," all in Spanish.

We have Spanish radio and TV stations, newspapers, books, and signs in many places.  Unfortunately, we have permitted the creation of an entire subculture in the US which watches Spanish TV, listens to Spanish radio, reads Spanish newspapers and books, and can even deal with the US Government in Spanish.  The questions is: Are they Americans?

This trend, plus the encouragement of the use of other languages in schools   or   providing   all   instructions   in Spanish at work or shopping, to assert "ethnic pride" is disturbing.    These   policies,   along   with   institutional manifestations of preference for some races, could tear the US apart.  Comments by Hispanic columnists to the effect **"just wait until the next century when we are in the majority, then we will take over,"** are not reassuring about the future of this country.

Unfortunately, there are many Americans with low English language skills, many of whom did not graduate from high school.  They have the highest unemployment rates and are the people employers could not promote due to poor word skills.   Also, there are large numbers of bilingual or non-English speaking households.

The encouragement of the use of any language other than American (English) is the gravest disservice we do to anyone who seriously desires to become an American.  The do-gooders who are pushing for such use are destroying the futures of those people and hastening the decline of the US.  If a person wishes to have a real future in the US, that person will be severely handicapped if unable to speak English.   If we create a country where one can grow up, go to college, and work all in a foreign language, then we will destroy the US,

which will not last through the next century.
This is not an impossible requirement, especially for the young.  As an example, when I lived in France, the daughter of a diplomat at the consulate attended a French school.  She was in about the seventh grade and had never studied French.  Half way through the school year, she was first in her class.  The younger children are the easier it is because of their limited vocabulary.

## Bilingual Stupidity

The goody-goody social engineers have wreaked havoc in this country.  The disastrous bilingualism school programs which started out with the Bilingual Education Act of 1968 with a $7.5 million budget grew to a typical Washington monster that now eats $10 billion a year.  And it is a **total failure!**

New York City reported that the immigrant children in its bilingual program ($300 million a year) did less well at every grade level than similar students who took their classes in English.  A 1990 study found that transitional bilingual education was basically no different from doing nothing at all for non-English speaking students.

The bilingual movement was supposed to be transitional, that is to get children quickly into the English-speaking mainstream.  New York noted that Korean and Russian-speaking children managed this rapidly.  Activists have been trying to keep Latino children apart culturally.

One of the more idiotic ideas that has come out of our crazy capital was a $1 million federal program for Cooke Elementary School in Washington, D. C., which is about half black and half Latino.  This experiment on live children called for about 80% teaching in Spanish in the lower grades then tapering off to about half in each Spanish and English.  How in the world did we get to the point where we were teaching nonimmigrant children in a foreign language?  There are too many vested interests in that $10 billion annual honey pot.  These people are destroying your country.

The key question for many of these immigrants is whether they really want to stay here or are they here temporarily only to make money and hopefully return home when conditions are better there or they have enough money.  In the latter case, we should not cater to their indifference and destroy our country.

In the particular case of the use of Spanish, we appear to have permitted large numbers of people to live in the US similar to living in Cuba or Mexico without enduring the miseries of their homelands. Is that good for the future of America? Changing our country for the convenience of foreigners defies the concept of assimilation.

There have been efforts to pass legislation making English the official language of the US. Montana is the most recent state to pass such a law. For one thing it relieves the state of having to print ballots and documents in other languages.

The social engineers are also loose as revisionist historians. "Standards" were developed for teaching history. Unbelievable nonsense emerged which even was denounced by the entire US Senate (a miracle in itself). They destroy any heroism or meaning in American history and would make our children feel negative about our country.

These radical young historians start with America not being a Western-based nation but the convergence of three cultures (Indian, black, and European) of equal value except that the Europeans were worse. Their whole diatribe is dishonest and propagandistic and would turn history books into a broad assault against American and Western culture.

### Possible Actions

• Continue bilingual programs.

• Continue English as a second language programs to help newcomers.

• Stop all bilingual programs and immerse all newcomers in English so they can more rapidly join American society.

• Ban **all** foreign language television and radio stations in the US. Probably the fastest way to learn a foreign language except by living with foreign speakers is by watching and listening to television.

• Pass a law proclaiming that English is the language of the US and that no other language will be used in government documents or actions.

·  Check any new history books that your children are to use and see if you recognize the world portrayed therein.

---

If you think English should be the official language of our federal, state, and local governments in America, you may wish to join U. S. English, which was created in 1983 by the late Senator S. I. Hayakawa of California.

U. S. English, Inc.
818 Connecticut Avenue, N. W.
Washington, D. C. 20006
Tel. (202) 833-0100       Fax: (202) 833-0108

---

## Victim Status

Another problem is that an increasing number of ethnic groups have claimed victim status in recent years. Their claims for justice or compensation for past discrimination have often been rewarded with preferential treatment in education, government, or business.

Now, majority Americans are labelled racists and discriminated against by these new tribalists. Government has sanctioned minority set-asides, racial quotas, and race-norming tests. These mock the dream of Martin Luther King of equality under the law which was fulfilled by the legislation of the 1960s.

The new racists ask not for equal treatment, but they demand compensatory privileges for past discrimination. Douglas Wilder, the former black governor of Virginia who was often travelling in Africa, announced in Nigeria that the West owed billions of dollars in reparations to Africa due to the slave trade.

Representative John Conyers of Michigan proposed that Washington pay $4 trillion to descendants of slaves, that would be $133,000 for every black man, woman, and child in the country. We have racial gerrymandering to guarantee that a minority candidate will be elected to office. One district in the Carolinas is many miles long and less than a mile wide in places to be sure the "proper" candidate is elected.

The new tribalism is repugnant racism. Demanding

group privileges instead of individual rights and responsibilities will split America and threaten our national cohesion. We are not the same country we were a half century ago, and if we continue to emphasize that we are African-Americans, Hispanic-Americans, hyphenated Americans, we will not likely be a country in another half century.

Fortunately, there are some ethnic leaders who tell their people, particularly the young, to quit their crying and get to work and earn their future, that self-respect and pride are earned not announced or issued by government. But as long as some people can make it by stealing, pushing drugs, or living on welfare, the future is not very bright.

It appears that a new generation of bigots is coming of age. It used to be that the more schooling a person had, the more likely he was to be tolerant. Now the surveys show that the young generation is either racist or disposed to racism. The reasons are not clear but the first is their ignorance of recent American history. They know little about the civil rights struggle. A second reason is apparently affirmative action which has generated feelings of reverse discrimination.

All forms of affirmative action were under scrutiny in early 1995 by the new Republican majority in Congress. California was in the process of putting the issue on the 1996 ballot. Presidential candidates were attacking it and the Supreme Court was poised to make a ruling in the summer on a 13-year-old program involving billions of dollars in contracts which gave a bonus to disadvantaged businesses.

Affirmative action evidently never had any real support among the electorate. The tragedy was that it fell into the hands of judges and bureaucrats who transformed it into a system of proportional representation by race. It became top-down social engineering without the consent of the governed and was soon enforced by intimidation and censorship.

Any dissent became bigotry and opposition was racist. The wall of secrecy was finally broken, partly by radio talk shows. Rather than being a temper tantrum by white males, it appeared to be a national revulsion against the politics of quotas, preferences, and group rights. Affirmative action infuriated whites who otherwise would have allied with blacks for racial justice.

Assimilation has not done well lately in America. Racism is alive and rampant. The melting pot has lumps in it which do not seem to melt and blend in to the whole.

## MINORITIES

The melting pot has always dealt with minorities; perhaps it should be called a blender. The settlers and immigrants who came from England were a minority. The people who came from other countries in Europe did not speak English and were minorities in the US. There are probably representatives in the US population from every national group in the world (and there are currently 185 members in the UN). As an example, there are 127 national groups who call it home in Fairfax County, Virginia, outside Washington, D.C.

The European immigrants tended to lose their overt identity, unless you could distinguish them by their names, and were lumped under the unusual label, Caucasian (evidently referring to that peaceful area, the Caucasus where there were only four wars raging recently: Christians against Muslims in Azerbaijan, two fronts in Georgia, and the mess in Chechnya).

The blacks were unfortunately labelled by their skin color and came from Africa, although we also have blacks coming from the Caribbean now, particularly those who fled terrorist Haiti trying to get to Florida. The Asians were also demarcated by race. The last major grouping is Hispanic, which may be less racial than linguistic, those who speak Spanish, coming from Central and South America (Brazil being the exception since it is Portuguese-speaking).

### Blacks

The ancestors of most of America's black citizens did not come here as immigrants but were brought here as slaves when the country was being exploited under colonial rule. After the Emancipation Proclamation in 1863, they were free but there was still considerable discrimination and segregation. Civil rights were assured by various legislative acts during the 1960s, but there were still many social problems and much still to be done.

Between 1940 and 1970, over 5 million blacks left the South and moved to the urban North in America's greatest mass migration. The interesting advice to young blacks now who want a better life is: Go south.

The US Army was one of the most advanced places for blacks and they rose to many key positions including Chairman of the Joint Chiefs of Staff. (It should be noted that General

Colin Powell's successor was an immigrant from Eastern Europe, General John Shalikashvili.)

Blacks are top executives, serve in the Congress, run major cities, and hold major positions in all walks of life. However, the typical black family earns much less than the typical white family and poverty and unemployment rates are high. Over 60% of black families are headed by a single female, 40% of black children live in poverty (compared with 17% of white children), and black-on-black crime is killing many of the young.

Some strong voices of dissent are being heard from the black intellectuals who are challenging the tide of black "progress." (See *Challenging the Civil Rights Establishment: Profiles of a New Black Vanguard,* by Joseph G. Conti and Brad Stetson, Greenwood Publishing Group, Inc., Westport, Conn., 1993, and an article by the authors in *The Atlanta Journal/The Atlanta Constitution,* 26 September 1993, p. F1.) These thinkers, the New Black Vanguard, are a dissident voice among black intellectuals and activists, and they are tired, along with many other Americans, of the lack of common sense in race discussions in the US.

Their message is directed at the black community, not at government and politicians. They are not demanding more government aid through more welfare, forced integration, affirmative action, and "race-norming" of test scores normally seen as in the black interest. In fact, to oppose them is considered racist if not racially insensitive for both whites and blacks, but a particularly sinister betrayal by blacks. The New Black Vanguard is not in total agreement, but it does have some basic disagreement with the civil rights ideology.

"1. **The New Black Vanguard rejects the deterministic notion that race unavoidably conditions individual thinking.**" They reject the charge that airing opposing opinions serves whites not blacks and contend that open discourse is needed to advance black interests. They provide some good examples of where the leadership and the black community differ on some key issues: preferential treatment: leaders, Yes -- black public, No; death penalty: leaders, No -- black public, Yes; forced school busing: leaders, Yes -- black public, No. The hiding of the diversity permits the civil rights groups to solicit financial support.

"2.  The New Black Vanguard argues that a chilling
silence has been spread around a ghetto-specific culture by
black advocates who fear that discussions about it will play
into the hands of enemies of the black community." They
describe the collapse of the black family. About 2% of black
babies were born out of wedlock in 1959, now it is over 60%.
They charge that the civil rights establishment discourages
discussion of personal responsibility, the reverse side of social
entitlement. Thomas Sowell, a newspaper columnist and
senior fellow at the Hoover Institution at Stanford University,
stated: "Once you start talking about personal
responsibility, you jeopardize the whole poverty industry,
which thrives by turning collective guilt into dollars and
cents." For a black to talk about "value" or "character" invites
being called an Uncle Tom.

"3.  The New Black Vanguard maintains that racism
is not a sufficient cause for ghetto poverty and other social
problems experienced by the black poor, though the belief
that it is effectively demotivates the poor." They find it
difficult to correlate the disparities between blacks and whites
and the emergence of the black middle class. Sowell asks, why
should a young black work hard if he thinks whitey is just
going to ambush him anyway? He added, "There have always
been racists, but there has not always been racial hype on the
scale that we are seeing."

"4.  The New Black Vanguard objects on moral and
pragmatic grounds to the civil rights leadership's reliance
on the political capital of white guilt." They feel that it has
been ineffective and kept poor blacks from critical evaluation
and self-improvement. Shelby Steel, professor of English at
San Jose State University, stated, "For every white I have met
who is a racist, I have met another 20 or more who have seen
me as an equal."

"5.  De-emphasizing racism as the generator of
black poverty, the New Black Vanguard ascribes the
proliferation of the black underclass to other causes;
including structural changes in urban economies, the
effects of welfare work-disincentives and elements of a
ghetto-specific culture." They feel the welfare benefits of the
1960s, even though well intentioned, were a disaster for inner-

city blacks and were the cause of family decomposition and urban unrest.  They note that 80% of black economic progress between 1940 and 1980 was before 1965, the ballooning of the "poverty industry."   Robert L. Woodson, founder of the National Center for Neighborhood Enterprise observed, "You cannot have programs that treat people as impotent children and then expect them to act like responsible adults."

"6.  The New Black Vanguard contests the practical relevance to the poor, as well as the morality, of preferential treatment policies based on race."   They question its economic effectiveness because it keeps business owners away due to the liabilities; it is indeterminate with no apparent end; and it leaves a stigma of self-doubt.

"7.  The New Black Vanguard emphasizes the importance of non-racial strategies to enhance the status of minorities, especially the development of human capital, mediating structures and neighborhood enterprise."   They do have an extensive positive agenda including: welfare reform, more use of the family and church, school vouchers, free enterprise zones, tenant management, a youth subminimum wage, etc.

As Glenn Loury, a political economist at Boston University said, "Respect has to be earned.  Respect can't be demanded or brokered as the quid pro quo for peace, where whites say, 'I'll respect you if you don't riot.'"
These dissidents draw their strength from their inner resources.  They support the advice such "as Clarence Thomas remembers his grandfather  giving him: 'Study  hard, work to improve  yourself and always do what's right.'"
It appears that there are at least some in the black community who are taking a realistic view of their situation. With leaders like these, hopefully they will be able to rebuild the family and break the ghetto mentality.  No doubt, it will be a long hard road and they need your help.

## Hispanics

According to the Census Bureau, Hispanics will eclipse blacks as the largest minority group in the US by 2010.  They are  expected  to  increase  from  their  present  9%  of  the population to 14% by 2010 and 23% by 2050. Blacks with 12% now will increase to over 13 % in 2010 and 16% in 2050. The Hispanic explosion is projected to result from a baby boom, accounting for about two-thirds of the increase with immigration accounting for the remaining third. Teen birth rates continue to increase with Hispanic teenagers playing a major role. Part of the problem is their religious and cultural mores. According to religious teachings, if you carry a condom, you plan to sin.

Also, many Hispanics think birth control is meant to reduce the number of Hispanics. Hispanic mothers do not like to talk to their daughters about sex assuming that if you mention sex, you condone the action. Hispanic women have the highest birth rate of any major racial or ethnic group.

The effect on the US will be enormous and will bring changes from the classrooms to the Congress. Most of the impact will be in New York, Florida, Texas, the Southwest, and California.

The non-Hispanic white share of the US population is projected to fall to 53% by 2050, almost evenly divided with the minorities. The impact can be incalculable since the non-Hispanic whites have created and dominated America's politics, economy, and culture throughout its history. We have a preview of this situation in Miami and Los Angeles.

The backlash has already started. A large majority of Americans is unhappy with immigrants, particularly Hispanics, in these tough economic times, reflecting concern about jobs. Sentiment against illegal immigrants is white hot in California where Mexicans continue to flow across the border. It is estimated that half the illegal immigrants in the US live in California. The California government estimates that 2 million of its 31.5 million residents are illegal and that it spends $5 billion annually to educate the children of illegal aliens in public schools, to provide health care and other services, and to house their criminals in state prisons.

Although undocumented immigrants are not eligible legally for welfare, their US-born children are eligible the same as any citizen. This includes the country's fastest-growing welfare program, Aid to Families with Dependent Children. There is much fraud including a booming market in counterfeit documents.

The state government searched for ways to stem the flow of undocumented immigrants and to reduce the heavy burden on the already severely strained California economy, suffering from the recession and the drastic cutbacks in defense and aerospace.

Governor Pete Wilson stated, "We are compelled to cut aid to the needy, blind, disabled and elderly in California in order to comply with federal mandates to provide services to illegal immigrants."

He declared that California's quality of life and economic recovery were "under siege" and called for Washington to eliminate citizenship rights for US-born children of illegal immigrants, to create a "tamper-proof" identification card for legal immigrants, and to deny education and health care to those who enter illegally.

He even called for the Mexican Army to guard the border and keep their people from crossing illegally. That was not likely since it is a political issue in Mexico. The root problem is low wages and not enough jobs in Mexico; until that changes, hopefully under NAFTA, the people will continue to migrate north.

The Mexican problem has been exported to the US for years. The people are caught in a circle of economic hopelessness. They have low job skills because they have little education.

In the US, Hispanics are three times more likely than non-Hispanic whites to live in poverty. There are 22.1 million Hispanics in the US and 29% live in poverty according to the Census Bureau. That makes them 18% of the poor even though they are 9% of the population. It is even worse for children: Hispanic children are 21.5% of poor children yet are only 12% of the child population.

This is a tragic problem of people who cannot find a decent living at home so they look abroad for opportunity. Some 3 million Mexicans were legalized by the Immigration Reform and Control Act of 1986, but there are still many, in the millions, illegally in the US and they continue to cross every night.

It is not only Mexicans; there are many other Latins who are flocking to the US, but the Mexicans are by far the largest group followed by people from El Salvador and Guatemala. The tragedy is that, by their very large numbers, their high birth rate, and their failure or lack of desire to assimilate, they threaten the very fabric of America.

## Asians

Asian-Americans are a much smaller minority, now about 3% of the population. However, they are the fastest growing racial group and should increase to 10% by the middle of the next century. The end of the Viet-Nam War brought us the "boat people" as many fled from the Communist regimes in Southeast Asia. The Vietnamese tended to be the more educated and have been fairly successful in adapting to a very different culture. It has been more difficult for the people from Cambodia and Laos, who tended to be less educated and have fewer skills.

California has been the favorite home for most of the Asian immigrants, except for the Chinese and Thais, many of whom have settled in New York. Many of these people are college graduates. Also, there is generally a strong sense of family and they support each other rather than look for outside aid.

Asian illegal immigration received notoriety in the summer of 1993 when several ships were detected carrying Chinese to the US. The story that unfolded was a horror story of people spending great amounts of money to be smuggled into the US where they would work in sweat shops and live as virtual slaves to pay off their debts to the smugglers.

The stories read like old Hollywood movies. One rusty scow left Fujian province in November 1991. It limped into Mombasa, Kenya in October 1992. The scow could go no farther; the Chinese people smuggler won a ship called the *Golden Venture* in a poker game. The 200 Chinese on board continued their odyssey on the *Golden Venture* which US officials tracked to South Africa where they tried to board it. They got the wrong boat and they lost track of it in the Atlantic.

The *Golden Venture*, what an ironic name for such a voyage, reappeared when the crew mutinied and ran it aground off New York City in June 1993. The Chinese struggled through the 53-degree surf toward the blinking lights of the "beautiful country," their description of America. Eight died beneath the waves in the pre-dawn darkness.

A chain of smuggler ships stretched across the Pacific that same summer. Five ships were floating off San Francisco and three were blocked by the US Coast Guard off Mexico.

The US did not want them to land because they could apply for political asylum.  The US government asked Mexico to take them in and fly them back to China.

There was a standoff of weeks while the two governments negotiated a solution for those Chinese who had been on the ships for months at sea.  Finally, Mexico allowed the ships in and the Chinese were flown back to China and about 40 people were facing smuggling charges in Mexico.

The stories for the various Chinese immigrants were about the same.  They agreed to pay from $15,000 to $35,000 to smugglers, called "snakeheads," to get them to the US: a downpayment of $5,000 or more with the balance to be paid from wages in the US.  These people became indentured almost for five years or more to pay off their debt while they live in horrible conditions.

Immigration officials believe that the snakeheads are affiliated with more than 20 different criminal triads, Chinese crime syndicates which have been smuggling Chinese across to America since the California gold rush, and they smuggle between 50,000 and 80,000 Chinese into the US annually.

There are also Indian and Pakistani smuggling operations but they are not as large as those of the Chinese gangs.  But they keep coming; there are probably 20 ships, crowded with illegal aliens, on the high seas bound for the US with visions of wonderful things in their new world.  "What do they know of the US?" asks a Western diplomat in Beijing. "Just that the streets are paved with gold.  Everyone knows this."

## DISILLUSIONMENT

There are a number of reasons why Americans are not as happy as one might have imagined after the end of the Cold War.  With a population of 260 million now and projected to grow to 392 million by 2050, no one can see where the jobs will come from to handle that growth and maintain the standard of living.

Some days it seemed the worst possible thing was to be a white male.  There were all kinds of affirmative action programs to provide equal opportunity to minorities. Government contracts were awarded to immigrants.  All forms of quotas and business set asides were in place.  Now there was a backlash against such inequal programs.

The nation's cities were a shambles. Cities like New York now keep their problems at home, with the homeless, the drug addicts, and the mentally ill in the same neighborhoods with everyone else, a product of Great Society optimism in the 1960s. Now there is national debate over how to return civility and order to cities. The cities have turned the streets over to the minority and protect them against the residents who are the majority.

The recession was called the "silent depression" by some. In their view, the economy had been depressed since 1973. In 1990, the Census Bureau reported that gross median family income finally surpassed 1973. Real weekly income of workers in 1990 was 19.1% below the level reached in 1973, but family incomes had been maintained by wives going to work. The problem was not all high taxes, it was low income.

Welfare was out of control. It was not only the loss of jobs. A culture of poverty had emerged, with a pattern of dependent, irresponsible antisocial behavior which came from the perverse incentives of the welfare system.

Crime was out of hand with our capital, Washington, the murder capital of the world. Way out of proportion to their percentage of the population, blacks and Hispanics led the crime spree. Senseless killings, particularly the seemingly random, execution-type murders and carjackings were very disconcerting. The populace wondered what kind of monsters have we created in this free land?

In southern California, we have caution signs on the road -- typical yellow signs with black silhouettes, except these show a running family: a father, a mother, and a small daughter. They represent illegal immigrants at risk as they might sprint through vehicles on the interstate to avoid a checkpoint. Immigrants are so numerous that we have to put signs up to be careful just like we do for deer crossing the highway. Americans are fed up with taking in the poor of the world.

We were able to absorb immigrants before, but now the nation's economy is weak, mainly from waging the world's battle against Communism for 45 years. The US does not have the resources to care for the floods of poor people arriving daily. It cannot even take care of its own decaying infrastructure, much less handle the poverty of the inner cities, which is made worse by millions of illegal immigrants. Also, there are severe social problems which include the growing violence resulting from poverty and anger. Thus, Americans have every reason and the right to say No to massive immigration.

After the Chinese boat people, the immigrant sheik linked to the World Trade Center bombing, and the Mexican problem in California, President Clinton cracked down on immigration. He attacked alien smuggling and put more patrols on the borders, particularly on the south. "We cannot and will not surrender our border to those who wish to exploit our history of compassion and justice," he said.

In 1995, Clinton sought authority to confiscate business assets of companies that employ illegal immigrants. He also sought means for quick-response checks of social Security cards and data banks to verify workers' status.

Georgia Anne Geyer, the Washington columnist, summed it up well as she praised the president for having the intelligence and guts to move to control illegal immigration. **Americans have finally awakened. "They have realized that not only their land and their economy are at stake with uncontrolled immigration, but their very culture and national life."**

Our social laissez faire approach to immigration has resulted in a change in the rhetoric of the pro-immigration lobby from it being a privilege to come to the US to it being a "right." She attacked America's sloppiness in the primary duty of the nation state to control its security and maintain its sovereignty.

Dominican New York activist Moises Perez proclaimed on "60 Minutes" that "Anyone who wants to emigrate has a right to be in this city. Documented or undocumented, you have a right to be in this country."

It is this "outrageous philosophy," she believes, that finally woke up Americans, "not to any 'threat' of legal immigration (which we all want to an appropriate extent) but to the profound threat of people and ideas that would tear apart the most successful and prosperous culture the world has known."

Americans are a little naive, somewhat simplistic, and want to be loved. They do not understand the *realpolitik* of why, after they spend their money to feed starving masses in Somalia, the ingrates turn on their soldiers, killing them, and dragging their bodies through the streets. They had trouble with thugs preventing our UN peace engineers from landing in

Haiti. They abhor what is going on in Bosnia, but do not want American boys killed there while Europe will not get off its backside. Americans, some days, would like to tell the world to go to hell.

Domestically, the situation was not looking better. Each week, another large corporation announced layoffs of additional thousands of workers. The harder people tried, they could not seem to get ahead. The literacy skills in the US reflected that pessimism. From the Education Secretary, "90 million adults in this country do not have the literacy skill they need to function in our increasingly complex economic system," that is 47% of our 191 million adults.

Some 40 million have only the lowest level of skills. Young adults (21 to 25 years old) were 11% to 14% lower than in the 1985 survey. The report blamed "shifting demographics of the population group, particularly the number of people speaking English as a second language." The minorities were more likely to be in the lowest levels.

A whole new group of experts or consultants had evolved dealing with work place diversity and multi-culturalism. By the year 2000, one-half of all workers will be over 35, half will be women, a third will be non-white, and only 45% will be white men, down from 51%.

Americans saw the cost of health care skyrocket, much faster than the cost of living. They saw lawyers dominating the system: they have most of the seats in the Congress, they write the laws, then they are the judges who enforce them. The US has more lawyers than any other country in the world and has become a litigious society with too many people trying to sue others.

The justice system seemed to have gone crazy. A person could go to jail for a minor offense, yet murderers were back on the streets in weeks. The death penalty had been reimposed but it was another bad joke. People sat on death row for years and only a small percentage were ever executed. Its deterrent effect was evidently zero.

Radical lawyers, like Catharine MacKinnon the University of Michigan law professor (mentioned earlier for her good work in Bosnia), have carried feminism to the extreme of censorship. Pro-censorship forces now dominate most legal academic meetings and law journals. They threaten to reduce our First Amendment rights. Such lawyers are a much greater threat to our country than any amount of pornography. (See "Censors on the left," by John Leo, *US News & World Report,* 4 October 1993, p. 30.)

Americans sent supposedly good people to Congress, but they seemed to become scoundrels who voted themselves pay raises, perks, and flitted around the world on taxpayers' money. Washington did not seem to be in tune with America. The 1994 elections showed the people's displeasure but it was not clear that the politicians received the message.

Americans were disillusioned in that they felt that after they had done so much, in their view, for the rest of the world, the world had taken advantage of their generosity and that, as a result, the great land they had built was slowly being destroyed.

## EQUAL BUT SEPARATE

A single mother in California struggling to make a future wrote a powerful commentary, "My daughter is disadvantaged just because she is white." Her daughter played with Hispanic, African-American, Vietnamese, and Laotian children.

Her daughter goes to the lousy neighborhood school while the Hispanic children across the street are taken by bus to the best school in the county. Two Asian girls next door go to a science "magnet" school; the white daughter is not eligible for "magnet" schools.

The family of her Hispanic friends has been speaking English for two generations, but when those children go to school, they are offered instruction in their "native" language. There is money in California for Spanish teachers but not enough to hire regular teachers to reduce "classroom crowding that is a statewide embarrassment."

Many of the children in her daughter's kindergarten class could not speak English, tell you their name or age in English, or any other language, or do simple tasks. Much of the teacher's time was spent on remedial skills that should have been learned at home. The parents of this mother were not taught in their native French or German when they were children. They proudly worked on their English.

She asked, does all this "federal assistance really provide an advantage to the disadvantaged? Will a high-schooler who has never had to learn English ever score well on the SAT exam?" Are we building a culture of dependence rather than relying on their own resources? Should we allow being disadvantaged "to become a way of life?"

Another columnist wrote that "Afrocentrism is more a trap than liberation." A former teacher was hired by the District of Columbia Board of Education and paid over $248,000 over three years to write a curriculum for elementary schools in Afrocentrism. Seven teachers worked on the project and they were educated at "an unlicensed and unaccredited Pan-African University, founded by the head of the project, whose master's degree is from the same university, which, as it happened, she founded."

The goal was "to increase self-esteem and expand information for black children," but she kept it veiled in secrecy because other teachers might "steal" her ideas. Her secret methods included "showing genuine love, concern for and identification with students." She was going to infuse the curriculum with African history and culture and add "special programs in the arts, the martial arts and African languages." It was not clear how this would help any child in our high-tech culture.

Young blacks are often intimidated by other blacks who accuse them of "acting white" if they try hard such as with their studies. Rigid black consciousness can prove to be more negative than liberating because it undercuts individual initiative. "It's easier to be 'African-American' than to organize oneself on one's own terms and around one's own aspirations" (Shelby Steele).

A mass of laws has been passed to protect the human rights and civil rights of citizens in this country. Every possible legal measure has been taken to assure equality among our citizens.

Nevertheless, the different groups, to an extent, live in separate worlds. Many cross over easily and interact with other groups; others never seem to mentally leave their side of the fence.

## WHAT IS AMERICA?

America is certainly different things to different people. But it certainly must still be the land of opportunity or millions of people would not go to such great lengths, danger, and expense to come here. The justice system may be flawed, but it sure beats a knock on the door at night.

We may be in the doldrums now, but it is still one of

the few places where a person can start with nothing and with sweat and brains make a fortune.

America is a perspective. It is a philosophy that the individual is more important than the state. It is a feeling that man should be free but that freedom carries obligations. It is a country that would prefer to stay in splendid isolation behind its borders, but knows that it cannot because it is a world economy now and because so many other peoples look to America for help and leadership.

The America that rose to great heights was based on values, a sense of morality. Whether it came from religious training or the family, our people had a strong sense of right and wrong. But over the last half century, American morality has been separated from responsibility. That split has been seen elsewhere also such as in Rwanda and Serbia. Morality is the key issue of our times and now when the world desperately wants us to lead, we have little moral leadership to offer.

André Malraux, the Minister of Cultural Affairs of France, described the United States as: "The only nation that has waged war but not worshipped it, that has won the greatest power in the world but not sought it, that has wrought the greatest weapon of death, but has not wished to wield it ... may (America) inspire men with dreams worthy of its action."

General Creighton Abrams, who commanded the US forces in Viet-Nam and was Chief of Staff of the US Army, added, "America is a dream come true. It was conceived as an ideal but born and sustained through action -- and action in this context is just another word for service. As long as we remember that and pass it on to those who follow us, America and all that it means to us and a hopeful world will endure."

## WHERE ARE WE GOING?   (Where do we want to go?)

The two questions are appropriate at this critical time in America, plus the follow-on question, Is where we are headed where we want to go? The optimists would say that we are a strong and diverse country which has always been able to cope with adversity and that we will meet the challenge again.

Let us hope they are right. The pessimists though see a few trends that if not checked may lead to the end of the great social experiment.

## Population Growth

First is **population growth**. Population growth is not automatically bad, but our growth is primarily in the minorities and the poor, the two most unproductive sectors of our society. Their growth only accentuates the divisiveness in our society and the lowering of our overall literacy and productivity levels.

## Possible Actions

* A pause in immigration.

* Deportation of many illegal aliens.

* All undocumented aliens could be immediately deported.

* A major effort in education among the poor so that we can increase their opportunities for work and reduce their birth rates.

* Children of illegal aliens could no longer be treated as citizens. They could also be deported.

* Stronger family planning programs.

* Ban on children born out of wedlock.

* Require licenses to have babies.

## Drugs and Crime

Second is **drugs** and **crime**. The two seem inseparable. It is puzzling how all those poor, unemployed people can be using drugs. Where do they get the money to buy them? It appears that most of it comes from stealing from **you** and me.

The court system, again our beloved lawyers, has become so totally frozen that it is completely incompetent to deal with the problem. It is a right to own weapons in this country but it is not a right to carry them to school or to use them illegally, and there is absolutely no right for a person to have an automatic weapon.

This country has to get serious or there may not be any

country as we know it by the middle of the next century. About half of all Americans say they know someone who became addicted to an illegal drug and nearly half of our people have had to change their lifestyle, such as where or when they shopped or where they lived, due to drug problems.

Attacking the supply of drugs has been a total failure. It is a problem of **demand** for illegal substances. We have an entire generation of individuals to educate with prevention and treatment.

Building more prisons and hiring more police are not the answer. We lead the world with people in prison and the criminals already outgun the police. About 1.9 million AK-47 automatic rifles were imported from China between 1989 and 1991 alone. This is just one of many automatic weapons which are currently in the hands of hoodlums.

Obviously, the prospect of going to prison is no deterrent to these people now. What is needed is to change their perspective: where the danger of being arrested is more threatening to them than the continuation of their activities with guns and drugs. We must take back the control of our country from the criminals. It can be done; look at Singapore and Turkey -- get busted for drugs and you are executed!

The international aspect is that most drugs come from afar: South Asia (Pakistan and Afghanistan), Colombia, and Southeast Asia (the Golden Triangle of Laos, Thailand, and Myanmar).

Officials estimate that about 70% of the cocaine enters the US from Mexico. Some 19 clandestine air strips were reported around Mexacali in the Imperial Valley south of the border servicing southern California. More than half of all that cocaine that moves into the US via Mexico enters through the Imperial Valley accounting for most of the supply to Los Angeles. Mexicans have joined with the Colombian cartels and the corruption has reached the highest levels in the Mexican government.

Heroin use is increasing in many parts of the US, with some crack users, including younger ones switching to heroin due to its price and availability. Some 60% of the heroin originates from Myanmar (old Burma). How to deal with these questionable governments is a major problem for the US Government.

Or should drugs be legalized? That would suddenly change the mob role much as happened after the repeal of prohibition. There is so much money involved that corruption is rampant. High level officials in Mexico are now accused of being part of the cartels and there is no telling how many US officials are on the take.

## Possible Actions

• Make all automatic weapons like the AK-47 illegal.

• The government could declare a national emergency and send troops into our major cities. Anyone illegally in possession of a weapon outside of his home or in possession of, using, selling, or transporting drugs would be arrested, held without bail, tried immediately before a military court and sentenced to military labor units at various military installations around the country, where they could be gainfully utilized cleaning up environmental problems, working in the national forests, or some work useful to society, or if necessary making little rocks out of big ones (Alabama has brought back the chain gangs).

• Anyone caught bringing drugs into the country or arranging therefor could also be tried by military courts and subject to execution with only Presidential review of the courts' verdicts within 30 days.

• Legalize drugs and put these people under controlled programs.

## Family

The deterioration of the **family** may be the most destructive of all in the long run. A major effort must be made to rebuild the family structure. An enormous percentage of black children are raised in a matriarchic society, with an unfortunate number who grow up with the objective to have a baby and get on welfare like mother. That is not fair to the millions of black or other women who are trying hard to make a living and raise their children to be good citizens. The welfare system encourages much of this.

There are many, like William J. Bennett the former Secretary of Education and drug czar, who want to get the federal government out of the welfare business completely, stop the dependence on government, stop subsidizing illegitimacy. They would fund it by the private sector, churches, and backed up by government only as a last resort. AFDC is running over $25 billion annually. Many see it as undermining the family because it is generally available only to single parents, mostly women, thereby encouraging illegitimacy, dropping out of school, amoral lifestyle, and multi-generational dependency. Many are upset over welfare continuing from one generation to the next.

There is something wrong with a system where a woman will not bring her children's father into her house because of endangering her welfare check. Also, she will not take a low-paying job because she can make more on welfare. The system is broken. It needs fixing.

A major effort must be made to stop the having of children out of wedlock. That is difficult because of rights. But is it a "right" to have a baby? When the rest of us have to pay for it and it is going to grow up to be a dangerous animal, maybe it is not a right but a responsibility. Babies having babies may not be the problem but it certainly does not add to the well-being of this country.

> In general, all teen-agers should be encouraged not to get pregnant.
>
> -- Dr. Richard Ward, *New England Journal of Medicine*,
> concluding that teen-agers are almost twice as likely as
> older women to deliver premature babies

Should teenagers be allowed to have babies at an age where it is even illegal to marry in some states and where they are too young to drive and to drink? Just because they want a cuddly little "toy" to love does not mean they should be allowed to eat up our taxes and damage our country. Most of them are on welfare and when the children are a little older and not so cuddly, the record shows child abuse and increased problems.

Women on welfare having babies is ridiculous and an insult to the taxpayers who are paying for her! Maybe women should get Norplant the day they sign up for benefits. Even Mayor Marion Barry of Washington, D. C. has suggested it. Others have even proposed sterilization of welfare mothers after one child. We have families in our nation's capital with their third generation on welfare and drugs and members in and

222    You and the New World Order

out of prison.

Newt Gingrich, the Speaker of the House of Representatives, made a good point in that it is less a matter of regulating their lives than getting them out of poverty. This is a core values issue which requires a major transformation in their lives from education to self esteem. **But contraception is needed early along with self esteem!**

A child is an investment of 20 years or more. We require a license to get married and a license to drive a car; perhaps we should require a license to have a baby which is potentially a much greater threat to society.

If a Kennedy has 10 children, it is not a drag on society, (unless you are a Republican) even though it adds to the numbers, because they can take care of them. But a poor unwed teenager who starts out on welfare and delivers 5 or 10 babies along her drug strewn path is a definite drag on society. We pay for them and many of her ill gotten offspring become criminals or like her.

Since the welfare agencies have failed in handling abused and unwanted children, is it time to bring back the orphanages or group homes or whatever name is used? Perhaps for long enough to establish efficient placement of these young ones. There are increased editorials calling for them due to the limit on foster homes and the increase in child abuse.

We have permitted the growth of a culture of fatherlessness -- the "superfluous father." According to the U. S. Census Bureau, over 80% of children lived with their father and mother in 1960; by 1990 it was under 60%. In 1950, 6% of kids lived with their mother only; that rose to 24%, 19 million children, by 1994.

Single parents have become commonplace in the US and even glamorized on television. We now have 30% of all American families -- 63% of black households -- headed by single parents, most of them women.

These fatherless children are five times more likely to be poor, twice as likely to drop out of high school, and very likely to end up in foster care or juvenile justice facilities. The girls are three times more likely to be unwed teen mothers, and the boys are much more likely to be unemployed, incarcerated, and uninvolved with their own children.

David Blankenhorn, chairman of the National Fatherhood Initiative, stated, **"Fatherless is the engine**

**driving our most urgent social problems, from crime to adolescent pregnancy to domestic violence.** "

He pointed out in his book, *Fatherless America*, that the main result of this culture gone awry is "the spread of me-first egotism hostile to all except the most puerile understandings of personal happiness."

There is a loss in children's well-being and an increase in male violence, particularly against women. This results in a fragmentation of society into isolated individuals who are estranged from the bonds of family, community, and nation. These are our new urban animals.

With about 25% of US babies born each year to unwed mothers who run their households alone, Blankenhorn has recommendations to create a stronger national focus on the value of fatherhood:

* Civic groups should ask every man to pledge that every child deserves a father and that marriage is the pathway to effective fatherhood.

* The president should issue an annual report on the state of fatherhood.

* Men should create Fathers' Clubs in their communities.

* Community organizers and veterans of the poor people's and civil rights movements should help build a grass-roots movement to empower families and strengthen community life.

* Policies should encourage a higher percentage of married couples in public housing.

* Religious leaders should speak up and act on behalf of marriage.

* States should prohibit sale of sperm from sperm banks to unmarried women and limit artificial insemination to infertile married couples.

* Famous pro athletes should support the importance of fatherhood.

\*    Prominent family scholars should write better high school textbooks about marriage and fatherhood.

New Jersey Governor Christine Todd Whitman got in trouble when she said she had heard of a game called "jewels in the crown" that young black males have to see how many children they can sire out of wedlock. This is a cultural problem and it is not just among blacks since teenage pregnancies are increasing even more among white unmarried girls.

It is clear that we need a philosophical change in this country about the importance of the father to the family. If we do not, we are in danger of this growing band of animals which have no feeling for people, community, or our nation and could do great damage to our society.

Blankenhorn's book was published by the Institute for American Values and reprinted by Basic Books. You might be able to contact him at the National Fatherhood Initiative, 600 Eden Road, Building E, Lancaster, PA 17601.

A "**culture of illegitimacy**" has evolved in America. Yet in Western European countries, where teen sex activity is as high as in the US, their rates of teen pregnancy and parenthood are one half to one sixth the US rates. So it appears there is room to tighten our ethics and morals.

Also, current contraceptive methods are inadequate. There have been so many lawsuits and negative publicity about various devices or systems such as the IUD, that only one US pharmaceutical company conducts any research on improving birth control methods and the US Government spends only $38 million a year for such research. The IUD, for example, is 10 to 20 times more popular in Europe.

Sterilization is actually the most used contraception in the US. Norplant and Depo-Provena have dropped in popularity. We need to rehabilitate the pill and the IUD and expand research into better systems.

Finally, as these children grow older, they must not be permitted to run wild and endanger society. Parents need to be held accountable for these beings they force on the world.

Governor George Allen of Virginia signed a new law by which parents could be brought to court and face stiff fines if they fail to help schools discipline their children. With the gangs and wild teenagers loose, those responsible for these young people need to be held liable for their actions.

## Possible Actions

• Unwed mothers could be banned from welfare so that they learn they must be responsible for their actions. A stigma could be regenerated on such actions.

• Place women on welfare on Norplant or something similar.

• Selective sterilization could be required.

• Orphanages might be needed -- private sector only, not government.

• It could be made illegal to have a baby without the means to raise it to adulthood. Having a baby does not have to be a right. Unauthorized babies could be taken by the state for adoption.

• If that fails, then a requirement for abortions might be necessary for a time until some degree of responsibility can be regenerated in this country. The pro-life radicals would not like this, but we put dogs and cats to sleep if we cannot find them proper homes. Why should we allow babies to be brought into a world with three strikes against them and let them become wild animals and a threat to society?

• Require a license to have a baby.

• Reform welfare to bring the fathers back into the families. It takes two to make a baby; two should be held responsible.

• Get the government out of welfare. Let the private sector and churches handle it. Give them tax incentives. Provide government funds as last resort.

• A priority education program to stress use of the IUD and birth control pills.

- Urge the US Government to encourage research for better contraception methods.

- Hold parents responsible for the actions of their children.

The Flower Children of the 1960s and 70s, who we mindlessly followed at the time of Viet-Nam, have finally grown up. **Funny how as the older the son gets the wiser his father gets! And young radicals become middle-aged conservatives!** Now Newt Gingrich gets massive applause when he calls for a return to Victorian values and to bring back "shame" to curb illegitimacy and other immoral behavior.

> *The baby boomers want vastly more caution for their children than they experienced for themselves.*
>
> -- Newt Gingrich

**It is time to rebuild the sense of values and moral responsibility in our country.** You might want to stress that at all levels starting with your schools, businesses, and local politicians up to the highest levels of government.

## Civic Bonds

A recent study about the problems of democracy in Italy holds some key lessons for America. Starting in 1970, Italy turned over unprecedented powers to 20 regional governments. Now there is the efficient, democratic north and a brooding, stagnated south.

Robert Putnam, a Harvard politics professor studied the mystery and published his results in *Making Democracy Work: Civic Traditions in Modern Italy* (Princeton University Press). He found that **civic bonds** cannot be legislated from the top. They must be developed horizontally and, without webs of trust, a democratic community will fail.

He concluded that Boy Scouts, Rotary clubs, PTAs, etc. are more important for democracy than a Congress or a White House. Northern Italy had developed **networks of civic engagement** through various societies, guilds, cooperatives, unions, and clubs. Those civic associations built mutual trust, were an integral part of the social fabric, and democracy flourished.

However, in the south, "Mutual distrust and defection, vertical dependence and exploitation, isolation and disorder, criminality and backwardness have reinforced one another in ... interminable vicious circles...". In the south, the Mafia dominated a system controlled from the top by fear and selfishness and the natural networks had not grown, so democracy did not grow and that mistrust even stifled economic development.

These conclusions should be quite troublesome to many Americans who see our networks of trust ravaged by crime, bureaucratic elitism, class divisions, and racial mistrust. Governing is difficult and cannot be faked. "Without norms of reciprocity and networks of civic engagement... amoral familialism, clientelism, lawlessness, ineffective government, and economic stagnation seem likelier than successful democratization and economic development." He concluded, "Building social capital will not be easy, but it is the key to making democracy work."

With the growth of government and business, our "third sector" -- charities and voluntary organizations -- has lost its vigor. The number of people who attend public meetings on town or school affairs has declined by a third. Union membership has fallen a third. PTA participation has dropped over 40%. Volunteers for Boy Scouts are down 26% and for the Red Cross 61%.

These attachments breed the habits of trust that make up our "social capital" which makes possible cooperation for mutual benefits which sustain a free society. They are the bonding force, the social glue, that unites the diverse elements of our people into a cohesive social identity. The family and neighborhood and community organizations are vital to character formation and crucial to the success of democracy.

With both parents, if there are two parents, working now to try to make ends meet, there is more pressure on the family and less time for PTA, for Little League, for scouts, for clubs, and for community activity. We need to make time for volunteerism. We need to build back those vital activities which play a key role in the strength of the community and the building of the young people.

We saw extensive civil disobedience in 1968 and a **"legitimation of violence"** by those who felt that their views raised them above the law. It has erupted again occasionally, such as with some anti-abortion freaks who commit murder, the lunatic bombing in Oklahoma City, and it festers under our minority communities.

This country was built on the basis of law and it must not forsake that cardinal trait of our society. Our leadership must face the difficult problems we have and impose the actions that are the best for the country, not the best for politics, votes, or pressure groups.

## The Media and Pressure Groups

That brings us to the dismal subject of the power of television and the lesser power of the rest of the media. Television showed us in Viet-Nam that it was all powerful. Even though Tet was a Viet Cong defeat, American television executives decided it was an American defeat and proceeded to create the facts to prove it. Nearly 75% of Americans believe the media are elitist, negative, adversarial, insensitive, and arrogant and that they get in the way of society solving its problems.

Top reporters are highly paid stars who think they can run the country better than anyone in office. Cynicism is the vogue. Balanced reporting would get them fired. They mold opinion.

Another aspect of the power of television is what your children watch. The boob tube has become a baby sitter for an entire generation. What they see on television is what they want to do. A poll by Children Now told us that most children say that what they see on television encouraged them to have sex too soon, to lie, to show disrespect to their parents, and to engage in aggressive behavior.

There is too much sex and violence in children's shows or children see it in other shows because of lack of parental supervision. Kids told us that trash like "The Simpsons" and "Married... with Children" encouraged disrespect toward parents. Even the kids think television should teach them values, teach them right from wrong, not show people getting away with deceitful behavior or physical aggression.

Finally, be leery of all you receive from the media. There is a difference between **public opinion** and what is presented by **interest groups** or **pressure groups**. Public opinion is at best a nebulous idea of what the people are thinking about on an issue, some times reflected in public opinion "polls." Interest groups are advocates for a position. Organized interest groups have multiplied to the point where they now clog the arteries of democracy in what Jonathan Rauch calls "demosclerosis," the political equivalent of arteriosclerosis -- a potentially fatal problem.

Most pressure is for budget money, but not all. It can be to ban textbooks in your local schools, block your legal right to abortions, or to support specific foreign governments. Public officials, particularly congressmen, are more often responding to pressure than to public opinion because it is more organized, focused, and threatening to their political lives.

The effectiveness of pressure groups or lobbies depends on their efficiency. If they can threaten lawmakers with the loss of their next election, they can be very effective. Many lobbies monitor congressional hearings and can have constituents phone in their displeasure before a member even gets back to his office. When that constituent is a large campaign contributor or controls large contributions, he can put a lot of pressure on a congressman. Unfortunately, there is some truth in the cynical statement that we have the best Congress that money can buy.

## Possible Actions

• Take part in the activities and organizations of your children.

• Take part in your community, county, and state government. Attend council meetings. Vote.

• Hold your government officials accountable.

• Join a political party and take part. Our young people are the most ignorant about politics in decades. Encourage your children to learn about the political system and to take part in it.

• Supervise what your children watch on television. Do not let them watch so much of the harmful garbage. Teach them to read.

• Emphasize morality. Teach your children right and

wrong. Try to get other people to do the same.

• Do not trust the media to give you the truth. Search out the facts from diverse sources.

• Be aware of pressure groups and move to have your views heard if you do not agree with theirs.

Freedom of choice is the American way. Many Americans are fed up with groups trying to impose their beliefs, some of them using police state tactics and terror.

One of the failures of leadership is a failure of confidence. Any great accomplishment by a leader reflects more confidence than the facts would warrant. Confidence is a trait that top executives have in common with great military commanders, great artists, and brilliant political leaders. It is a trait of societies as well as individuals. Every great civilization has shown confidence in itself.

If leaders lack such confidence, they can waffle by avoiding decisions by going to committees, public opinion polls, statistics, information processing systems to delay a decision. When the facts are in, the leader must act, sort of like the little girl who told her teacher she was going to draw a picture of God. The teacher told her, "But, Mary, no one knows what God looks like;" and Mary replied confidently, "They will when I get through."

Americans need to decide to rebuild this wonderful country and then do it. **You** can do **your share** by telling your local and national officials what **you** would like them to do and also by taking an **active role yourself** or supporting those who do. Intelligent policies do not just appear; they are generated by ordinary human beings who decide to act.

---

*The great tragedy in America today is not the waste of our natural resources. The real tragedy is the waste of our human resources.*

-- Oliver Wendell Holmes

# Chapter 10

# HOW TO BRING ORDER OUT OF THE

# NEW WORLD DISORDER

*Now we can see a new world coming into view. A world in which there is the very real prospect of a new world order... in which the principles of justice and fair play protect the weak against the strong.*

-- President George Bush

*There is no new world. There never is.*

-- Charles Krauthammer

     The old world order was collapsing as the Soviet Empire was disintegrating and Saddam Hussein's forces were sitting in Kuwait on 23 August 1990 when President Bush called Brent Scowcroft, his National Security Advisor. They spent four hours talking that morning and fishing. They caught three bluefish and came up with the foreign policy phrase, "the new world order."

     Scowcroft and the president developed several precepts for their view of foreign affairs. America needed to maintain a strong military and should not be afraid to use it. Europe should remain central to US policy due to long-standing political and economic bonds across the Atlantic. As the only superpower, the US was the only state capable of mobilizing resources and motivating people in other countries to solve international problems. The eviction of Iraq from Kuwait was the example of the Bush/Scowcroft new world order.

     The world order was new, but it was not clear exactly what it was. Harvard professor Samuel Huntington saw "a more jungle-like world of multiple dangers, hidden traps, unpleasant surprises and moral ambiguities" instead of the black and white, bipolar world of the Cold War.

     Les Aspin, while still in the Congress before becoming Defense Secretary, said, "This ambiguous, complicated and changing security environment is not a comfortable one for

Americans.  The post-Soviet world bumper sticker, 'Less Threatening, More Complicated' offers no clear-cut guidance.... The Persian Gulf war highlighted the most important aspects of the new era -- the spread of nuclear weapons, terrorism and regional powers." but it did not resolve them.

But Bush was soon turned out of office by the governor of an inland state, Arkansas, who promised to focus on domestic problems like a laser beam and who belittled Bush's preoccupation with international affairs.  President Bill Clinton was soon up to his neck in the alligators of the international swamp.  He was soon spending a great deal of time on the former Soviet Union, Bosnia, Somalia, and Haiti.

There is general agreement on what should constitute the international order.  It should be free of any major war; there should be economic growth without disastrous environmental damage; and there should be some minimum amount of human rights.  However, there is considerable disagreement concerning the appropriate ways to reach these objectives.

The term "world order" is inevitably a concept with ideological overtones.  Now that the major world ideological conflict has been resolved with the death of Communism, this should be a time to try for more world consensus.  It should be widely accepted that there is a major crisis in the territorial sovereign state -- the nation state -- in its traditional form.

World government is no where on the horizon, but if we consider the European Community growing into the European Union as an example, there is an opportunity for more states to delegate some of their authority upwards, no doubt in an erratic fashion and with recurrent reassertions of national sovereignty.  The international system as we know it will remain pluralistic and unmanageable well into the next century with states playing the leading role but probably increasingly having that role reduced.

Regardless of specifics, it is a new world order, because the major ideological dispute of the century has been removed. The significance of that dispute on the nation state system was important because of the bipolar nature it forced on the world; it in effect divided the world into two large blocs which restricted the actions of individual nation states which constantly had to consider the ramifications of their actions in terms of how they would be perceived by the two superpowers. The end of the superpower confrontation rejuvenated the independence of action of the other states. The result has been disorder and that should be the status for the future. The freedom from the smothering influence of the Cold War unleashed pentup hatreds, grievances, and designs. This was reflected in the numerous small wars or border actions around the world.

Nevertheless, there was still an opportunity for morality in the world, even though the Serb-Croat actions in Bosnia might cause disbelief. The US intervention in Somalia was a great humanitarian effort; it was unfortunate that the UN was drawn into tribal warfare. There probably is no pure humanitarianism; the world is a tough place and sometimes shooting is necessary.

Higher morality on the part of the international community was called for in dealing with Bosnia. Rewarding aggression by agreeing to divide Bosnia and total indifference to "ethnic cleansing" were most disturbing and made one wonder whether Europe and the US really learned anything from World War II. This was the worst example of appeasement since Neville Chamberlain and it may come back to haunt the Europeans.

It is interesting that someone like Charles Krauthammer would bring back the old Viet-Nam rubric that, "Sometimes you do indeed have to destroy the village in order to save it." It is unbelievable after the years of the radical leftists and their divisive rantings, he should add, "How much better off Cambodia, for example, would have been had the US prevailed in its Indochina campaign and the communists never come to power." Hindsight is so clear! However, he did come up with one beautiful sentence, **"There is no immaculate intervention."**

Thus, we have a new world order of sovereign nation states freer than before to do what they wish and restrained only by their susceptibility to pressure from the international community or by direct action from the UN or another state.

The UN was created to do what we do not want to do. There is a **need** for actions by some authority higher than the individual nation states. There is an **opportunity** in this new world order for a greatly expanded role for the United Nations.

There are **only two alternatives:** either give the UN the means to accomplish its missions or else dissolve it and do it ourselves. (True, the UN could be disbanded, BUT it would have to be replaced by a similar body.) If we ignore this opportunity, then we will have to assume the role of the world's policeman, or the world will degenerate into an even more disorderly place than it is and that will have **dire consequences for American interests worldwide.**

## UNITED NATIONS FORCE

The UN was the creation of the powers in an already dividing world after a major war that defeated Germany and Japan. It clearly represented the power structure of that period. Times have changed and the first order of business should be a revamping of the UN. Germany and Japan should be brought into the mainstream of its power structure. The UN has only limited power because it has no army, no taxing authority, and thus no sovereignty. **The UN needs its own army.**

To man police checkpoints in a quiet zone, ad hoc forces, such as the UN has been compelled to use, can do the job. However, in a situation such as in Somalia where the relatively quiet job of escorting food convoys turned into military operations against clans, such forces are not adequate. They are not properly organized, trained, or supported.

Every UN peacekeeping force that has been deployed has been hastily thrown together from contingents from all over the world, with no common tactics or equipment, different languages and customs, no training together, and sporadic support. It is only through the perseverance and dedication of these fine people that the UN has been as successful as it has.

There are **two approaches** to building a UN Force (UNF); they could be combined or executed sequentially. The **first** would be to **recruit full units, probably at battalion size.** One possibility would be Gurkha battalions from Nepal. I observed them in Malaya in 1958 during the emergency and I carried one of their *kukris*, their traditional knives, thereafter and during two tours in Viet-Nam. They are fine soldiers and would be loyal to their officers and to the UN. Some of their officers could be seconded from other countries, including the US.

There are possibly other sources of full battalion size units from national armies such as Turkey, Jordan, or maybe the French Foreign Legion. The reason for starting with complete units is because that would provide troops with organization, resources, training, tactics, support, and esprit and tradition. It will take considerable time to build those from scratch. The providing nation would furnish replacement personnel and supplies for the unit.

The UNF should be built up with homogeneous units, including combined arms with tanks, armored cars, artillery, and aviation and with full logistics support units up to at least a division size or about 20,000 men initially. The UNF could be based in the US at some of the current US Army posts, some of which are being cut back or closed, or it could be based in Germany where the US Army has been vacating casernes with the drawdown there.

**The other approach would be to recruit the UNF from the bottom up.** Then it would truly be the UN's force. The drawbacks are that it would take much longer to build an effective force and it would be much more expensive. Complete supply systems would need to be created as well as ongoing training for replacements.

The experience of the French Foreign Legion would probably be a good starting point for how to develop such a force. It would take a long time to build cohesive, well trained, disciplined units with a sense of esprit, but in the long run they would probably be the best UN soldiers.

Again, this force could be based in the US or Europe. With the recession and military cutbacks in most countries of the world, there are many potential volunteers who already have military experience. Recruiting men with experience would accelerate the readiness of the units.

Since the expected size required for any UNF is difficult to predict, there will always be a requirement for national contingents to augment the UNF. Intercontinental transportation will have to be provided by the US or other countries with such capabilities. Likewise for air support, large numbers of helicopters including gunships, some communications and other logistics requirements, and any specialized needs.

If the UN had its own elite force, that would enhance the prestige of the UN around the world. One of the major problems is that we have tolerated thugs and petty warlords and even governments to interfere with UN peacekeeping troops. That must be brought to a thundering halt. Such people need to be stomped so that the word around the world becomes that no one would dare to confront a UN blue beret.

Such nonsense as we have seen in Bosnia where UN troops were held hostage, food convoys were extorted and blocked and UN helicopters were forced to land and be searched, in Somalia where UN food convoys were also harassed and UN troops were ambushed and killed, in Haiti where UN non-combat troops were blocked from landing, and the Israeli contempt for the UN in general and its troops firing on UN forces in Lebanon, is intolerable. The UN was created to do what the major states do not want to do. The major powers have a choice: either give the UN the means to do its job properly or else they should dissolve it and do it themselves, which means most of the burden would fall on the US.

## UN TRUSTEESHIP SYSTEM

Certain tasks are too large for any UN force to handle, such as the Korean War and the operation to liberate Kuwait. These were major military operations and needed the capability and experience of a major power. The three major current UN operations all have aspects that make them too complicated and extensive for a realistic UN operation.

The mess in the former Yugoslavia is a war using modern equipment and cannot be handled by a UN force, and it needs long term supervision. As we have noted earlier, Somalia is not really a state and it needs long term help. Haiti has been a disaster for years and remains one of the poorest countries in the world and has suffered from corrupt government for much too long. These are not problems that will likely have reasonable solutions developed by the participants themselves, even though there was some headway made in Haiti.

UN peacekeeping forces are designed to police agreements that have already been made, not to impose settlements or build nations. Since it is unrealistic to expect any **UN force to be able to deal with these rather intractable problems,** another means is needed. Fortunately, such **a means already exists in the UN structure.**

It is the **International Trusteeship System** and **The Trusteeship Council.** Some modification to the UN Charter would be required to deal with states, but the changed world situation should permit a **new category** of **"states in which there is no present effective or responsible government or which in their threatened situation require the protection of the United Nations."**

Somalia does not have a government and is not likely to have one. Haiti never has had a responsible government, having been ruled by "presidents for life" and thugs and criminals such as the *Tontons Macoute*. The leaders of Serbia and Croatia should be tried as war criminals and their countries do not deserve legal status at this time due to their aggression against Bosnia. The remnants of Yugoslavia, Serbia, Montenegro, and the two provinces plus Croatia and Bosnia-Hercegovina should be placed under UN Trusteeship.

The UN Trusteeship System calls for an "**administering authority**" to administer trust territories. That administering authority may be one or more states or the UN itself. The advantage of placing these troubled areas under the Trusteeship System would be that a competent military and political authority could be placed in charge of the country to impose peace and then develop and install effective government, all under UN supervision. After effective government was installed, the UN would pass sovereignty to it and reinstate it in the UN.

In the case of Somalia, the OAU (Organization of African Unity) should first be asked for recommendations as to who should be designated as the administering authority. The current president is President Hosni Mubarak of Egypt, which could play a major military role if needed. The administering authority would not necessarily have to come from the OAU itself.

For Haiti, the OAS (Organization of American States) should be consulted. Because of language, the OAS might want to invite France to be the administering authority, otherwise Brazil or Argentina come to mind.

To straighten out the mess in the former Yugoslavia, there should be consultations with the EU (European Union), NATO (North Atlantic Treaty Organization), the CSCE (Conference on Security and Cooperation in Europe), or the OECD (Organization for Economic Cooperation and Development). The CSCE was involved early there and its role in human rights makes it a key player in this field. The administering authority should be a European state or organization.

**Use of the Trusteeship System would permit the members of the UN to designate rogue states as incompetent to protect the rights of their inhabitants and assert the right of the world community to protect those**

**people and provide them with decent government.**
This would be the greatest step forward in human rights
in history. Too many people have had to live in silent misery
under despots and tyrants. America should lead the march for
this advancement so that world policing is not by one powerful
state, but by the UN members finally acting responsibly on
behalf of mankind.

## UN INTERNATIONAL COURT

The world needs a **permanent international court** to
deal with crimes that violate international law or human rights
and are not being dealt with properly by national courts. The
International Court of Justice only has jurisdiction in cases
involving states. Either the UN Charter should be amended to
change the jurisdiction of the ICJ to include individuals or the
UN should establish a separate court. The Inter-Parliamentary
Union conference of politicians from 114 parliaments called
for such a court in April 1995.

The war criminals of World War II were tried by
special tribunals established by the victorious powers. There
was wide agreement that Slobodan Milosevic of Serbia, Franjo
Tudjman of Croatia, and Radovan Karadzic the Bosnian Serb
leader, should be brought to trial for their crimes. The UN
established a tribunal but it has made very little progress. The
US should demonstrate its leadership by forcing the issue and
leading a campaign for a permanent international court.

There are hundreds, if not thousands, of people in
Serbia and Croatia who should be brought to justice for the
rape of Bosnia. The UN, which earlier announced a reward for
the arrest of Mohammed Farrah Aidid in Somalia,  should
bring him before a court to decide  the fate of this warlord.

Human rights have received much deserved prominence
in recent years, but they are still blatantly violated in many
places and those victims have no recourse to any authority. A
UN international court would bring a chance for decency to the
people of the world. **The US must lead.**

## THE NEW WORLD ORDER

As Henry Kissinger observed, world orders are in
constant change and of shortening duration. The Peace of
Westphalia in 1648 resulted in an order that lasted 150 years.

The Congress of Vienna in 1815 created an order for 100 years. The Cold War order lasted 45 years. He does not believe the form of the new world order will be visible until well into the next century. The Wilsonian ideals of collective security, democracy, rule of law, and ethnic self-determination will be less practical. The growth of democracy will continue but will be more difficult. The state preceded the nation in most of the world and minorities and majorities tend to be permanent. Politics become a struggle for domination in such societies, and there is rarely the concept of a loyal opposition.

US leaders liked to claim they were struggling in the name of principle not interest. America will have to be more pragmatic and articulate its national interests. This will require more *realpolitik*, which is alien to American tradition.

American policy toward Russia will need to be based on permanent interests. The changes in Russian domestic politics will complicate that. Russia, like the old Soviet Union, is an empire which is disintegrating. They will continue to be involved with the "near abroad," the former Soviet republics. The challenge will be to keep the Russian Army at home and not develop new Russian imperialism. Germany and Russia must not be permitted to become too close as partners or too distant as adversaries.

America must continue involved with Europe. We must be careful not to fall into what Boris Yeltsin called a Cold Peace.

We have seen the growing military expenditures in Asia, particularly in China. Japanese defense expenditures will increase further and as China looms more powerful, Japan may pursue a nuclear capability. Pragmatism will likely be called for with China, since human rights have come to dominate our relationship, something we did not do with the Soviet Union.

Chinese perception that American actions are an effort to impose our values could lead to their conclusion that the US has no national interest in an Asian balance of power and would reduce their desire for accommodation. We need agreement on a global strategy.

The historical differences among civilizations are reappearing as the main source of world conflict, according to Samuel P. Huntington. Since governments and groups are less able to mobilize support and form coalitions based on ideology, they will increasingly try to gain support by religious and

ethnic appeals.
Some claim US foreign policy stopped with the
November 1994 election. Forget the new world order and
assertive multilateralism. The new foreign policy is
neomercantilism, the art of the possible, anything of tangible
benefit for the US public. The emphasis would be on issues
that can gain bipartisan support, led by trade, and including a
new security order for Europe, peace efforts in the Middle East,
and fighting proliferation, terrorism, and international crime.
Hillary Clinton reminds her husband that voters she
talks to simply do not care about foreign policy. If **you** care,
maybe **you** should let her or him know.
The US has no clear foreign policy now. Clinton has
threatened and backed down, moved in and pulled out. We do
need a national debate about what should be our international
role in the 21st Century. Where and for what purpose should
we use our military forces abroad? What are the US national
interests?
Yes, the UN is beset with diverse interests. Yes,
Bosnia revealed the weakness and lack of decisiveness of both
the UN and "an increasingly effeminate Western Europe."
Therefore, we should not bind ourselves too rigidly to them.
We should support them when we agree, but we should be
ready to take the lead. To do that, we have to know where we
want to go.

## THE US MUST ACT LIKE A MAJOR POWER

The post-Cold War has fallen into the hands of
functionaries, not visionaries. The age of national heroes has
been replaced by an era of political leaders. The rape of
Bosnia has shown us that the UN and Europe are either unable
or reluctant to play a role in the new world order.
**The entire world looks to the US as the symbol of
hope and for leadership.** We may not have campaigned for
this role but we have been unanimously elected and we cannot
hide from it. We cannot pull a General Sherman and refuse to
serve.
Bosnia, Somalia, and to a lesser extent Haiti could be
the bench marks in the history of post-Cold War collective
action against massive violations of international and
humanitarian law. This can be a defining moment as to
whether or not the 21st Century will see progress in collective

action for peace and justice, or escalation of racial and religious bigotry, persecution, and slaughter. The challenge can be met without falling into a "quagmire."

Western cowardice toward the disaster in Bosnia has unleashed religious intolerance and militant nationalism on a scale in Europe not seen since the Nazis. An additional outcome and a potential direct threat to America was the galvanizing effect it had on Islamic zealotry. The only beneficiaries are the Islamic fundamentalists who already hate the West and its liberal values. It will be cruel irony if the Bosnians, who are a secular and well-educated European people, become the rallying point for Islamic radicals and their terrorist impulses.

Atrocities against the Muslims in Bosnia may cause the US to be a major target for Islamic fundamentalist terror. We have already had the bombing of the World Trade Center and attempts on US air liners in the Pacific. We need to work to avoid such attacks. The true irony is that US interests are with the Muslim World not against it. Only our sometimes overly domestic and therefore misguided policies toward Israel by our politicians have clouded our interests.

Thus at the end of the 20th Century, Western indifference and inaction have set the stage for a relapse into the violent politics of tribalism, militant nationalism, and religious fundamentalism and intolerance which we thought had ended with the death of Communism and the victory of democracy. We must preclude that from happening or else history will judge us harshly.

We played a major role in shaping much of the world we are now stuck with: we played a key role in creating the UN, we helped rebuild Europe, we were there as the colonial empires died and the colonies became the numerous new states in the UN, we were there during the crazy times between Somalia and Ethiopia, we were in Haiti, we supported Yugoslavia. If we were part of the problem, then we must be part of the solution.

The world yearns for a leader, not a tyrant, not a dictator. We have many flaws in our society, but the millions who want to come here vote with their feet that it sure beats a lot of others. We do not have to export our ways to everyone else; they have their own ideas on how they might like to live. What they want is a chance to try. We cannot wait for Europe; let them follow us. **If we lead, the world will follow.**

This country was blessed with fertile soil so we have helped feed the world. This country was blessed with brilliant forefathers who gave us a great Constitution and sense of freedom; we must share that with the poor and oppressed of the world. This country built a great military force to defend democracy; we must now use it to protect mankind. This country has been reluctantly pushed into the position of world prominence; **it is our duty to lead.**

We must be true to our heritage. We would have failed those who went before us, many of whom are buried in cemeteries around the world from Arlington to Normandy. Whether it is our destiny or whether we were dragged into this position, it makes no difference, we are there. We should seize the chance as an opportunity to make the world safe for democracy and at the same time make it a better world for all mankind.

---

*Where the spark of freedom flickers, we must fight for a flame of light.*

-- In a letter home from an Army
Sergeant killed at Christmas in Viet-Nam

---

It is better to light one small candle than to curse the darkness.

# AFTERWORD

There are many problems both in our country and all around the world. As we become more numerous both in number of countries and number of people, these problems only seem to grow.

Many of the domestic problems are rooted in the family and the home. Politicians will have a difficult time solving them. The families will have to take responsibility for their members. A renaissance of the family, including making fathers and mothers responsible for their children, and an overall reestablishment of a sense of responsibility for one's actions, not leaving everything to government, will be required to alleviate some of our worst domestic difficulties.

The international scene is somewhat similar to the domestic in that we seem to have more irresponsible states now. These will have to be dealt with by politicians who must wisely assess our vital national interests and lead our government in the efforts to make the community of nations a safe place before we are drawn into new wars.

In both cases, **you** the citizen are the key. **You** run the families. **You** are responsible for the children. **You** elect the officials who determine your local policies as well as our national interests and lead our country. It is up to **you** to make sure we have good people in office, not just politicians. It is **your money** they are spending. Those are **your children** they send to battle to die. It is **your country** that they are either leading to a better future or taking down a path to disaster. So, ultimately, **you, we the people are responsible.**

I hope you found this book interesting. I would appreciate hearing your comments and particularly any successes you have. Call me at **(702) 356-0905** or fax me at **(702) 356-0967**. Good luck, **our country and the world are in your hands.**

# Glossary

**AFDC:** Aid to Families with Dependent Children.

**AIDS:** Acquired Immune Deficiency Syndrome.

**ANC:** African National Congress.

**ARMSCOR:** Arms Corporation established by the South African Government.

**ASEAN:** Association of Southeast Asian Nations (Brunei, Indonesia, Malaysia, the Philippines, Singapore, and Thailand).

**CENTO:** Central Treaty Organization (United Kingdom, Turkey, Pakistan, and Iran plus US support).

**CIA:** Central Intelligence Agency.

**CIS:** Commonwealth of Independent States (after the USSR).

**COMECON:** Council for Mutual Economic Assistance (Bulgaria, Czechoslovakia, Hungary, Poland, Romania and the USSR, later joined by Albania and East Germany).

**CSCE:** Conference on Security and Cooperation in Europe.

**EC:** European Community.

**EU:** European Union.

**FAO:** Food and Agriculture Organization (UN).

**GATT:** General Agreement on Tariffs and Trade.

**GDP:** Gross Domestic Product.

**GNP:** Gross National Product.

**Hamas:** Radical Palestinian group opposed to agreement with Israel.

**Hezbollah:** Radical Muslim faction based in Lebanon backed by Iran.

**HIV:** Human Immunodeficiency Virus.

**IAEA:** International Atomic Energy Agency.

**ICBM:** Intercontinental Ballistic Missile.

**ICJ:** International Court of Justice.

**IMF:** International Monetary Fund.

**Intifada:** Palestinian uprising

in the occupied territories that started on 8 December 1987.

**INF:** Intermediate-Range Nuclear Forces (an arms reduction treaty in 1987).

**IRA:** Irish Republican Army.

**IRBM:** Intermediate Range Ballistic Missiles.

**IUD:** Intra-Uterine Device.

**Kaabah:** Holy Muslim shrine in Mecca.

**Kach:** Radical Israeli group formed by late Meir Kahane who had earlier formed the Jewish Defense League in the US.

**KGB:** *Komite Gosudarstvennoy Bezopasnosti* (Committee for State Security), Soviet intelligence agency that started as CHEKA in 1917 and evolved through other designations: GPU, OGPU, NKVD, NKGB, MGB, MVD.

**Knesset:** Israeli Parliament.

**KT:** Kiloton (equivalent explosive power of 1,000 tons of TNT).

**LDCs:** Less Developed Countries.

**Likud:** Israeli political party of Menachem Begin and

Yitzak Shamir.

**LOBS:** Limited Orbit Ballistic System.

**MCTR:** Missile Control Technology Regime.

**MIRV:** Multiple Independently-targeted Reentry Vehicles (in nuclear warheads).

**Mossad:** Israeli intelligence service.

**MT:** Megaton (equivalent explosive power of 1,000,000 tons of TNT).

**Mujahedin:** Muslim freedom fighters (name for fighters against the Iranian regime and also those who came from many countries to fight against the Communist government in Afghanistan).

**NAFTA:** North American Free Trade Agreement.

**NATO:** North Atlantic Treaty Organization.

**NGOs:** Non-Governmental Organizations.

**NPT:** Nuclear Non Proliferation Treaty.

**OAS:** Organization of American States.

**OAU:** Organization of African

Unity.

**OECD:** Organization for Economic Cooperation and Development (Europe).

**OPEC:** Organization of Petroleum Exporting Countries.

**PLO:** Palestine Liberation Organization.

**PTA:** Parent Teachers Association.

**SAC:** Strategic Air Command (US Air Force).

**SALT 1 & 2:** Strategic Arms Limitations Treaties.

**SEATO:** Southeast Asia Treaty Organization (US, UK, France, Australia, New Zealand, Thailand, Pakistan, and the Philippines).

**SLBMs:** Submarine Launched Ballistic Missiles.

**SS-18:** Soviet ICBM, *Satan,* 6,600 mile range, 10 MIRVs, 500 KT warheads.

**SS-19:** Soviet ICBM, *Stiletto,* 6,000 mile range, 6 MIRVs, 550 KT warheads.

**SS-20:** Soviet IRBM, *Saber,* 3,000 mile range, 3 MIRVs, 150 KT warheads.

**SS-24:** Soviet ICBM, *Scapel,* 6,000 mile range, 10 MIRVs, 100 KT warheads, rail-based, some in silos, solid fuel.

**SS-25:** Soviet ICBM, *Sickle,* 6,300 miles range, single warhead of 750 KT, road-mobile, solid fuel.

**START 1 & 2:** Strategic Arms Reduction Treaties.

**UN:** The United Nations Organization based in New York City.

**UNESCO:** United Nations Educational, Scientific, and Cultural Organization.

**UNITA:** National Union for the Total Independence of Angola.

**UNTAC:** United Nations Transitional Authority in Cambodia.

**WTO:** World Trade Organization. Successor to the GATT.

# Resource Directory

The following listed sources by Richard Hobbs are available from ColDoc Publishing. There is an order form at the end of the book.

## Books

**THE MYTH OF VICTORY What Is Victory In War?** Foreword by Admiral Arleigh Burke, former Chief of Naval Operations and founder of The Center for Strategic and International Studies in Washington. This book examines the need for reconciliation between the democratic dislike of war and the appropriate use of the military instrument in world politics. It questions whether the results obtained in war are worth the expenditures made and contends that victory gained from total war is illusory and not commensurate with the terrible cost. (Originally published by Frederick Praeger at Westview Press)

ISBN: 0-89158-388-2, hardcover, 6 x 9, 566 pages, $39.95.

**WORLD WAR IV China's Quest for Power in the 21st Century** The Soviet Union had imploded and Communism was discredited yet China and North Korea tried to hold back the clock. The rest of the world was reducing its armaments; why then was China expanding all areas of its military forces? What are China's motives and what are its objectives for the future? The book is set in the year 2012 and sketches a scenario of a possible version of the new world order. The historical part of the book concerning the humiliation of the Middle Kingdom and the growth of Red China is factual up to date. The future is projection of either what China and the other countries were already doing or could do.

ISBN: 0-9647788-7-4 (not yet published) 8.5 x 11, 221 pages, $19.95.

**THE NEW WORLD ORDER Tribalism, Nationalism, and Religious Fundamentalism** The end of the Cold War introduced a new world order, but it is not yet clearly defined. The relative stability we knew even with a balance of terror has given way to a ferocious new tribalism such as we see in the disintegration of the old Yugoslavia. Terrorism and wars are rampant. It is a very disorderly world. America is also in disarray. The world needs a leader and the United States is the only candidate.

ISBN: 0-9647788-1-5 (Not yet published) 8.5 x 11, 218 pages, $19.95.

**YOU AND THE NEW WORLD ORDER How You Can Influence the Alarming and Growing International and Domestic Problems** This book takes *The New World Order* above and makes it into a citizens' handbook by determining some of the options available and possible actions that could be taken to address some of these enormous problems. After a brief review of how we got into this mess, it addresses tribalism, nationalism, religion, the nation state, the United Nations, war crimes, overpopulation, famine, disease, unemployment, migration, terrorism, war, and the mess in America, including guns, drugs, crime, welfare, and minorities. It asks where are we going? and where do we want to go? and asks you, the citizen, to take part in determining that future.

ISBN: 0-9647788-6-6 Softcover, 5.5 x 8.5, 256 pages, $19.95.

## Special Studies

**SS101 The Old World Order** This study is a review of the post-World War II period covering bipolar world, neutralism and nonalignment, the Cold War, and the world order during the Cold War which had a degree of stability but a dilemma for the superpowers between being the world's policemen or supporting the United Nations.

27 pages, $9.95

**SS102 The Evil Empire** This study reviews the growth of the Russian Empire and eventually the Soviet Empire with its extension into Eastern Europe and its influence in peripheral states.

26 pages, $9.95

**SS103 The End of Empire — The Soviet Disunion** This study reviews the demise of the Soviet Union covering the arms race, Cold War resurgence, the collapse, and looks at why including the role of Star Wars and finally the significance of the demise to the world.

26 pages, $9.95

**SS104    The Common-wealth of Independent States** This study looks at the republics that emerged from the former Soviet Union, their difficulties, the potential for a new Russian Empire, and the significance of the Commonwealth of Independent States to the rest of the world.

18 pages, $9.95

SS101 through SS104 are chapters 1-4 of *The New World Order* and are condensed together as Chapter 2 of *You and the New World Order.*

**SS105    The Threat of War** This study is a brief review of the war potential in the world covering conventional war capabilities of the major countries of the world with tables listing strengths of armed forces and major weapons systems. It also covers nuclear capabilities around the world, the problems of nuclear waste and the outlook for nuclear war. It ends with the major current threats in the world.

35 pages, $12.95

SS105 is chapter 5 of *The New World Order* and was partially incorporated into chapter 8 of *You and the New World Order.*

To place an order for any of the above, see the order blank on the last page.

# INDEX

# Order Form

✳ Fax orders: (702) 356-0967

☎ Telephone orders: (702) 356-0905 (9 to 5 Pacific time)

✉ Postal orders: ColDoc Publishing, Richard Hobbs,
  P. O. Box 50682-C, Sparks, Nevada 89435-0682, USA

**Please send the following books:**

I understand that I may return any books for a full refund
-- for any reason, no questions asked.

_____

_____

_____

❑    Please send update information to me **FREE.**

Company name: _____

Name: _____

Address: _____

City:_____State: _____ Zip: _____-_____

Telephone: (_____) _____

**Sales tax:**
Please add 7% for books shipped to Nevada addresses.

**Shipping:**
Book rate: $3.00 for the first book and 75 cents for each
additional book  (Surface shipping may take three to four
weeks)
Air Mail: $4.50 per book

**Payment:**
❑    Check
❑    Credit Card: ❑ Visa  ❑ MasterCard  ❑ AMEX  ❑ Discover

Card Number: _____

Name on card: _____Exp. date: ___/___